Medieval Britain

By Denis Richards
A History of Britain

Volume 1 Britain and the Ancient World
James A. Bolton and Denis Richards

Volume 2 Medieval Britain

Volume 3 Britain under the Tudors and Stuarts
Denis Richards

Volume 4 Britain 1714–1851
Denis Richards and Anthony Quick

Volume 5 Britain 1851–1945
Denis Richards and Anthony Quick

Volume 6 Twentieth Century Britain
Denis Richards and Anthony Quick

An Illustrated History of Modern Europe, 1789–1945
Denis Richards

An Illustrated History of Modern Britain, 1783–1964
Denis Richards and J. W. Hunt

Royal Air Force, 1935–45
A history in three volumes
Denis Richards and Hilary St George Saunders

Offspring of the 'Vic'
A history of Morley College
Denis Richards

Medieval Britain

Denis Richards M.A.

Formerly Principal of Morley College and Longman Fellow,
University of Sussex

Arnold D. Ellis M.A.

Assistant Master, Shrewsbury School

LONGMAN

LONGMAN GROUP LIMITED
London
Associated companies, branches and representatives
throughout the world

© Longman Group Ltd. 1973

First published 1973
ISBN 0 582 31487 9

Filmset by Photoprint Plates Ltd., Rayleigh, Essex, and
printed in Hong Kong by Sheck Wah Tong Printing Press

Contents

Maps and Diagrams

Acknowledgements

The author and publisher are grateful to the following for permission to reproduce photographs:

Aerofilms Ltd., pages 153 and 202; J. Allan Cash, page 12; Ashmolean Museum, page 40; Batsford Books Ltd., pages 195 right, 263, 270 and 276; Bibliothèque Nationale Paris, pages 131, 181, 189 right and 267; Bibliothèque Royale Bruxelles, page 232; The Bodleian Library, pages 41, 97, 103, 121 left, 176 left, 176 right, 217 and 253; The Trustees of the British Museum, pages 15, 25, 46, 55, 78, 102, 137, 139, 157 right, 166, 167, 173, 182, 193, 223, 227, 230, 233, 240, 241, 246 left, 246 right, 252, 256, 259 and 281; British Tourist Authority, page 29; British Travel Association, pages 206 and 255; Cambridge University Press, reproduced from Beresford and St. Joseph *Medieval Britain*, page 98; Corpus Christi College, Cambridge, page 112; Country Life, page 208; Courtauld Institute of Art, pages 134 and 135, photo Laurence Stone, page 141; The Dean and Chapter of Durham, pages 58 left, 107 and 229; Department of the Environment Edinburgh Crown ©, pages 49 and 283; Rt. Hon. Sir Alec Douglas Home, page 157 left; Henry E. Huntington Library and Art Gallery, page 249; The Illustrated London News, page 71; J. K. St. Joseph, page 220; Keeper of the Records of Scotland and Controller of H.M.S.O. Crown ©, page 159; A. F. Kersting, pages 129, 185 and 275; Kofler-Tuniger, page 123; Mansell Collection, pages 37, 237 and 282; Ministry of Public Buildings and Works Crown ©, pages 152 and 216; National Museum of Antiquaries Scotland, page 45; National Monuments Record Crown ©, pages 170, 189 left, 215 (W. H. Godfrey), 239 and 263 left; National Portrait Gallery, pages 195, 263 right and 270; Sydney W. Newbery, page 224; Phaidon Press Ltd., pages 84 and 85; Public Record Office London, page 95; Royal Commission on Historical Monuments Crown ©, page 213; Royal Library Windsor by gracious permission of H.M. Queen Elizabeth, page 162; Science Museum, pages 242 and 280; Society of Antiquaries, page 19; Thames and Hudson, reproduced from R. T. Stoll and J. Roubier *Architecture and Sculpture in Early Britain*, pages 33, 51, 57, 61, 110 left, 110 right, Halliday *Cultural History of England*, photo Martin Hurliman, page 198; Topix, page 14; Trinity College Cambridge, pages 104, 105, 121 right and 226; Trinity College Dublin, pages 54, and 201; Universitetets Oldsaksamling, page 35 left and right; Victoria and Albert Museum, page 257; Barbara Wagstaff, page 24; Walkers Art Gallery, page 113; The Warburg Institute; pages 99 and 145; The Dean and Chapter of Westminster, page 103, Reece Winstone, pages 58 right and 209; G. Bernard Wood, page 234.

Foreword to Teachers

This book is intended mainly for pupils between the ages of twelve and fourteen. It completes the six-volume History of Britain which began with the publication of *Britain Under the Tudors and Stuarts* in 1958.

Since that date the study of history in schools has undergone many changes, of which the increased emphasis on project work and on the study of historical 'patches' are two of the most interesting and rewarding. Neither of these developments, however, seems to make it less desirable for the pupil to have some knowledge of a lengthier sweep of history, both for reasons of general education and to help him set his more detailed studies within their historical context. To what extent 'period' history should be the staple fare in class, or to what extent it may more usefully be studied by way of supplementary reading to projects and patches, is to some degree a matter of opinion. In either case, the pupil will no doubt be helped by possessing a text which outlines the history of the country or countries concerned over a fairly extensive period.

A further and most welcome development in recent years has been the increased attention given, even with very young pupils, to the documentary basis of history. Owing to the length of this book it has not been possible to include any documents, but a selection of source material will shortly be published as a companion volume.

It has been the policy in this series to offer rather detailed narratives, and it may well be that some teachers will need or prefer to use only a part of this book. For those who wish to follow the whole period in outline, but at shorter length than by way of the complete volume, the chapters most convenient to omit will probably be those on Anglo-Saxon Civilisation (6, 7 and 8), Domesday Book and the Medieval Manor (11), Medieval Architecture (21), Priests, Monks and Friars (22), Towns and Trade (23), and Language, Literature and Art (24). For teachers on the other hand who want to give as much time as possible to the social and artistic aspects, it might perhaps be the best plan to concentrate on those chapters, and to reduce the length of the period by omitting either some of the pre-Conquest chapters (e.g. 2 and 5), or else chapters 25–26 on the Fifteenth Century.

I should like to thank my old friend and collaborator J. W. Hunt very much for his most helpful comments on an early draft of the first half of this book.

D.R.

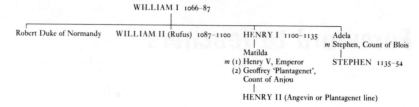

THE NORMAN KINGS OF ENGLAND

WILLIAM I 1066–87

Robert Duke of Normandy   WILLIAM II (Rufus) 1087–1100   HENRY I 1100–1135   Adela
m Stephen, Count of Blois

Matilda
m (1) Henry V, Emperor   STEPHEN 1135–54
(2) Geoffrey 'Plantagenet',
Count of Anjou

HENRY II (Angevin or Plantagenet line)

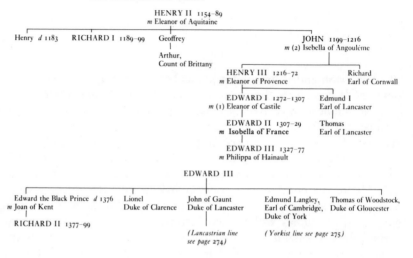

THE PLANTAGENET KINGS

HENRY II 1154–89
m Eleanor of Aquitaine

Henry *d* 1183   RICHARD I 1189–99   Geoffrey   JOHN 1199–1216
m (2) Isebella of Angoulême

Arthur,
Count of Brittany

HENRY III 1216–72   Richard
m Eleanor of Provence   Earl of Cornwall

EDWARD I 1272–1307   Edmund I
m (1) Eleanor of Castile   Earl of Lancaster

EDWARD II 1307–29   Thomas
m Isobella of France   Earl of Lancaster

EDWARD III 1327–77
m Philippa of Hainault

EDWARD III

Edward the Black Prince *d* 1376   Lionel   John of Gaunt   Edmund Langley,   Thomas of Woodstock,
m Joan of Kent   Duke of Clarence   Duke of Lancaster   Earl of Cambridge,   Duke of Gloucester
Duke of York

RICHARD II 1377–99

(Lancastrian line   *(Yorkist line see page 275)*
see page 274)

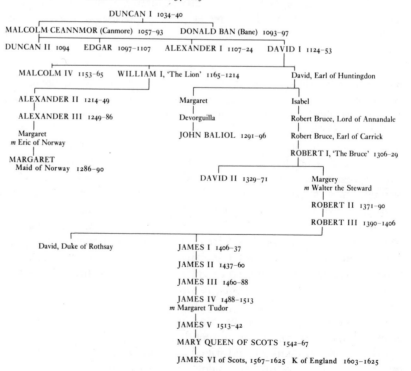

KINGS OF SCOTS 1034–1625

DUNCAN I 1034–40

MALCOLM CEANNMOR (Canmore) 1057–93   DONALD BAN (Bane) 1093–97

DUNCAN II 1094   EDGAR 1097–1107   ALEXANDER I 1107–24   DAVID I 1124–53

MALCOLM IV 1153–65   WILLIAM I, 'The Lion' 1165–1214   David, Earl of Huntingdon

ALEXANDER II 1214–49   Margaret   Isabel

ALEXANDER III 1249–86   Devorguilla   Robert Bruce, Lord of Annandale

Margaret   JOHN BALIOL 1291–96   Robert Bruce, Earl of Carrick
m Eric of Norway

MARGARET   ROBERT I, 'The Bruce' 1306–29
Maid of Norway 1286–90

DAVID II 1329–71   Margery
m Walter the Steward

ROBERT II 1371–90

ROBERT III 1390–1406

David, Duke of Rothsay   JAMES I 1406–37

JAMES II 1437–60

JAMES III 1460–88

JAMES IV 1488–1513
m Margaret Tudor

JAMES V 1513–42

MARY QUEEN OF SCOTS 1542–67

JAMES VI of Scots, 1567–1625 K of England 1603–1625

1 The Decay of Roman Britain

Four centuries are a long time in a country's history. Going back four centuries from now, we should find ourselves in the glorious – and highly dangerous and inconvenient – days of the first Queen Elizabeth. Within this stretch of four hundred years from the Elizabethan age to our own, there have occurred nearly all the developments which most affect us today – things such as the progress to democratic government, the rapid growth of population, towns and industry, and all the wealth of scientific invention from the steam engine to the hydrogen bomb. In comparison with this modern epoch and its crowded happenings, the four centuries of Roman Britain mean little to us. Yet they, too, saw great advances in civilisation – advances which we may still glimpse when we motor along a former Roman road, trace the great cross-country march of Hadrian's Wall, or gaze respectfully at the Roman baths in Bath.

Unfortunately these advances did not for the most part survive Roman Britain. They disappeared during the period of invasion and settlement by the Anglo-Saxons. These newcomers did not preserve or for the most part use the Roman achievements – they neglected or destroyed them. That is why, although we still have plenty of medieval cathedrals, we have no complete Roman temples; and why, although we inhabit most of the town sites of Roman Britain, the actual Roman buildings are now usually no more than ruins, foundations, or oddments of stone and brick in the local museum.

We can date the beginning of Roman Britain from the formal conquest started by the Emperor Claudius in A.D. 43. Before this, however, there were Julius Caesar's two expeditions, in 55 and 54 B.C., followed by many years of increasing trade and other contacts between the Roman Empire and the various British chiefs. Once they had started properly in A.D. 43, it took the Romans about forty years to subdue the tribes between the South coast and the River Tay, including those in Wales.

Even then, however, Roman control was far from complete. It did not touch either Cornwall or most of the Scottish Highlands. On its northern border, it was always threatened. Around A.D. 142 the Romans built a wall of turf – the Antonine Wall – to block the narrow stretch of land between the Forth and the Clyde, but this line they could not hold. After about forty years they withdrew their frontier further south, to the much stronger stone-built wall erected earlier between the Tyne and

the Solway Firth after the visit of the Emperor Hadrian. But though Roman military occupation finally covered nearly all Britain up to Hadrian's Wall and even parts beyond it, by no means all this area became 'Romanised' in its ways of life. In the north-west beyond the Trent, Roman civilisation was largely confined to a few strong points, and in Wales it made little impact except in the southern part.

What was the nature of this Roman civilisation in Britain? The word 'civilisation' comes from the Latin 'civis' meaning a citizen; and to the Romans it was something largely bound up with town life. In Britain the Romans founded or developed over forty towns. Four of these – which we know as Colchester, Gloucester, Lincoln and York – were 'colonies' built mainly for time-expired veterans from the legions. From the first, these were places in which all the townspeople were Roman citizens with special rights of local self-government. Of the other towns, fourteen or so were tribal capitals. Some of these were new, others enlarged from pre-Roman hut settlements. When fully built, they finally varied in size from large towns of 200 acres like Venta of the Belgae (Winchester) to small towns of some 50 acres like Venta of the Silures (Caerwent). In population they probably varied between 15,000 and 2,000 inhabitants. At first only the officials and their families in these towns enjoyed Roman citizenship. Later, Roman citizenship was extended to nearly all inhabitants of the Empire who were not slaves.

Apart from the colonies and the tribal capitals there were other towns such as Bath and Rochester, and there was what finally became the biggest and most 'Romanised' town of all – Londinium (London). This was enlarged from a pre-Roman town; and its importance as a centre of communication and trade, with docks and a bridge over the Thames, made it by the fourth century A.D. the official capital. But of whatever type, Roman towns normally had certain common features. They followed a master-plan usually based on a grid of streets laid out in criss-cross fashion. There was the forum at the centre, with town hall, law courts, market place, possibly temples. Round the edges of the town were the walls, often not built till the town was a century or more old, and in the walls were great fortified gateways. Near the outskirts was usually a very large amphitheatre for cock-fighting, bear-baiting, acrobatic shows, and the like, plus gladiatorial combats or man versus beasts contests when they could be afforded. Some of the larger towns

Roman civilisation in Britain

Towns

Hadrian's Wall *A stretch of the Wall in Northumberland as it may be seen to-day. Built in the main between A.D. 122 and 128, the Wall was 15 feet high and broad enough for soldiers to march along the top. It had a small fort or castle at every Roman mile—79 in all—and 16 larger forts at wider intervals. In front, to the North, a ditch ran along most of its length; while behind the Wall, to the South, ran a Roman road, with a further ditch behind that. The purpose of the Wall was to maintain military control over the tribes on both sides, rather than simply to keep out intruders from the North.*

The palace at Fishbourne *A model reconstructing the probable appearance of the palace the remains of which have recently been excavated at Fishbourne, near Chichester. It may have belonged to Cogidubnus who was one of the British kings or chiefs who cooperated with the Romans during their invasion, and was well rewarded for his help. This very large palace is evidence of wealth and security in the first century of Roman rule in Britain.*

also had a theatre and all had public baths. Most of the shops and houses were timber-built, with a crude greenish semi-transparent glass for windows; and the better houses had a hypocaust or heating-plant circulating warm air under the floor of the main rooms.

The countryside

In the countryside the Romans made their mark chiefly by the building of roads and bridges. Beyond this the larger landowners sometimes arranged their estates on the pattern of a Roman villa. *Villa* in Latin means farm, and the landowner's house was always the centre of a working farm. As the years went on such farm houses tended to become

Roman villas

larger and more luxurious and to employ the hypocaust system of heating. At Lullingstone, in Kent, the remains of a large Roman villa include some very elaborate and beautiful mosaic flooring and – an addition of the fourth century A.D. – a Christian chapel. A villa of this kind shows us how the wealthier Britons might try to imitate the pattern of Roman Mediterranean life.

Extent of 'Romanisation'

Geography and climate were the main factors in deciding which areas became the most Romanised. Southern Britain, being dry and fertile, offered the richer soils for cultivation, and so here there de-

Treasure denied to the invaders *This fine Roman silver dish [part of a dinner service] was among the precious objects turned up by a plough at Mildenhall in Suffolk in 1939. These objects had presumably been buried to save them from the invading Anglo-Saxons. To-day this 'Mildenhall Treasure' is one of the most prized exhibits in the British Museum.*

veloped in many places a settled villa life which reached its greatest prosperity in the third and fourth centuries. The North and the West were areas of military control marked by forts and roads – areas which, as the fourth century went on, the legions found harder and harder to defend from marauding groups of Picts, Scots or Saxons. A glance at the Ordnance Survey map of Roman Britain will show where the main villa settlement took place: on the Hampshire uplands, on the Cotswolds, in the area round Bath, where soil and climate were favourable. Elsewhere, settlement was patchy, especially on the heavier damper soils of the Midlands. In the West, on Salisbury Plain and on the Marlborough Downs, many native Celtic villages remained hardly touched by the impact of the Romans.

Roman Britain, then, was a province with several towns and with a rural life affected in some areas by Roman ideas – even to the extent of growing vines in the South. It was a country which, despite its huge stretches of forest, fen and wild hills and moorland, also enjoyed over a fair part a settled agriculture. It had a trade in agricultural products and in articles of clothing made from wool or leather, and within it there was mining for coal, iron, lead, copper, tin, silver and even gold. From the second century A.D. onwards it was a country where one of the religions followed by a part of its people was Christianity.

None of this, however, went very deep. From the third century it seems that town life in Britain began to decay. The theatre at Verulamium became used as a rubbish dump; and the extensions to London Wall were built from the materials of derelict houses. Despite many attempts to give the towns fresh vigour, prosperity gradually deserted them and centred in the villas. In unsettled times towns were too obvious a target for attack; and in unsettled times the trade and easy communication with the surrounding countryside, which were their life-blood, withered away.

On the whole, then, the British remained little touched by Roman habits. The Celtic languages survived the four centuries of Latin superiority, and even the Celtic gods maintained a hold. Celtic art forms, too, persisted, with their curving intricate patterns, very different from the Roman representations of human beings and of animals. Beneath the top dressing of the Roman occupation, there was always the basic soil of Celtic Britain. For its survival, Romano-British civilisation really depended on the presence of powerful Roman military forces. Without these it was liable to collapse at any time.

When and why were these forces withdrawn? For the answer, we have to look at the Roman Empire as a whole. All through its history, the Emperors had fought to establish and defend some kind of frontier across Germany and Central Europe against the various peoples whom the Romans termed 'barbarians'.[1] For most of the first two and a half centuries A.D. they managed to maintain the Imperial defences well beyond the Rhine and the Danube; but in the middle of the third century the Franks and the Alemanni from Germany penetrated the Rhineland area, and the Romans withdrew their frontier in that part of the world to the Rhine – Danube line itself. Here they preserved it in some sort of fashion, despite repeated inroads by invaders, until it finally collapsed early in the fifth century A.D. under the continuous pressure of the barbarian tribes.

These tribes came from areas which stretched from Scandinavia right through Germany and central Europe into the Balkans, south Russia and central Asia. The more distant invaders, like the nomadic Huns of central Asia, were driven by food shortage and a growing population to move westwards in search of fresh lands and easily-won supplies. The tribes to the west of these, like the nomadic Goths – who later split into Visigoths (West Goths) and Ostrogoths (East Goths) – had behind them the pressure of the Huns. And those nearest to the Rhine, like the Franks of North Germany and the Alemanni of South Germany, though they had in many cases a settled agriculture, also moved westwards, partly forced by the pressure of the tribes to the east of them, partly drawn by the wealth and attraction of the Roman Empire.

[1] Perhaps from their speech, which to many Roman ears merely sounded like bar-bar.

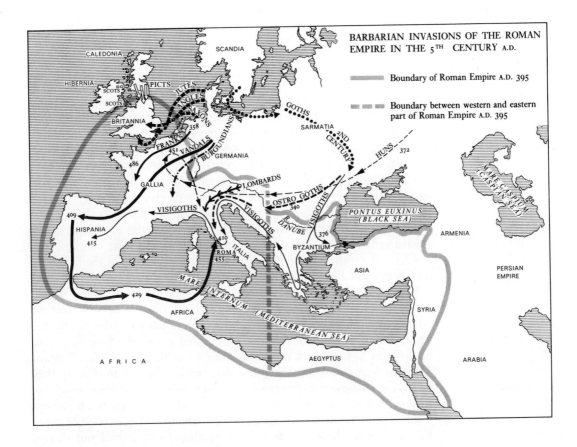

BARBARIAN INVASIONS OF THE ROMAN EMPIRE IN THE 5TH CENTURY A.D.

These nearest Germanic tribes began by fighting against Rome and ended by fighting for her. Outstanding warriors, they became recruited into the Roman armies, either as individuals or in groups. In the course of the third and fourth centuries A.D., many of them took their place within the Roman frontiers, and some of their leading soldiers rose to very high positions in the Roman armies. Long before the collapse of the Roman Empire in the West in the fifth century A.D., there was a partial 'take-over' of the Empire by the nearest Germanic tribes.

Barbarians within the Empire

As time went on the Roman Empire found it more and more difficult to resist these pressures. Things were not made easier by the constant struggle among the successful Roman generals to seize the imperial throne for themselves. From time to time a strong ruler like Diocletian (who made the last determined attempt to wipe out Christianity) reorganised the Empire and improved its chances of survival; and in the fourth century A.D. a very drastic change was made by Constantine the Great, the first Christian emperor. Recognising the unsuitability of Rome as a base from which to organise the defence of so vast an Empire, he founded a new capital much better placed to control Asia and south-east Europe. This was New Rome, or Constantinople, built around the old town of Byzantium on the Bosporus – a site dominating many

Roman counter-measures

routes leading east and west. This measure preserved the eastern half of the Roman Empire for another thousand years, but could not prevent the downfall of the western part.

In the last years of the fourth century and in the first half of the fifth, the Empire in the West finally succumbed. By A.D. 375 the brutal and barbaric Huns had reached South Russia, and with the Huns behind them the Goths pressed ever more strongly on the Roman defences. The Visigoths forced the Roman government to admit them within the frontiers as allies, and then under their King, Alaric, began to dominate the Empire. The Roman Empire became practically split into two halves, East and West; and the Emperors claiming authority in each part cheerfully employed barbarian leaders against the other. In A.D. 410 Alaric and his Visigoths sacked Rome; forty years later the Huns, under their dreaded leader Attila, swept across Europe and were checked only at Chalons, on the Marne, by a Roman general, Aetius, at the head of a mixed army of Romans and barbarians.

What happened to the Roman Empire in the West as a whole, happened on a smaller scale to Roman Britain. Britain had to withstand attacks by three main groups of enemies: the Picts from the North, the Scots (the inhabitants of Ireland, who raided across the Irish Sea), and the various Saxon tribes who came across the North Sea. The Romans did their best to counter these assaults. During the fourth century they built, for instance, forts round the coast from the Isle of Wight to Yorkshire to act as centres for local forces and as bases for naval patrols. They also put into service special ships which a writer called 'Pictae'. Fast and light, these vessels were camouflaged – their hull and rigging were painted green, and the rowers wore the same colour. In charge of this coast the Romans put an officer called the Count of the Saxon Shore, while another called the Duke of Britain became responsible for the defences against the Picts. Forts similar to those of the Saxon Shore were also built on parts of the Welsh coast – at Caernarvon and Holyhead for example – to keep off the invaders from Ireland.

As if there was not enough trouble from outside, there were also frequent internal disputes to weaken the Roman hold on Britain. More than once, rulers who were sent from Rome to govern Britain took up arms against the Imperial government. During one of these occasions, the Picts poured into the north of Roman Britain. They were driven out, but never subdued. In 368 the Picts, Scots and Saxons all attacked at the same time and succeeded in killing the Count of the Saxon Shore and destroying the army of the Duke of Britain. Again the Romans restored the situation; but in 383 another disloyal general took troops from Britain to fight against the Emperor, and the Picts once more breached Hadrian's Wall. This marked the end of it as a frontier defence. Stilicho, a general of barbarian descent sent from Rome to expel the raiders, based the defence of the north on the garrison at York, and left the Wall to its enemies.

In 400 a Roman court poet described triumphantly how Stilicho had

The Empire in the West over-run

The invaders of Britain

Roman defences

Concerted barbarian attack, A.D. 368

Hadrian's Wall abandoned, A.D. 383

The legions leave

Late Roman coins *These tiny fifth-century bronze coins, known as 'minimissimi', show how materials were becoming scarcer and the authorities in Britain poorer at that time. On the left, for comparison, a modern British half-penny of the pre-decimal coinage. More than fifty minimissimi are needed to cover this coin (right).*

freed Britain from her invaders. Only two years later, however, he had to withdraw forces to Italy to deal with the Gothic invasions there. These troops never returned to Britain. The remaining military forces in Britain then set up their own rulers, only for the last of these, another Constantine, to depart with several regiments to seek his fortune in Gaul. This left Britain almost defenceless. In 410 those who strove to carry on Roman rule sent an appeal to Honorius, the Emperor in the West. He was struggling himself against foes nearer home and answered that he could offer no further aid.

It may be that direct Roman rule was re-established for a few years around A.D. 430, but this cannot be proved. If it was, it was probably only in the south-eastern parts of the island. The Britons were left to defend themselves against attacks which gradually became more frequent and more overwhelming. When their appeals in 446 to the prefect in Gaul, Aetius, went unanswered, the centuries-old link with Rome was at last shattered. In the struggle against the barbarians the Britons would have no help from their former masters.

The end of Roman Britain

2 The Coming of the Anglo-Saxons

The 5th-century
countryside

To follow the Anglo-Saxon invasion of Roman Britain, we must forget the English countryside of today – the neat lines of fields and hedgerow, the parkland, fences, ditches and roads. Instead we must picture huge areas of swamp, marshland, forest and heath, pierced only by rough, narrow tracks. There were still brown bears in Northumbria when the Anglians arrived; wild boars provided food and sport; and the flocks and herds of the Midlands had to be protected against wolves. Among the great tracts of marshland which confronted the invaders were the fens of eastern England, the Pevensey and Romney marshes, and the marshland between Athelney and Glastonbury where King Alfred later took refuge from the Danes. The thick woodlands also held out dangers to the newcomers. There were few paths, and many wild beasts, in the forests of North Essex, the Weald, Sherwood, Galtres, Arden, Dean, and Wyre.

How the invaders
came

For the most part the Anglo-Saxon invaders entered the country by the river mouths. They moved inland either on the streams or by using tracks such as the Icknield Way which ran along the uplands above the heavy clay soils. They settled where the ground was clear, and the battles that they fought were not only against the Britons but also against the nature of the land. They came not in large armies but in boatloads, and their coming was spread over many years. Although the first great English historian, the monk Bede, placed the earliest settlement in A.D. 449, that date is by no means certain. What is certain is that invasion and settlement went on continuously but in a haphazard way during the second half of the fifth century and through most of the sixth. All told, it took about a century and a half for the greater part of Roman Britain to become England.

Evidence concerning
invasions

The details of this great movement are far from clear. They have to be pieced together, using such sources as archaeology (now powerfully aided by air photography), place-names, and a small number of written accounts.

Anglo-Saxon
accounts

The written sources may be Anglo-Saxon, British, or continental. On the Anglo-Saxon side there is no account of the invasions written at the time, but there are two later accounts which outline the traditional story of the settlement of Kent, Sussex and Wessex. The earlier of these is the *Ecclesiastical History of the English Nation* written by Bede in his monastery at Jarrow in the first half of the eighth century. It is possible

Bede's 'Ecclesiastical
History' (8th century)

that for his version of events he drew on some sixth-century annals which were also used by those who compiled the second great Anglo-Saxon account – *The Anglo-Saxon Chronicle* started during the reign of Alfred. The references in these Anglo-Saxon accounts to the years of invasion are scrappy, but they do provide some dates, some names, and some order of events.

Anglo-Saxon Chronicle (9th century onwards)

On the British side, the main piece of literary evidence is the work of a Welsh monk, St. Gildas, who lived during or very soon after the events of which he wrote. He seems to have been born towards the end of the fifth century and his greatest work, *The Overthrow of Britain*, was written around the middle of the sixth. It became the chief source on which Bede drew for his own later account. Gildas's intention was not really to write history but to attack the sins of his own people: the ferocities of the Saxons, he claimed, were God's punishment for British misdeeds. Nevertheless from Gildas a great deal can be learnt about the events that were taking, or had recently taken, place.

British accounts: Gildas: 'Overthrow of Britain' (6th century)

As a source of evidence, archaeology is probably more important than the written accounts for this early period, but it rarely provides precise dates or the exact order of events. Archaeology is the study of the material remains of the past and its value depends on the material available. On the British side there is very little: some Christian tombstones from the West country, a small number of tiny, badly-shaped coins, but nothing to give much shape to the story.

Evidence from archaeology

Archaeologists have of course excavated a number of towns and villas which flourished during the Roman period, but what these excavations reveal suggests on the whole slow disrepair and decay rather than Gildas's story of wholesale ravage and destruction. The Anglo-Saxon invaders did not like towns, and were not used to them. For long the newcomers built only of wood, and wooden buildings do not survive for any length of time. Hence the bulk of the archaeological evidence on the Anglo-Saxon side comes not from towns but from their cemeteries, from the objects that were buried with their owners: objects varying from a dish, a pot, or a brooch to the great treasure of the Sutton Hoo burial ship, probably the tomb of an East Anglian king of the sixth century.

From such remains we can, for instance, work out what were the earliest areas of settlement, but though we can place things in time-order the dates are usually vague. In the same way, the study of air-photographs and of place-names helps us to discover general trends, but not exact dates. Air photography often reveals, beneath the growing crops, the pattern of past settlements; while the study of place-names can often tell us, for example, where groups of Britons remained in areas generally settled by the invading tribes. From all these sources together the main outline of the story can be traced, even if most of the detail remains lacking or in dispute.

Evidence from air photography and place-names

Bede mentions three tribes as making up the invaders – the Angles, the Saxons, and the Jutes. He gives to each group special areas of

Angles, Saxons, and Jutes

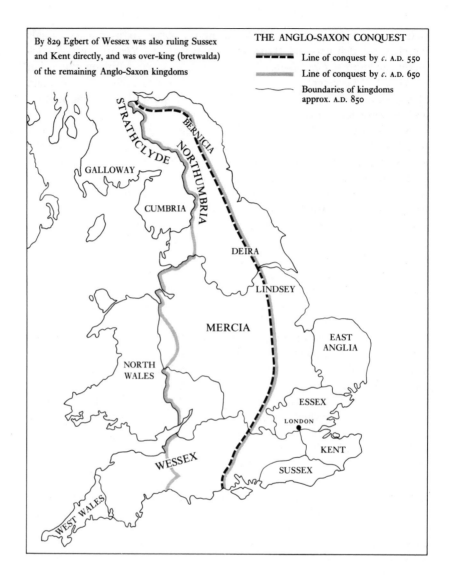

By 829 Egbert of Wessex was also ruling Sussex and Kent directly, and was over-king (bretwalda) of the remaining Anglo-Saxon kingdoms

THE ANGLO-SAXON CONQUEST
Line of conquest by *c.* A.D. 550
Line of conquest by *c.* A.D. 650
Boundaries of kingdoms approx. A.D. 850

settlement – and in so doing probably over-simplifies the story to make it fit in with the conditions of his own time. All these tribes came from the general area of north-west Germany. The Angles or Anglians, the most northerly of the three peoples, probably came originally from the Angeln district in Schleswig and from the neighbouring islands, but had moved south and had mingled with the Saxons: it is probable that there were Anglo-Saxons on the Continent before they came to Britain. The Jutes are more of a mystery; very little is known for certain about them, and it is not now generally thought that Jutland as a place-name has any connection with them. Bede writes that they settled in Kent, the

THE COMING OF THE ANGLO-SAXONS

Isle of Wight and southern Hampshire, and it is true that the archaeological material found there is very different from that found elsewhere:
the Kentish jewellery, for example, which can be seen in the British
Museum is of a quality found nowhere else in England, and the Kentish
system of land division and inheritance was very different from that
which existed in the rest of the country. In these matters the civilisation
of Kent was very similar to that of the Franks across the Channel and it
is possible that the Jutes, if they in fact existed as a separate tribe, came
from the Rhineland.

The Jutes and Kent

It is certainly true that in the middle of the fifth century there was a
general stirring of the tribes throughout Western Europe: the Roman
Empire was decaying and could not resist the pressure of the tribes
across its frontiers. Far to the east the Huns and others were beginning
to press to the west, so starting a chain reaction of tribal movement.
The tribes on the low-lying north German coast were troubled not
only by this pressure but also by the encroachments of the sea upon
their terpen, or mounds above sea-level, and by over-crowding of these
dry areas. For such tribes Britain, at first a place to raid and plunder,
became a place of refuge and of settlement: for in Britain the population
was very small, and there was good land to be had for the taking.

Causes of the
invasions

The invaders crossed the North Sea in slim, pointed, open-deck
boats, often of thirty oars. For landfall or entry into the country they
made great use of the rivers and inlets of the east coast – especially the
Thames, the Wash, and the Humber. According to Bede, who follows
Gildas in this, they did not come first as enemies. He tells us the story
of Vortigern, the British tribal chieftain who after the collapse of Roman
power extended his sway over much of south-east England. Troubled
by attacks from the Picts, he sought the help of some Angles, or Saxons,
to whom he offered in return a place of settlement. This was a frequent
practice in the closing era of the Roman Empire in the west, and Bede's
story is quite possibly true. The newcomers, according to Bede, arrived
in A.D. 449 in three warships and in due course helped to fight and beat
the Picts. The first leaders, records Bede, were said to have been two
brothers, Hengest and Horsa. Reinforcements then came across to swell
the Anglo-Saxon numbers; but very soon, not content with their
rewards, they began to attack parts of Vortigern's kingdom and to over-
run much of south-east England. Horsa, says Bede, fell in battle against
the British, who seem to have resisted more strongly in some places
than in others.

The first invasions:
Bede's version

A little later, records Bede (again following Gildas), a Romano-
Briton, Ambrosius Aurelianus, won a series of battles against the
Saxons; and from an account written by Nennius, a Welsh monk of the
ninth century, emerges the figure of the British leader whom the Middle
Ages later took as the pattern of chivalry – King Arthur. Around
Arthur's life was to be spun a web of legend and romance; he is sup-
posed to have fought and won twelve battles, and his name is linked
with many different parts of the country, including Scotland. It has been

suggested that Arthur's success was based on the organisation of a cavalry force against which the Saxons, fighting on foot, were powerless. His last victory, on or near the unidentified Mons Badonicus, probably took place somewhere between 490 and 515, and is thought to have checked the invaders for fifty years. During this time the Anglo-Saxons tightened their grip upon the parts of the country that they had already won, farmed the land, cleared new holdings, and mingled with the remaining Britons in these areas.

Anglo-Saxon advance resumed

Eventually the Anglo-Saxon settlers managed to advance again and in the end seven main Anglo-Saxon kingdoms – the Heptarchy, as it has been called – covered most of modern England and the Lothian area of Scotland. They were Kent, Sussex, Essex, East Anglia, Mercia, Wessex and Northumbria. Something has already been said about the settlement in Kent. Sussex, or the South Saxon kingdom, was established by Aelle and his three sons, who, we are told in the Chronicle, landed near Selsey Bill in 477 and in 491 defeated the last group of Britons holding out in Pevensey. Aelle and his sons had fought their way eastwards along the coast; and the kingdom of Sussex, isolated behind the forest of the Weald and hemmed in by marshland on the east and by the sea on the west, remained coastal and cut off from the rest of the country. The origins of Essex, the East Saxon kingdom, are obscure and the population remained thin because of the forest and marshland. The Middle Saxons (whence Middlesex) failed to establish themselves as an independent kingdom and became part of Essex, while Surrey became dependent first on Kent and then on the West Saxon kingdom – Wessex.

The main kingdoms: Sussex Kent

Essex

East Anglia Mercia

Farther north, on the eastern side of the island, the East Anglians formed some sort of group comprising the North Folk (Norfolk) and

The Sutton Hoo burial: The ship's outline *In 1939 excavation of an ancient barrow or earth burial mound at Sutton Hoo near Woodbridge, in Suffolk, revealed in the sand the outline of a ship – the timbers had all perished but most of the rusted iron nails and bolts remained in position. Within the ship—a great rowing or sailing vessel 80 feet long—had been placed a great variety of objects, ranging from weapons, jewellery and royal emblems to a musical instrument and household utensils, and many of these still survived in damaged form. It seems that the ship was dragged up overland and buried, as the tomb of an East Anglian king of the mid-seventh century, and that in accordance with pagan custom it was furnished with objects and possessions of the king for his use in the after life. No human remains were found, so presumably the king's body was not available for burial. Two other ship-burials of this kind have been discovered in England, and several in Scandinavia.*

the South Folk (Suffolk). In the centre of the country Mercia, also an Anglian area of settlement, was to become one of the chief kingdoms with its royal headquarters at Tamworth. It probably arose from two streams of invasion, one from the Wash along such rivers as the Welland and Soar, the other from the Humber and up the Trent valley.

There is still some dispute about the routes by which settlers reached the upper Thames valley at Dorchester, for here have been found the settlements from which probably grew the kingdom of Wessex. In the middle of the seventh century, however, the Mercians seized this area and the kings of Wessex eventually set up a capital in Winchester, much farther south.

Wessex

The last and most northerly kingdom, Northumbria, came to the fore in the seventh century. It consisted of two parts, Deira and Bernicia, the first of which was settled by the Anglians in the late fifth century; Bernicia, which extended as far north as the Forth, was later colonised from Deira. Northumbria lay entirely north of the Humber, which was the greatest dividing line between the Anglo-Saxon invaders. South of this river was Lindsey (Lincolnshire), at first independent, later absorbed by Mercia.

Northumbria (Deira and Bernicia)

By the end of the sixth century the broad pattern of the settlement was complete. Britons still kept their independence in the highland fastnesses and remote areas of the north and west, but those who remained elsewhere were gradually absorbed into the Anglo-Saxon groups which surrounded them. How long that process took is not known, but gradually from the turmoil there emerged a new civilisation – an Anglo-Saxon or English one – to replace the destroyed civilisation of Roman Britain.

The pattern of settlement completed (c. A.D. 700)

The Sutton Hoo burial: A drinking horn and a shoulder clasp *Among the objects recovered from the burial ship were the crushed remains of seven silver-mounted drinking horns – two large and five small. One of the larger ones, made from the horns of the huge and now extinct aurochs, is shown here after restoration. A prized hunting trophy of the Saxon warrior, it is over 3 feet long and holds no less than six quarts. Above it, one of a pair of decorative shoulder-clasps of curved shape, each, as shown above, hinged about a central pin. They are of gold, ornamented with enamel and coloured glass. The designs at the end are of interlinked boars, whose bodies are made from garnets. The designs on the top of the plates have much in common with the 'carpet' pattern of decoration found later in illuminated manuscripts.*

3 The Return of Christianity

The Anglo-Saxon
invaders

The Anglo-Saxon invaders were warlike men, trained from youth to a life of fighting and adventure. They crossed the seas in long, slim ships, probably dragon-prowed, the steersman with his oar standing on the right – the starboard (steerboard) side – high above the rowers, and their shields lining the sides of the vessel. The later Vikings or sea-raiders, the Danes and the Norwegians (or Norsemen) used similar ships and in them made long and dangerous voyages to Greenland and even North America.

During the fifth and sixth centuries, these bold men in their strong ships reached Britain in large numbers. A glimpse of their habits and beliefs may be obtained from their legends and their later poems. For

Evidence from
Beowulf

example in *Beowulf*, the great Anglo-Saxon poem which was composed from an existing story round about A.D. 700 but not written down for another 300 years, one may read how the young warrior Beowulf overcomes the monster Grendel, who is disturbing the king of the Danes in his great hall, and how later he fights Grendel's mother, a sea-monster, in a dwelling at the bottom of a lake. Finally, when Beowulf is a king and an old man, he falls defending his country against a fiery dragon. In the course of all this, it is possible to learn much about Anglo-Saxon society; about the king, absolute lord of all his followers; about the great halls in which were held the feasts and the councils; about the ale-drinking and the exchange of gifts and other courtesies; about the poet in the hall chanting verses in celebration of famous fights and battles; about the fears and superstitions of those who lived days of peril on stormy seas or in cold lands. Beowulf asked that his body should be burned on a pyre on a high barrow visible to seafarers; so would the hero find his way lighted to the next world by his fame in the life that he was leaving.

Overlordship of the
kingdoms

These warrior peoples spent most of their first century in Britain fighting, first against the Britons and then amongst themselves. Gradually one kingdom gained a kind of supremacy, at first over its nearest neighbours, then over most of the country. This overlordship tended to pass from kingdom to kingdom: Bede lists seven such overlords who claimed supremacy in England south of the Humber, beginning with Aelle of Sussex and continuing through kings of the West Saxons, Kent and the East Angles. Bede's list ends with the kings of the later Northumbrian supremacy – Edwin, Oswald and Oswiu. After them came the supremacy of Mercia and then of Wessex.

Later chronicles record the names applied to these overlords – Bret-walda or 'Britain-ruler' – and something of the kings themselves. They became rulers not simply because of their royal birth, but because they were thought suitable for the task, and were acclaimed so by the great men of the kingdom: the crown did not have to pass to their sons but usually went to the outstanding male within the royal family. Under the rule of kings appointed in this way the Anglo-Saxon settlements took shape. Meanwhile in the west the Britons lived their own lives, cut off by hatred and geography from the invaders and trying to avoid all contact with them.

'Bretwalda'

The Angles and the Saxons were pagan, as were most of the tribes that had helped to overthrow the Roman Empire in the west. They came from lands to which the Christian Church of the Empire had not yet sent missionaries. Something is known about the gods whom they worshipped, but not very much: undoubtedly they were gods to suit a warlike people. Woden (to the Scandinavian peoples, Odin) and Tiw were both war-gods, and Thunor (Thor) was the thunder-god. The first two gave their names to the days of the week, as did Frigg the wife of Woden. Woden was also given the name 'Grim' which means 'a masked one', and in this form his name can be found in the word 'Grims-dyke' by which ancient earthworks are known in various parts of the country. The names of the other gods can also be traced in place names and there is evidence of many centres of heathen worship: 'hearh', for example, meant 'hill-sanctuary' and can be traced in the place-name Harrow. Exactly how these gods were worshipped is a matter of debate, although there must have been shrines which were holy places and in which sacrifices took place to thank, or to beg the help of, the god. 'Giuli', which we call 'Yule', a festival at the turn of the year, seems to have been a time of special importance. Bede does not write very much about these matters; but other authors mention the Teutonic idea of Valhalla, the dwelling-place of the chosen, to which Woden gathered all those who fell in battle.

Anglo-Saxon religion

While these pagan cults were taking root in England, the Britons in their western sanctuaries carried on the Christian worship which had come to them during Roman times. They seem to have refused to have any direct contact with the Anglo-Saxon invaders, and made no effort to send missionaries to them. They did, however, send missionaries to other Celtic tribes, especially from Strathclyde. Just as St. Ninian, a Briton trained in Rome, had established a monastery at Whithorn on Wigtown Bay and converted the Picts of Galloway in the late fourth century, so in the sixth century St. Kentigern taught those living in the area where Glasgow now stands. British Christianity in Wales also produced great saints during the sixth century, men of godliness and devotion like St. David, the patron saint of Wales. Said to have been the son of a Welsh prince, David became archbishop of southern Wales and founded the great religious centre in Pembrokeshire, later called after him.

British Christianity

Missions to Celtic tribes:

St. Ninian and the Picts

St. David in Wales

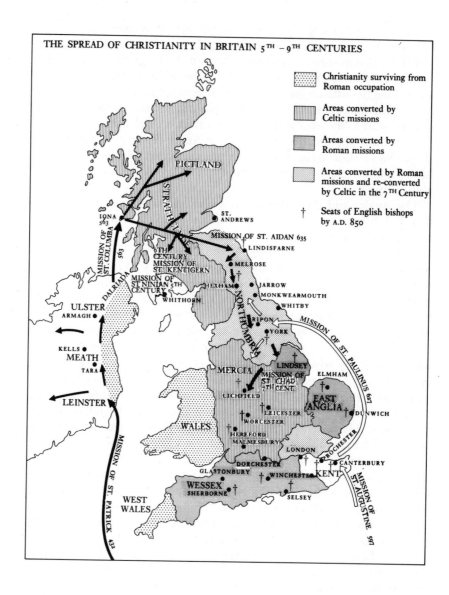

THE SPREAD OF CHRISTIANITY IN BRITAIN 5TH – 9TH CENTURIES

St. Patrick and the
conversion of Ireland
(5th century)

The man who converted many of the Irish during the fifth century
has become recognised as the patron saint of Ireland. St. Patrick, the
son of a romanised Briton, was seized as a youth by Scots raiding from
Ireland and carried off into captivity. He escaped and fled to Italy and
the south of France, became a priest, and then returned to Ireland as a
bishop and missionary. For thirty years he worked among his former
captors founding monasteries such as that of Armagh, and carrying the
Christian faith into areas it had not reached before. He seems to have
introduced Latin into Ireland as the language of the services, and
altogether he built up a flourishing Church that was later to make Ireland one of the great intellectual centres of Europe.

A Saxon crypt at Repton *This crypt, or underground chapel, was part*
of a monastery probably built around 700, and later rebuilt around
1000 after being largely destroyed by the Danes. Though only 17ft
Iona *The site of St Columba's Monastery, now occupied by the recently rebuilt*
Iona Cathedral.
Mercian kings were buried here. The crypt became forgotten after the
dissolution of the monasteries under Henry VIII, and was rediscovered
in the eighteenth century when a workman digging a grave fell into it.

The Irish church in its turn sent out missionaries, one of the most
famous being St. Columba, who after founding churches in Ireland
went to Iona, off the west coast of Scotland. Of royal birth, Columba
seems to have quarrelled with, and possibly even fought against, his
ruler in Irish Dalriada; at all events, in 563 he left there with a small
band of companions and settled in Scottish Dalriada, in the island of
Iona. There he founded a monastery whence he and his fellow monks

Irish missions:
St. Columba on Iona
(A.D. 563)

went out teaching and preaching over much of Scotland. It seems that among his triumphs was to convert the Pictish king Bruce and to persuade him to stay his hand against the Scots of Dalriada. Among the miracles with which he is credited, was to rid the river Ness of a monster.

Different practices of Roman and Celtic Christianity

Unfortunately the Church in these remote Celtic areas grew somewhat apart from the Church elsewhere. It did not adopt different beliefs, but it spread largely in the form of separate monastery and mission centres, whereas the main church developed on more tightly organised lines under much closer control by bishops, headed of course by the Bishop of Rome – the pope. As the Roman Empire in the West collapsed, this close organisation of the main Church from Rome helped to provide a framework for civilised life, and to carry some of the better principles of the Empire into the 'dark ages' of barbarian rule.

The Benedictine Rule

The Roman Church also gained strength at the end of the fifth century when St. Benedict of Subiaco, in Southern Italy, drew up his Rule of monastic life. This Rule (a fairly lengthy set of principles and regulations in seventy-three sections) laid down among other things that monks should take the vows of poverty, chastity, obedience, and stability (i.e., that they would remain bound to the monastery for life). A monastery was to be a self-contained community – though it might offer hospitality to travellers – and the monks' day was to be occupied by religious services, periods of study and meditation, and manual work. Benedict's Rule was widely adopted and a monastery he founded, Monte Cassino, became the model which was copied throughout Europe. But between these developments abroad and the church in Ireland stood the barrier of the barbarian invaders. The result was that the Celtic Church came to have certain practices different from those of the mother body. Irish monasteries were not run in the Benedictine way; the bishops were fewer and less powerful than on the Continent, and acted more independently of Rome; and there were differences in details such as the type of tonsure or haircut laid down for the priests. When the two traditions of Christianity began to meet in the same places there was bound to be some conflict between them.

Gregory the Great

In 590 Gregory I – Gregory the Great – was elected pope. The first monk to become head of the Church, he was a man of outstanding ability and energy, who built up territory for the Church in Italy and did all he could to make other Churches acknowledge the supremacy of Rome. Among many other things, he was very zealous about missionary activities. Bede relates how, some time in the 570s, Gregory had seen some English boy-slaves exposed for sale in Rome, and how he had been moved to try to convert the English peoples to Christianity. Whether this story is true or not, Gregory nourished the idea of conversion for a long time: he once set off on a mission himself, only to be recalled by the pope at the time. Finally, when he himself became pope, he gave

The mission of St. Augustine, 597

orders for a group of monks under a leader named Augustine to set off for England. Its members, who according to Bede could not speak English, were not at all happy about their task; and while still in Gaul they sent Augustine back to Rome to ask the pope to excuse them from it. But Gregory told them they should continue, and early in 597 – having picked up interpreters abroad – they were received at the court of Aethelberht, king of Kent.

This king's wife, Bertha, the daughter of the king of the Franks in Paris, was already a Christian, and she and her chaplain were using the little church of St. Martin in Canterbury for their worship. Aethelberht allowed Augustine and his companions to live and preach in Canterbury; and very soon, 'induced by the unspotted life of these holy men, and their delightful promises, which by many miracles, they proved to be most certain', the king agreed to be baptised. Thousands of his subjects rapidly followed suit, and by 604 a second Kentish church had been built at Rochester. To this area Augustine, whom Gregory had made archbishop, appointed a separate bishop. Meanwhile the mission, re-inforced by fresh priests from the Continent, carried its work beyond the boundaries of Kent into the lands of the East Angles and the East Saxons; and in East Saxon territory, in London, a church was built on the highest piece of ground and dedicated to St. Paul.

Augustine died in about 605 and was buried at Canterbury. With his death the churches that he had set up, and the monastery of St. Peter and St. Paul at Canterbury, almost collapsed; for his successors had to deal with new rulers who were pagan. That Christianity in England recovered and took on a new lease of life was largely the result of a second mission which in 625 went from the Kentish church into Northumbria.

The King of Northumbria at this time was Edwin, after whom Edinburgh may be named, and in 625 he married Aethelberht's daughter Aethelburh. She took with her, when she travelled north, a newly appointed bishop named Paulinus, who had earlier been sent by Gregory to join St. Augustine. Paulinus succeeded in baptising Edwin and many of his followers, but only in 627 after long discussions and the calling of a formal council by the king. At this council the pagan high-priest, Coifi, pointed out that as he himself had not prospered greatly from serving the old religion, there might be good reason to change! His speech was followed by that of another of the king's chief men, who offered a poetic comparison: he compared the life of man on earth to the flight of a sparrow through a lighted hall at night, coming from the unknown and returning to it. If the teaching of Paulinus, said this counsellor, could lighten the darkness of man's unknown, it would seem fit to be followed. Thus Bede recounts the story and elsewhere he tells of Paulinus's missionary work throughout Northumbria and Lindsey, giving an eye-witness's description of him – 'a man tall of stature, a little stooping, with black hair and a thin face, a hooked and thin nose, his aspect both venerable and awe-inspiring'.

Once again, however, success was not to be lasting. In 632 Edwin fell in battle near Hatfield Chase against the heathen Penda of Mercia, who was fighting in alliance with Cadwallon, King of Gwynedd in Wales

The conversion of Kent

Christianity in East Anglia and Essex

Relapse in Kent

Paulinus and the conversion of Northumbria. Edwin's Council, 627

Defeat of Edwin by Penda of Mercia, 632: set-back to Christianity

– one of the remaining regions under British rule. Penda then became King of Mercia, and with his ally invaded and laid waste much of Northumbria. This violently set back Christianity there, and Paulinus and Queen Aethelburh fled to Kent.

For a year the Northumbrian regions of Deira and Bernicia fell apart, but in 634 a new leader was able to re-unite them. This was Oswald, nephew of Edwin and son of a previous king; his small army defeated and killed Cadwallon at Rowley Burn, near Hexham. According to Bede, Oswald, who was a Christian, raised a wooden cross just before the battle began and held it with his own hands, while earth was piled round the base to keep it firm. His army then knelt and prayed before it. From this, the place of the victory became known as Heavenfield; and near the Roman Wall to the north of Corbridge a great wooden cross has been placed in modern times to mark the site of the battle.

Oswald and his brother Oswiu had recently returned from exile. When forced to flee from Northumbria they had taken refuge on the island of Iona, off the west coast of Scotland, where St. Columba had set up his monastery. There they had been won over to Christianity; and when Oswald returned to Northumbria he asked for missionaries from Iona – from the Celtic Church – to come into his kingdom. The greatest of these was the monk and bishop St. Aidan, who fixed his headquarters at Lindisfarne, on Holy Island, a place cut off from the Northumbrian coast at high tide. He was described by Bede, who considered the Celtic churchmen to be somewhat in error, as 'a man of the greatest gentleness, godliness and moderation, and possessing the zeal of God, although not entirely according to knowledge'.

This time Christianity had come to stay, and Oswald's work was carried on by Oswiu after the death of the former in battle in 642 against Penda of Mercia. Oswiu at first succeeded to only one half of the Northumbrian kingdom, but by 654 he was able to defeat all his enemies including Penda who was slain in a battle near Leeds, and to establish his rule not only over all Northumbria but over part of Mercia as well. Under him, Christianity of the Celtic tradition spread slowly southwards. Mercia was converted by two brothers Cedd and Chad, and Cedd worked also among the East Saxons, who had turned from the Christianity brought to them earlier.

The renewed spread of Christianity soon brought into conflict the missionaries from the Celtic centres and those who had been sent directly from Rome or Canterbury. Though not the most important, one of the most irksome differences between the Celtic and the Roman practices was that they did not celebrate the greatest Christian festival, Easter, at quite the same time. In an age when Christian worship was coming to mean so much, this could be very inconvenient; and the problem hit home to Oswiu, since he followed the Celtic custom and his wife the Roman. To discuss this and other differences and to settle the growing disputes among the clergy of Northumbria, many of whom had taken to the Roman ways, Oswiu in 663 called a Synod, or council, at

Revival of Christianity in Northumbria under Oswald

St. Aidan at Lindisfarne

Defeat of Penda by Oswiu, 654

Conversion of Mercia: SS. Cedd and Chad

Clash between Roman and Celtic practices

Synod of Whitby, 663 (or 664)

An early Saxon church *St Peter-on-the-Wall, Bradwell-on-Sea, Essex. This little church was probably built as far back as 654–664 by St Cedd, who was then bishop of the East Saxons. Cedd had originally been sent from Lindisfarne to convert the Mercians, but later worked among the East Saxons and set up the first churches in Essex. This one, far out on the Blackwater estuary, he built largely of bricks and other materials from the old Roman fortress of Othona nearby. What we see here is only the nave of the church – in its original form it also had a chancel with a rounded end – an apse. In the eighteenth century the building became a barn, but it was restored to church use in 1920.*

Whitby, the site of a noted 'double' monastery, i.e. one with male and female sections. Those who attended the Synod included Bishop Colman of York and Bishop Cedd on the Celtic side, while the main spokesman for the Roman traditions was the Roman-trained Wilfrid, then abbot of a monastery at Ripon. Wilfrid was a man of great power who later had a stormy career as bishop of York – whence he was expelled, to travel afar in England and North Germany, ceaselessly preaching the faith and setting up fresh Christian centres. At Whitby his arguments won the day, and Oswiu announced that he accepted them. After this, it was not long before the Roman practices became standard throughout the English kingdoms.

St. Wilfrid

In 669 the pope appointed Theodore of Tarsus, who had done outstanding work for the Church in Asia Minor, to be Archbishop of Canterbury. He became the greatest organiser of the Church in England. Bede says that he made a tour of all the Anglo-Saxon kingdoms, carrying out reforms and giving orders about Easter and the monastic rule. Certainly he seems to have established the superior authority of Canterbury over all the other Sees. He summoned and presided over Church councils – that at Hertford in 672 was the first to include Church leaders from all the chief English kingdoms – and by the time of his death he had brought unity to the English Church. Celtic influences still remained – as may be seen from the fact that the great shrine and cathedral of Durham grew up round the final resting-place of the bones of St. Cuthbert, the seventh-century bishop of Lindisfarne. Nevertheless, by the eighth century the authority of Rome was generally recognised, even though the Celtic practices lingered in Scotland and Wales for two centuries or more. A few districts apart, the whole island was now Christian, and its people were members of a great Church covering most of Europe. To this body, the Church with the pope at Rome as its head, Britain was to owe most of her advances in civilisation for many centuries to come.

Theodore of Tarsus, Archbishop of Canterbury, 669–90

Church organisation and unity

4 The Viking Invaders and King Alfred

The first Viking raids

At some date between 786 and 802 three ships put in to shore at Portland, now in the county of Dorset, but then in the kingdom of the West Saxons. They were of a type not seen by the Anglo-Saxons in Britain for many years: long, slim, shallow, dragon-prowed with shields fixed to the bulwarks, and each vessel perhaps carrying a single, brightly-striped sail. Such ships the Angles and Saxons themselves had once used. Settled in Britain, however, most of them had forgotten their seacraft and become farmers, clearing the ground and carving out holdings from the forest.

From the three ships there landed armed men wearing helmets and speaking a strange language. When the king's reeve or chief official from Dorchester rode up to ask their business, they attacked and killed him. Then they put to sea again, carrying back to their homeland tales of an undefended coastline which promised easy booty. Such was one of the first recorded Viking raids on Western Europe.

The same few years around the end of the eighth century witnessed other isolated attacks, notably on the coasts of what are now Northumberland, Scotland, Ireland and Wales. Monasteries such as those of Lindisfarne (in A.D. 793) and Iona (in 802 and 806) were raided and plundered, the monks killed or carried off as captives. From this time on, fear of the 'wicking' men grew as their ships sailed farther and farther, seeking riches from places as distant as Labrador and Constantinople, Seville and Novgorod.[1]

The Viking routes:

– the Swedes

– the Norwegians

The Vikings came from all parts of the Baltic lands, and especially from the countries we call Sweden, Norway and Denmark. They followed three main routes, those from Sweden tending to move eastwards while the others moved west. To the east, the Swedes attacked the Slav territory of what was later called Russia. To the west, the Norwegians, who were the first to attack the British Isles, made perhaps the most adventurous journeys, for they voyaged to Iceland, Greenland, and North America. Their main route took them round the North of Scotland by way of the Orkneys and Shetlands, which they occupied at an early date. Then they moved down to the Irish Sea, occupying the Hebrides and much of the Western Scottish coast, landing on the Isle of Man, and making settlements in Ireland, where Norse kings founded the

---

[1] The word Viking has been derived from two words, either the Old English *wic*, a camp, or else *vik*, a creek or inlet. The word has nothing to do with 'kings'.

cities of Dublin, Cork, Limerick, and Wicklow. They also raided the coastlands of north-west England and of Wales. Their movements can still be traced through place-names: off the Pembrokeshire coast, for example, the two islands of Skokholm and Skomer gained their names in this time of Norse invasion.

The third route, that followed by the Danes, took the Vikings to the east and south coasts of England, to Ireland, and to the north-west coasts of Europe. Later, the settlement of large hosts under famous chiefs led to the establishment of two big Danish-ruled areas or Dane-laws, one in eastern England, the other in Normandy.

– the Danes

Cart from the Oseberg ship *The cart found in the Oseberg ship seems to have been used for religious purposes. It is 5·5 metres long, including the shafts, and 1·5 metres wide. It is richly carved with human and animal figures, probably representing scenes from the Scandinavian myths.*

A Viking ship reconstructed *This, the most spectacular of the three or four Viking ships to be recovered, was found and excavated at Oseberg on Oslo Fiord in 1904. It dates from about 800. It had been covered by a burial mound, and was in many thousands of small distorted pieces. Among the articles found with the ship were ship's accessories such as oars, together with a cart, sleighs, kitchen utensils, beds, tents and the skeletons of oxen, horses (at least ten) and women (two). The ship itself, made largely of oak, was about 21 metres long and nearly 6 metres wide (at its broadest point). It would have held about 35 men, and was of a kind suitable only for coastal cruising in fine weather. Perhaps it was the state vessel of a Viking chieftain.*

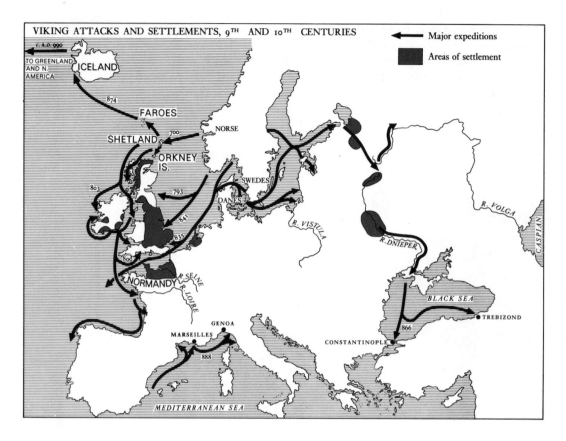

VIKING ATTACKS AND SETTLEMENTS, 9TH AND 10TH CENTURIES

Major expeditions

Areas of settlement

Causes of Viking expeditions

It is not possible to give one simple explanation of why the Vikings left their own lands in search first of plunder and later of new homes. There may have been famine, and there was certainly a shortage of easily worked land. To take part in an expedition of this kind became, too, almost a part of the education of Scandinavian youth – something in which he gained experience of fighting and qualified as a true man. Moreover, at the beginning of the ninth century Charlemagne's troops were campaigning against the pagan German tribes, and in the course of their activities they came near to the southern borders of Denmark. All these things made for an unsettled state of affairs; but in addition the habit of raiding caught on, especially when it bought success. After the defeat of the Frisian fisher tribes by Charlemagne, there were few ships capable of opposing the Viking craft: they held undisputed command of the seas and could go where they liked. Out of raids which became more and more frequent grew the idea of finding fresh homes in lands which seemed rich and fairly empty, and so later the great hosts settled down to farm and to trade in the territories they had invaded.

Eighth-century England: the dominance of Mercia

In the mid-eighth century, before these raids began, the leading position among the Anglo-Saxon kingdoms had passed to Mercia. This saw its greatest days during the reign of Offa II. His power was such

The Emperor Charlemagne *This bronze statu-ette, from the Carnavalet Museum, Paris, dates from Charlemagne's own time or shortly after-wards. Charlemagne (Charles the Great), King of the Franks, became also King of the Lombards and ruled a territory which covered the modern France, Belgium, Holland, Germany west of the Rhine, and most of Italy. His favourite capital was at Aachen (Aix-la-Chapelle), in Germany near the Belgian border. On Christmas Day 800 Pope Leo III crowned him Roman Emperor, thereby reviving a Roman Empire in the West – the organisation which came to be called the Holy Roman Empire. A great ruler, Charlemagne was the dominant figure in Western Europe in his time, and gave great encouragement to art and education (e.g., by attracting to his service the scholar Alcuin from York). Strongly religious, he imposed the death penalty for such violations of Church law as eating meat on Friday. At one church, he arranged for 400 monks and clergy to pray continually for his salvation, working in three shifts night and day.*

that he even disposed of land in Kent and Sussex without referring to the local kings. For a large part of his reign he dominated England south of the Humber; and when one of his daughters married the King of Northumbria, his influence spread there too. From calling himself 'Rex Merciorum' (King of the Mercians) in his earliest charters, he began to use in 774 the title 'Rex Anglorum' (King of the English). Moreover his fame extended to the Continent, where he negotiated with Charlemagne on almost equal terms, and made a commercial agreement between the two realms. In Rome, too, he made his wishes felt; resenting the supremacy in Church matters of Canterbury, in the kingdom of Kent, he persuaded the pope to agree to the creation of a new arch-bishopric at Lichfield, in Mercia. Perhaps the most striking evidence of his power, however, was the building of Offa's Dyke, the great earth-work which marked the western boundaries of his kingdom and enabled his soldiers to keep watch over Wales beyond. Offa's Dyke ran for over a hundred miles through the Welsh borderlands; and seventy miles of it in one fashion or another still survive – a monument to his authority and achievement.

The glory of Mercia faded under Offa's successors, and supremacy passed to Wessex by the victory of Egbert of Wessex over the Mercians at the battle of Ellendun, near Swindon, in 825. Egbert went on to

Offa II

The rise of Wessex under Egbert – Ellendun, 825

dominate all southern England, linking Kent, Surrey and Sussex with Wessex, and then in 829 to conquer Mercia itself and proclaim himself 'Rex Merciorum'. Northumbria too at this time acknowledged his overlordship. These northern successes, however, were short-lived. Mercia rapidly recovered its independence, and Egbert's lasting conquests proved to be Kent and the adjoining provinces, and – despite later revolts – the British stronghold of Cornwall.

Danish raids
intensified

After the year 833, when Charlemagne's empire began to fall apart owing to the quarrels of his successor Louis I and Louis' sons, the Danes were more and more tempted to descend on western Europe by the lack of serious opposition. Their raids across the North Sea became more frequent, better organised, and longer lasting. In 835 came the first landing in England to be undoubtedly made by Danes rather than Norwegians. 'In this year', records the Anglo-Saxon Chronicle, 'heathen men ravaged Sheppey'. During the next thirty years, there were more than a dozen such recorded invasions, and doubtless many more that were unrecorded.

Danes winter in
England, 850

Landing of the
'Great Army', 865

During the year 850, the Danish invaders for the first time wintered in south-eastern England, in Thanet. Fifteen years later there arrived the first great host which sought not only plunder but lasting conquest and settlement. For ten years the Great Army, as the Saxons called it, terrorised the land; moving across the country on horses which they seized in East Anglia, fighting battles wherever the English mustered a force to meet them, and setting up subject kings in the areas which they conquered. Northumbria, Mercia and East Anglia (whose King Edmund, killed or executed by the Danes in 870, was soon revered as a martyr) all came under their control, and were divided up amongst them.

The Danes attack
Wessex

Ashdown, 871

The only kingdom able to resist continuously was Wessex. By 870 the Danes were at Reading, and pressing further west; but in the following year, which saw eight or nine battles, they suffered at least one big defeat, at Ashdown in Berkshire. This was the work of the Wessex forces under King Aethelred and his younger brother Alfred. Shortly afterwards Aethelred died, leaving sons who were still only boys; and to Alfred, now acclaimed king, fell the hard task of holding off the fierce invaders.

Succession of Alfred,
871

Alfred's youth

King Alfred seems to have been one of the most able and admirable rulers in the whole of English history. Born at Wantage in 849, he was twice taken on pilgrimage to Rome as a small boy, and this experience no doubt gave him a broader outlook than that of many rulers of his time. He loyally supported his three brothers, who all wore the crown of the West Saxons before him, and when he succeeded to the throne at the age of twenty-two he was already a tried warrior and statesman. All his determination and skill in battle, however, could not at first drive the Danes from his much-harried kingdom. To free the territory of Wessex, he was also obliged to buy them off with a sum of money

The Great Army
splits, 874

– *Danegeld*, as such payments later became called.

In 874 the Danes' Great Army at last split. While part of the host ravaged Northumbria and Strathclyde or settled in Yorkshire, the other half remained to trouble the Midlands and the south. In 876 its leader Guthrum left East Anglia and broke right through Wessex to Wareham and Poole, where he was soon joined by fellow-Danes from France, Wales and Ireland. Eventually Alfred managed to overcome this threat, and the Danes departed from his kingdom. Most of their army then occupied themselves in carving up Mercia. Guthrum, however, remained with a force at Gloucester, near the Wessex border; and from Gloucester in the opening days of 878 he suddenly struck south. A swift move took him to Chippenham, in the heart of Alfred's kingdom, and large areas of Wessex fell into his hands.

Guthrum in South Wessex, 876

Guthrum attacks again, 878

This was the crisis of Alfred's reign. Though for a time almost powerless, he refused to surrender, and withdrew into the Somerset-shire marshland. Later, after other Wessex forces had beaten off a Danish landing on the North Devon coast, Alfred established himself on the Somersetshire 'island' of Athelney, some forty feet higher than the surrounding swamps. Here he managed, by secret contacts with distant parts of Wessex, to organise a fresh campaign; and here legend – but not history – tells us that one day, musing over his plans in a hut, he allowed the cakes to burn.[1]

Alfred at Athelney

It was from this hiding-place that in the spring of 878 Alfred emerged to link up with forces secretly mustered from various parts of his king-dom. At 'Ethandun', on the Salisbury plain probably near the modern village of Edington, the two armies clashed, and Alfred won a great victory. Pursuing the Danes to their camp, he blockaded them there, forcing them to accept humiliating terms. Guthrum agreed to be baptised and to lead his forces from Wessex. Shortly afterwards the ceremony took place, with Alfred standing as Guthrum's godfather and later feasting with him at Wedmore. In the summer Guthrum and his men then departed for Mercia and finally East Anglia.

Ethandun, 878

Wedmore

Eight years later, after fruitless Danish attacks from other directions followed by a West Saxon occupation of London in 886, Alfred and Guthrum made a peace laying down a boundary between Saxon England and the Danish territory or 'Danelaw'. It ran along the Thames, then up the Lea, and then in a straight line to Bedford, and so along the Ouse to Watling Street. To the south and west of this line the land was under the control of the king of Wessex, for there was no one to rival his power.

Boundary treaty with Guthrum, 886

Once again before the end of Alfred's reign a Danish host came from the sea, some 300 ships crossing the Channel from Boulogne. The Danish settlers already in England helped these new invaders, even if

---

[1] The story probably derives from twelfth-century sources connected with St. Neot, who lived in the century after Alfred. St. Neot apparently told how Alfred, unrecog-nised in a cottage, had been bidden by the housewife to turn over the loaves. Later this developed into the 'burning the cakes' story and in this form it was inserted in 1574 into the first printed life of Alfred – the life probably written in Alfred's own reign by his servant Bishop Asser.

The Alfred jewel *This gold and enamel jewel, found at Athelney in Somerset in the seventeenth century, is now in the Ashmolean Museum, Oxford. It probably dates from around 880–900 and it bears an Anglo-Saxon inscription meaning 'Alfred ordered me to be made'.*

Further Danish invasion, 892–6

rather half-heartedly, and this enabled them to raid deep into Mercia, which the ealdorman Aethelred, married to one of Alfred's daughters, was now holding in allegiance to Alfred. For four years the Danes raided different parts of the country from their base in Essex. Finally, however, Alfred forced them from their camp on the River Lea, probably by diverting the course of the river. In the following year, these new invaders left the country.

Strengthening of Wessex defences

Alfred could not have saved his kingdom from the Danes had he not reorganised and strengthened the Wessex military forces. Grasping one of the main principles of island defence, that it is better, and often easier, to prevent an enemy from landing than to defeat him when he has landed, he built a fleet. Earlier Wessex kings had owned naval vessels, but Alfred seems to have built larger numbers of them and used them to much greater effect. Some of them were also, according to the Anglo-Saxon Chronicle, of his own design:

Alfred's navy

'Then King Alfred ordered long ships to be built to counter the Danish ships: they were twice as long as the Danish light ships. Some had sixty oars, and some had even more. They were swifter, steadier, and higher than the others. They were shaped neither in the Frisian manner nor in the Danish, but as it seemed to him that they might be most useful.'

The 'burhs'

Inland, Alfred greatly strengthened the kingdom by building up a series of garrison centres, fortified places or 'burhs' as they were called. Sometimes they were built on the sites of Roman fortresses, as at Bath, Winchester, and Chichester; but generally they were created according to the lie of the land as at Wallingford, Cricklade, Shaftesbury, and Oxford. All told, there were finally about thirty of these, most of them near the kingdom's frontiers. In time of need, folk from the surrounding countryside could take shelter in these burhs, the garrisons of which

✝ ÐEOS BOC SCEAL TO WIOGORA CEASTRE ·:·

ÆLFRED kyning hateð gretan Wærferð biscep his wordum luf-
lice 7 freondlice · 7 ðe cyðan hate ðæt me com swiðe oft on ge-
mynd · hwelce wiotan iu wæron giond angel cynn · ægðer ge godcundra
hada ge woruldcundra · 7 hu gesæliglica tida ða wæron giond angel
cynn · 7 hu ða kyningas ðe ðone onwald hæfdon ðæs folces gode 7 his
ærendwrecum hersumedon · 7 hie ægðer ge hiora sibbe · ge hiora

Alfred's translation of 'Pastoral Care' This is the beginning of Alfred's translation
into Anglo-Saxon of Pope Gregory's work on Pastoral Care. The words in
capitals on the top line mean 'This book is for Worcester'. The manuscript is now
in the Bodleian Library, Oxford.

were mainly provided by residents and local land-holders in proportion
to the amount of land they held. To some extent this imitated the Danes'
own custom of building a fortified strong-point as a base from which
to mount raiding parties.

Besides building burhs, Alfred reorganised the *fyrd*, or general
fighting force in which all the peasantry were liable to serve at call.
Owing to the needs of agriculture, the normal liability was for a very
short period of service and for local defence only; but Alfred secured
longer service, and at greater distances from the men's homes, by
calling up only half of this body at a time. 'The King', says the Anglo-
Saxon Chronicle, 'divided his forces into two parts, so that half were
always at home and half in the field, not counting those men whose duty
it was to garrison the burhs.' Other features of Alfred's work in defence
included strengthening the authority of his thegns or nobles (many of
whom provided military service and fighting men as a condition of
land-holding), and greatly increasing the use of horses to make parts of
his army more mobile. By means such as these Alfred created a military
system which, primitive and clumsy though it still was, the Danes could
not overcome.

Reorganisation of fyrd

Horses

The special glory of Alfred's reign, however, was that, despite the
long and desperate struggle to preserve Wessex from the Danes, the
king still gave constant thought and care to matters other than warfare.
He firmly supported the Church, the main civilising influence of the
time, and was passionately eager to restore the culture of Wessex to the
level of before the Danish invasions. Well-educated clergy and leading
men were, he thought, the first need, so he persuaded a number of distinguished scholars from west Mercia and the Continent to come into
his kingdom and act as teachers. One of these, Bishop Asser, wrote a
life of the king which is the most detailed source of first-hand in-

Alfred's cultural achievements

Education

Translation into
Anglo-Saxon

*The Anglo-Saxon
Chronicle*

formation about him.[1] Having learnt Latin from Asser, Alfred also encouraged, supervised or took part in the translation of several Latin works into Anglo-Saxon. These included two works of religious instruction by St. Gregory and the *Ecclesiastical History* of Bede. *The Anglo-Saxon Chronicle*, which outlined the history of England till Alfred's time and was kept up for some 250 years afterwards, also appears to date from his reign, though what share the king had in starting or encouraging it is uncertain. In his last years Alfred was concerned with the translation from the Latin of two famous works of philosophy.

Alfred's legal code

To help keep order in his kingdom and in the areas outside Wessex under his control, Alfred issued his own Code or system of laws, based mainly on earlier codes of Wessex, Kent and Mercia. His main intention, like that of most rulers for centuries to come, was not to frame new laws, but to remove contradictions and points of doubt and to declare clearly what the law was. In his preface to the Code he wrote:

I, then, Alfred, King, gathered these laws together and commanded many of those to be written which our forefathers held, those which to me seemed good; and many of those which seemed to me not good, I rejected them by the advice of my Councillors and ordained otherwise; and in other cases I have ordered changes to be made. I dared not be so bold as to set down many of my own in writing, for it was unknown to me how that would please those that should come after us. But of those laws dating from the time of Ine or Offa or Ethelbert, I gathered together here such as seemed to me best, and the others I rejected. Then I, Alfred, king of the West Saxons, showed all these to my Councillors, and they then said that it pleased them all to observe them.

Alfred's character

Alfred seems to have been a man of most attractive character. He served his brothers loyally before becoming king himself, and was in turn loyally served by his own family and others. Brave in battle, he was merciful afterwards: no wanton massacres stain his name. Though acknowledged as a leader even beyond the bounds of his own kingdom, he was modest and fully prepared to work at tasks alongside men of lesser rank. His practical nature showed itself not only in his military reforms, but also in such details as the invention of a candle-clock and a reading lantern, and in the way that he inserted homely examples into the rather high-flown texts of the classical authors he helped to translate. There have been few kings in England who gave to their subjects so fine an example of common sense, conscientiousness, and civilised behaviour.

Alfred has been called the English Charlemagne, and many of his achievements can be compared with those of the great emperor of the West. Not only did he save the English civilisation of his day, but he also gave it new strength. By the time he died in 899 he had built a firm base from which his successors could advance to the reconquest of the Danelaw and the building up of a united, Christian England.

[1] Or so it is generally considered. Some scholars, however, think the work to be an eleventh-century forgery. The earliest known manuscript, which is thought to have been written after 1000, was burnt in the eighteenth century.

5 The Supremacy of Wessex

Alfred had saved Wessex, but he left to his successors no direct authority north of the Thames. They took it as their task to extend West Saxon rule over the lands conquered or dominated by the Danes. So well did they succeed that by 955 a single kingdom stretched from the Channel to the Forth – a kingdom in which all peoples and all lesser rulers recognised the supremacy of the king of Wessex.

The extension of West Saxon supremacy

This result was achieved only by half a century of patient effort, in the face of strong resistance from both Danes and Norsemen. The Danish armies had settled down on the land, retaining much of their military organisation but turning from war to farming and trade. They had split into various sections, who between them controlled eastern and much of central England, and they could not be subdued in one campaign. By stages, however, the rulers of Wessex pushed their frontier northwards and compelled the Danes group by group to recognise West Saxon supremacy.

A long task:

– against the Danes

As they moved north, the English came up against another enemy – the Norsemen. From the beginning of the tenth century Norwegians were sailing across from their first settlements in Ireland to north-west England. They occupied parts of the Wirral, Lancashire, and the Lake District, and they set up a Norse kingdom in York. These Norsemen were hostile to English and Danes alike. Not until 954, with the death of Eric 'Bloodaxe', expelled King of Norway and last Norse king of York, was their power broken.

– and Norwegians

The extension of West Saxon power northwards was helped by the alliance which Alfred had made with the West Mercians, who had not been overrun by the Danes. The West Mercian leader was the ealdorman Aethelred, who had married Alfred's daughter Aethelflaed. When Aethelred died in 911, his policy was carried on by his wife, whose position as ruler was recognised under the title of 'Lady of the Mercians'. She co-operated closely with her brother, Edward the Elder, Alfred's son and successor as king of the West Saxons; and thanks to this, progress was made in a joint campaign of reconquest against the Danes. Its first big success came in 910, when combined West Saxon and Mercian forces caught and defeated a raiding Danish army near Tettenhall in Staffordshire.

The Wessex – West Mercia alliance

Ealdorman Aethelred and Aethelflaed

Edward the Elder, King of Wessex, 899–924

Tettenhall, 910

Mercia had been in a very exposed position, with a long eastern border touching Danish lands and a western and north-western border

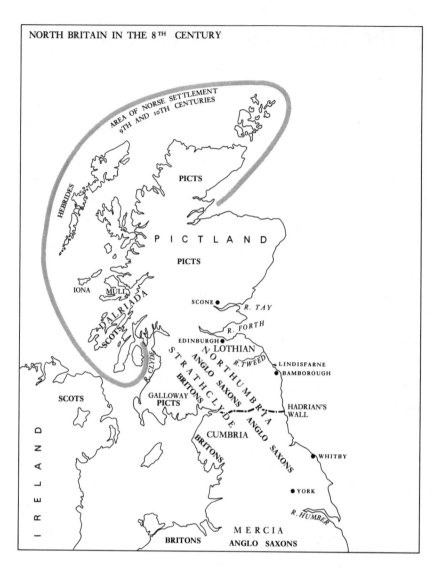

NORTH BRITAIN IN THE 8TH CENTURY

Aethelflaed's burhs

open to Norse attacks across the Irish Sea. Aethelflaed continued Alfred's policy of building fortified 'burhs' or defence centres. She ordered the construction of at least ten of these. Bridgnorth, for instance, was designed to guard the middle Severn; Stafford and Tamworth to cover Watling Street; and Runcorn to counter invasion up the Mersey estuary. In 917 the Danes of Derby and in 918 those of Leicester submitted to this remarkable woman, who seems to have taken a full share in the planning of her military expeditions, and to have led the Mercian host in person.

After Aethelflaed's death, Edward soon took control of her daughter and successor; and all the newly-won territories, and Mercia itself, came under his sway. He meanwhile had been pressing northwards from the London–Oxford area, which had earlier been handed over to him by

Aethelflaed, and he carried out the same policy of fortifying certain chosen places. As he advanced north between 911 and 918, he made strong points of – among other places – Buckingham, Bedford, Towcester, Lincoln, Nottingham and Stamford. While keeping the Danes in Essex and East Anglia well in check, he managed by 920 to push his frontier forward to Bakewell in the Peak District. Still further north, he also fortified Manchester. Beyond these limits, a number of independent rulers acknowledged his supremacy, amongst them the king of the Scots, the king of the Strathclyde Britons, the ruler of Bamburgh (northern Northumbria), the Norse king of York, and many of the princes of Wales. It was a fine heritage that, in 924, Edward the Elder handed on to his son Athelstan.

Edward's progress and burhs

His supremacy acknowledged

Athelstan, who frequently styled himself 'King of the English and ruler of all Britain', was one of the outstanding West Saxon monarchs, but there is little detailed evidence to supply the story of his reign. He quickly gained recognition as ruler of Mercia, where he had been brought up in the household of Aethelred and Aethelflaed. The high-water mark of his power was the victory that his West Saxon and Mercian forces won in 937 at 'Brunanburh' – a place as yet unidentified – against an alliance of the Scots, the Strathclyde Britons, and the Norsemen from Ireland.

Athelstan, 924–39

Brunanburh, 937

> With their hammered blades, the sons of Edward
> clove the shield-wall and hacked the linden bucklers,
> As was instinctive in them from their ancestry,
> to defend their land, their treasures, and their homes,
> In frequent battle against each enemy.[1]

Ten years earlier, after capturing York, Athelstan had received the homage of lesser rulers – the kings of Scotland and Strathclyde, and the lord of Bamburgh – at Eamont, just south of Penrith. The river here still marked the northern limit of the territories of the king of the West

[1] From a contemporary Old English poem, *The Battle of Brunanburh.*

The Monymusk reliquary *Kenneth MacAlpin, the King of Dalriada who vanquished the Picts and united Scotland north of the Forth, took this reliquary from Iona to his new religious centre at Dunkeld on the Tay. The casket, in the shape of an early Irish church, held the remains of St Columba. It is now in the Museum of Antiquities of Scotland.*

Saxons and the Mercians when Athelstan's brother Edmund succeeded him in 939. The border with the southern Welsh had been fixed on the Wye, and further south still, the Britons of Cornwall had been forced back behind the Tamar. Within the boundaries of Edmund's kingdom lived English, Danes, and Norse, and whether they could be held together or not depended very much on the personality of the king. In fact Edmund and his successor Eadred both had to deal with Norse rebellions, but once these risings had been put down all England south of the Tyne–Solway line recognised the authority of one ruler.

Edmund, Eadred and the struggle against the Norsemen

The sixteen-year reign of the next important king, Edgar, was almost wholly peaceful. In the words of the great historian of the Anglo-Saxon period, Sir Frank Stenton, 'It is a sign of Edgar's competence as a ruler, that his reign is singularly devoid of recorded incident.' Edgar's main achievements lay not in fresh conquests, but in the reform of the Church and the machinery of government.

Edgar, 959–75: his supremacy unchallenged

There was now no other power in the British Isles able to challenge the supremacy of the West Saxon king. The kingdom of Scotland had come into being between 844 and 860 when the two chief tribes, the Picts and the Scots (who had settled from Ireland), united under Kenneth MacAlpin. Nevertheless, the king of the Scots, as he was known, acknowledged allegiance to Athelstan at Eamont, and one of his successors later did the same to Edgar. Relations between the two kingdoms, however, were by no means firmly settled. In 945 Edmund tried to buy the friendship of Scotland by handing over Strathclyde, which he had conquered, to Malcolm, the Scottish king; and after 973 Edgar, also seeking for Scottish friendship, seems to have handed over Lothian, or the north-eastern part of the old kingdom of Northumbria, to Malcolm's successor Kenneth.

Growth of Scotland

In Wales and Ireland a number of native kings and princes still ruled their different territories. The Welsh princes were generally prepared to accept the supremacy of the English king, and sometimes to make active alliance with him. With the native Irish there were fewer links, for the Norse raiders had established themselves strongly on the east coast of Ireland. But none of these independent rulers could prevent the steady growth of West Saxon power.

Wales and Ireland

The rulers of Wessex were not concerned only with Britain. From the end of the ninth century they began to develop much more regular contacts with the Continent. Alfred, for example, normally sent a mission each year to the pope in Rome; foreigners visited his court; and one of his daughters married the Count of Flanders – the beginning of a long period of Anglo-Flemish friendship. Under Athelstan, such contacts grew rapidly. One of his sisters or half-sisters had already

Relations with the Continent

King Edgar's charter to Winchester Abbey *This is the frontispiece to the foundation charter granted by Edgar to the 'New Minster' at Winchester in 966. The king is shown between the Virgin and St Peter and holding the charter, which he presents to Christ enthroned above (from MS. in British Museum).*

married the king of the West Franks – the king of France – before Athelstan's accession. Afterwards, another married a great French noble, Hugh, Duke of France, whose son Hugh Capet was later to start a new line of French rulers; while a third married Otto I, one of the most famous of early German kings. These relationships led Athelstan at one time to send ships to help his nephew, Louis V of France, in warfare – the first time an English king is known to have sent naval support to a continental ally.[1] Athelstan also had links with another famous European king, Harold 'Fairhair' of Norway, who once sent him as a gift a wonderfully decorated warship with a purple sail, a row of gilded shields, and a gilded stem at prow and stern.

Perhaps Athelstan's most treasured gifts, however, came to him from Duke Hugh when the latter sought Athelstan's sister in marriage. According to one source, they included

perfumes, gems, horses, an onyx vase, a diadem set with jewels, the sword of Constantine the Great with a nail from the Cross in its hilt, the lance of Charlemagne with which the centurion had pierced our Lord's side, the standard of St. Maurice the Martyr, and fragments of the Cross and of the crown of thorns set in crystal.

9th-century Europe

Western Europe at this time was in a very confused state and its various rulers were well aware of the value of an English alliance. The empire of Charlemagne had split up under his less able successors into three main parts – the lands of the West Franks, the lands of the East Franks, and Italy – and in this disunited condition had to meet fierce attacks. The Vikings in the west, the Moslem armies in Spain and southern Italy, the Magyars in the east, all strove to wrest territory from Charlemagne's heirs. Since these could not defend all their lands, this period saw the rapid growth of feudalism in western Europe – a system in which the great local land-holders wielded much power in the absence of a strong central authority.[2] In 911 the French king ceded to the Norseman Rollo the town of Rouen and certain other places in north-west France which were later extended to become the duchy of Normandy – an event of some importance for the future of Britain.

The tasks of peace

Though links with the Continent were fast developing, Alfred's successors were of course much more occupied in conquering the Danelaw. They had also to provide good government for their newly won territories. Athelstan did much to deal with this problem, and he made laws, held councils, and issued many charters. But it was in the time of Edgar that the greatest progress was made in this way, as well as in the reform of the Church by St. Dunstan.[3] From Edgar's reign also dates the form of the Coronation Service, which was drawn up by Dunstan as Archbishop of Canterbury, and which was first used in Edgar's late coronation at Bath in 973.

---

[1] Actually the fleet gave Louis no proper help, and it returned having merely ravaged part of the coast on the other side of the Channel.
[2] For an explanation of feudalism and the derivation of the word, see page 90.
[3] See pages 59–60.

A Celtic round tower *This tower at Aber-nethy, Perthshire, is one of the few that remain of this type of defence against the Vikings. Many such towers were built in the ninth–eleventh centuries by monks in Scotland and Ireland.*

At a meeting held at Chester after this coronation Edgar is said to have been rowed on the Dee by a group of other kings from Scotland, Strathclyde, and Wales, while he himself sat at the helm.[1] Whether this story is true or not, it illustrates something that had been going on throughout the tenth century – the fact that the kings of Wessex had slowly built the framework of a larger kingdom, and had made all the other kings in the lands around acknowledge their supremacy. There was little idea, as yet, of 'England' as a single state, but there was be-ginning to grow the idea of a united 'English' people, recognising one over-ruler, and looking to him as the supreme source of law, order, and defence. It was upon this rapidly developing West Saxon monarchy that there now fell, towards the end of the tenth century, the full force of renewed Viking invasions.

Towards English unity

[1] This story appeared in the Norman period. The Anglo-Saxon Chronicle records that Edgar went with his fleet to Chester after his coronation, and that six kings came to swear allegiance to him there.

6 Anglo-Saxon Civilisation: I The Church, Learning and the Arts

1 Before the Viking Invasions

By far the greatest civilising influence on the warlike Anglo-Saxons was the Church. Not only did it convert them to Christianity and lay down standards of conduct, but it also tried to foster among them a respect for learning and the arts. It was within the Church that these revived, to reach heights unknown since the days of Roman Britain.

The language of the Church and of its services was Latin. A prime task of the Church was therefore to teach Latin to its future priests and monks. It had also, however, to teach intending clergy to read and write the ordinary language of the people – what we now call Anglo-Saxon or Old English; and it had to teach them enough simple mathematics and astronomy to calculate the date of Easter and other festivals. This meant that from the beginning the Church and education were closely linked.

There was probably a school in Canterbury soon after A.D. 600. From the late seventh century it was specially famous for the study of Roman law and Greek. These, however, were subjects for adults. For children accepted into monasteries the first stages were learning to read, to write, and to repeat from memory the Creed, the Lord's Prayer and the Psalms. Later the more able pupils studied such subjects as music for chanting, astronomy, logic and mathematics; and finally they came to grips with philosophy and theology.

For its services and for teaching and study the Church needed a good supply of books. At this time – and for many centuries afterwards – these had to be written out by hand, so copying became a very important task. At first, the texts were largely obtained from the Continent. They were brought back by people like Bede's teacher, Benedict Biscop, the

founder of the two linked monastic houses at Monkswearmouth and Jarrow. On six journeys abroad, Biscop collected manuscripts for these great Northumbrian monasteries. Another notable collector appears to have been St. Aldhelm, a scholar who studied at Canterbury and was

later bishop of Sherborne. Apparently Aldhelm used to ferret about on the quayside at Dover to discover if any manuscripts had been landed with the merchandise. Very early on, too, a cathedral school and a fine library were built up at York. One of the heads of this school,

Alcuin, acquired such fame as a scholar that Charlemagne persuaded him to leave York and work in Frankish territory. Here among other things he acted as adviser and tutor to Charlemagne and his family and created a library in the royal palace. Unfortunately the library which was the seat of Alcuin's labours at York, and which was said to be the greatest north of the Alps, perished in the first Danish invasions.

Since very few people in Anglo-Saxon England apart from the clergy could write – though many of the thegns could read – it took a long time for the different dialects of England to become written languages. When the Anglo-Saxon invaders came they brought with them a system of writing or alphabet which we call 'runic'[1]: It was probably used for writing on wood, for the symbols were formed by cutting different combinations of straight lines. About forty runic inscriptions survive, the most important being on the Ruthwell and Bewcastle crosses and

Writing

Runic inscriptions

Detail from Ruthwell cross *Many stone crosses were erected during the sixth–twelfth centuries and often they display superb carving. On this cross, from Ruthwell in Dumfriesshire, we see a carving of Christ on the right or broader side, and on the left or narrower side a flowing Celtic pattern of vines enclosing creatures feeding on the grapes.*

[1] 'Rune' and 'runic' come from a word in the Scandinavian languages meaning 'secret' or 'mystery' – for letters and writing were secret to people who could not read them.

on the Franks' Casket. Later the Anglo-Saxon tongue, or Old English, came to be written in an alphabet largely derived from the Roman. One of the earliest surviving pieces of this written Old English is the set of laws given by King Aethelbert to Kent around 602–603. Later codes of laws were also written down, and in the dialect of the kingdom concerned; after all, it was important that people should understand them. One reason why Alfred wanted his thegns to read was so that they could administer the laws correctly.

There must have been many songs and poems in the seventh and eighth centuries, but those that were not Christian were seldom written down. They were spread by minstrels, whose listeners in village street and thegn's hall delighted in tales of fighting, daring, and danger. The greatest Anglo-Saxon poem of all, 'Beowulf', gives a vivid impression of the sort of story the minstrels told. But as such stories were normally far removed from the lessons that the Church wished to teach, few examples have survived.

A different tradition began with the growth of Christian literature. Caedmon, the untaught oxherd of Whitby Abbey, is regarded as the first writer of Christian verse in English – though only one of his poems has come down to us. We know about him from Bede, who tells how Caedmon first composed a song unconsciously in his dreams. It was about the Creation; and later, encouraged by the Abbess Hild, he composed many other poems inspired by events in the Bible. Almost certainly it was English Christian poetry, too, that St. Aldhelm sang when he stood, as a chronicler records, on the bridge of Sherbornè like a professional minstrel, singing to the people in the hope that they would come and hear his sermons.

Perhaps the greatest of the surviving Old English Christian poems of this early period is *The Dream of the Rood*, some lines from which are carved on one side of the Ruthwell Cross. In this poem, as the poet regards a beautiful bejewelled cross, it comes to life and tells him how it was once a tree, and how it was cut down to make a gallows for Jesus. After the Crucifixion it was cast down, despised and bloody, and buried in a trench – only to be found again later, to be revered above all other trees and become a means of Grace for sinful man:

> Now I tower under Heaven in glory attired
> With healing for all that hold me in awe

In much Anglo-Saxon poetry, even pieces with a Christian message, there is repeated emphasis on suffering and hardship. Often there is a lament for the glories of the past – a feeling perhaps inspired by the sight of Roman ruins. Thus in the poem 'The Seafarer', probably composed in the eighth century,

My feet were nipped with cold and numbed by the ice bonds of frost: passionate care sighed in my heart: hunger within tore the spirit of one weary of the sea . . . . . . Gone are the days of old, and all the glory of the earthly kingdom. There are now no kings or emperors, or treasure-givers, as once there were . . . all this noble company is fallen, its joys vanished. . . .

Written Old English

Christian verse: Caedmon

The Dream of the Rood

The note of suffering

But even in these rather gloomy poems there is the Christian message of hope, and the occasional note of gaiety.

For its effects, Anglo-Saxon poetry did not employ rhyme, but depended very much on rhythm and alliteration – the use of several words or syllables close together beginning with the same letters or sounds:

> Then the Norsemen, the *sorry survivors* from the *spears*. . . .

The rhythm was often marked by a pause in the middle of the line, where perhaps a sound was struck on the accompanying harp:

> Then the Norsemen   the sorry survivors from the spears. . . .

More surprising than the existence of fine poetry among the seventh- and eighth-century Anglo-Saxons, however, was the writing of a great history – Bede's *Ecclesiastical History of the English Nation*. Like nearly all Bede's work, it was written in Latin, but he also wrote in English. His 'Ecclesiastical History' has endured not only because it is one of our fullest sources on early Anglo-Saxon England, but also because it is a work of wonderful skill, in which fragments of information from a great variety of sources have been woven together into a coherent story. Bede took quite exceptional care in gathering material, and in judging its true historical worth. A member of the monastery at Jarrow from the age of seven until his death at sixty-three, he seems never to have travelled beyond York and Lindisfarne, and for most of his material must have relied on the libraries built up by Biscop and others at Jarrow and Monkswearmouth. Outstanding as it was, however, Bede's was not the only work of history written at about this time.

One of the skills in which Anglo-Saxon England very early excelled was that of manuscript illumination. The text of the manuscript was written out; then the spaces were filled with small pictures or intricate patterns and the capital letters were elaborated, all in attractive and often brilliant colours. This was an art which the Church brought to the Anglo-Saxons, the work being done in the schools of craftsmanship which grew up at different times in different monasteries. The centre of the craft in the early days was Northumbria. The biographer of St. Wilfrid, Eddi, records that for his church at Ripon Wilfrid ordered 'the four gospels to be written out in letters of purest gold on purple parchment' and illuminated. He also ordered jewellers to construct for the books a case made of purest gold and set with precious gems. This order was probably executed abroad; but before long Northumbrian artists were capable of producing such superb manuscripts as the Lindisfarne Gospels, thought to have been written and illustrated by the monks of Lindisfarne around the year 700.[1] Later, the main centre shifted to Canterbury. Then came the Danish raids, which destroyed many beautiful books and often prevented work on new manuscripts. Not

Poetic technique

Historical writing

Bede

Manuscript illumination

The Lindisfarne Gospels

---

[1] They may be seen, as beautiful as ever, in the British Museum.

Left: St Matthew, Book of Kells *The Book of Kells, now in the Library of Trinity College, Dublin, is one of the most famous and beautiful of the early illuminated manuscripts. A copy of the Gospels, in Latin, together with some local records, it was written and painted during the eighth century in the monastery at Kells (Co. Meath). It is strongly akin in style to some of the great manuscripts of the period from Northumbria.*

Above: A 'carpet' from the Lindisfarne Gospels *The Lindisfarne Gospels, now in the British Museum, are thought to have been produced at Lindisfarne around* A.D. *700. They are among the earliest of the great Northumbrian illuminated manuscripts. Though these Gospels contain four full-page portraits of the Evangelists and various figures based on animals, perhaps their outstanding feature is the large number of decorations of a geometric or 'carpet-pattern' type, like the page illustrated above.*

until the more settled conditions and the monastic revival of the tenth century were the glories of the earlier Northumbrian period recaptured.

Sculpture

Another notable art in early Anglo-Saxon England was that of sculpture or carving, both in stone and wood. Little, however, has survived. Quite apart from destruction by the Danes, much was broken up when churches and monasteries and shrines were looted during the Reformation period of the sixteenth century, and further attacks were made on what was left during the Civil Wars and Commonwealth a hundred years later. Probably ninety per cent of what survived into the Middle Ages was destroyed in those two periods. What now remains is scattered in small pieces in churches throughout the country, and from it the passing of time has removed one of its main qualities. From written accounts we know that Anglo-Saxon sculpture in churches glowed with colour.

Crosses

The first great school of Anglo-Saxon sculpture arose in the north and east, and two splendid monuments of this remain in the Bewcastle and Ruthwell crosses. Both are covered with carving, that on the Ruthwell Cross being particularly fine. As in Ireland, such crosses may well have been put up to be centres of worship in areas lacking a church. The

The Franks' Casket

Franks' Casket, carved in whalebone, was also created in this early period. It shows a curious mixture of themes in its carving, for we can distinguish Romulus and Remus and Weland the Smith, as well as such Christian stories as the Adoration of the Magi.

Churches

The purpose of Anglo-Saxon sculpture was partly to instruct, but mainly to beautify churches. These churches were for the most part simple structures, tall, long and narrow. They must also have been rather dark, for their windows were few, small and high up. This at least helped to keep wind and weather from the congregation, for glass in windows was still rare.

From wood to stone

The earliest Anglo-Saxon churches, like the kings' and thegns' halls, were built of wood. None of these survive. The Christian missions of the late sixth and seventh centuries reintroduced building in stone, and from this period there are many surviving remains, though few complete buildings. At Canterbury there are foundations, at Hexham and Ripon fine crypts, at Brixworth in Northamptonshire the largest known Anglo-Saxon church. There is also an interesting early Anglo-Saxon church at Bradford-on-Avon (Wiltshire) originally commissioned by St. Aldhelm; and far out on the Blackwater estuary in Essex there still stands St. Cedd's little church at Bradwell, of which the west doorway and window at least are parts of the original structure, built in 654. These examples may not amount to very much, but they show that by the time of the Danish invasions the Anglo-Saxons had made progress in the art of building churches in stone. For supplies of this they were often indebted to local Roman ruins.

Types of church building:

– Basilican

In Anglo-Saxon church building there came to be two competing plans. The Roman missionaries brought with them the Roman plan based on the basilica or law court, a long rectangular building with an

Cross at Ahenny *The early high stone crosses are one of the glories of Ireland, where they were erected in greater numbers than anywhere else in the British Isles. In this example, from Tipperary, the arms of the cross are enclosed in a circle of stone, as is common with the Irish crosses. The base of the cross portrays a procession and a battle between animals.*

apse, or semi-circular recess, at one end; in churches an altar here took the place of the magistrate's seat. From Ireland and Iona, however, the Celtic missionaries brought ideas of a church with a lofty, fairly narrow rectangular nave (the main body of the church) and a small square-ended chancel (the part where the clergy officiate). Eventually the Celtic pattern became the basis for most English church building, for it suited better the need of the clergy for a special part of the church – the chancel – set slightly apart from the general congregation.

– Nave and Chancel

Among the crafts practised at an early date by the Anglo-Saxons, both for the Church and for the kings and wealthy thegns, was fine metalwork. In the British Museum can be seen some magnificent jewellery made in the sixth and seventh centuries in Kent, inlaid with garnets, blue and green glass, and white shells. From the Sutton Hoo burial ship came splendid pieces of Anglo-Saxon jewellery, as well as cups, dishes and plates; and one of the noted pieces of metal-work is the Alfred Jewel made in Wessex in the ninth century. Many generous gifts of gold-covered or silver crosses, candlesticks, cups and the like were made to churches and monasteries, but practically all these objects have disappeared. In the same way, many churches had wonderful vestments or robes for the clergy; but by their nature these were perishable, and only a few fragments are left to give us some idea of

Fine metalwork

Vestments

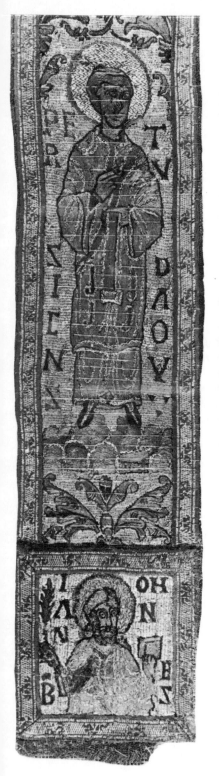

Left: Tenth-century embroidery *This piece forms part of a vestment presented by King Athelstan to the shrine of St Cuthbert in 934. The saint's shrine was then at Chester-le-Street, and the king stopped there on his way north to attack the Scots. The figure represents Peter the Deacon, secretary to Pope Gregory the Great.*

Above: A Saxon crypt at Repton *This underground chapel was part of a monastery probably built around 700, and later rebuilt around 1000 after being largely destroyed by the Danes. Though only 17ft square, the crypt is an outstanding example of Saxon architecture. Repton (in Derbyshire) was one of the chief centres of Mercia, and Mercian kings were buried here. The crypt became forgotten after the dissolution of the monasteries, and was rediscovered in the eighteenth century when a workman fell into it while digging a grave.*

them. Such were the quality of their workmanship and colour that English embroidery became famous throughout Western Europe and was later known – as were also fine English metalwork and ivory carving – by the name of 'opus anglicanum' ('English work').

Embroidery

2 The Tenth and Eleventh Centuries

Very many churches were sacked and their artistic treasures destroyed during the Viking invasions. The Norwegian raid in 793 when – in the words of the Anglo-Saxon Chronicle – 'the ravages of heathen men destroyed God's church on Lindisfarne, with plunder and slaughter', ushered in a new era of extreme violence and brutality, in which far more great art was ruined than created. We have seen how Alfred stemmed this tide, and how he and his successors recaptured the Danish conquests and laid the foundations of the later kingdom of England. And as the fighting died down and more settled conditions returned, so the Church regained its vigour and the arts once more flourished under its care.

Destruction by the Danes

The Danes were fairly quickly converted to Christianity; but their invasions had wrought great damage to the Church in its habits and organisation as well as in its buildings. It was Alfred who first inspired a revival of church and scholastic life. But it was under his successors, and particularly in the peaceful reign of Edgar (959–975), that this revival began to extend over the whole of England.

Recovery

That it did so was especially the work of three men – St. Dunstan, finally Archbishop of Canterbury; St. Oswald, finally Archbishop of York; and St. Aethelwold, finally Bishop of Winchester. Their first task was to set up again or reform the old monastic foundations, for many had become derelict, while in others the occupants had abandoned St. Benedict's rule and were living a comfortable and worldly life – accompanied, in many cases, by their wives. In addition, the three bishops founded several new monasteries, laid down a common form of religious observance, and trained a new generation of monks to carry on their work. This was a time when a great monastic reform movement was getting under way on the Continent, particularly in the monasteries of Cluny in Burgundy and Fleury on the Loire, and the three English reformers were in touch with these developments.

10th century reformers

Cluny and Fleury

The greatest of the three was probably Dunstan, who was also a statesman, the counsellor of four kings, and the deviser of much of the present coronation service. The son of a thegn of Somerset, he spent the early part of his life near Glastonbury, one of the most ancient of English religious centres – a place whose first wattle church was erected, according to legend, by Joseph of Arimathea shortly after the death of Christ.[1] As a monk, he became the friend of King Edmund

St. Dunstan, c. 909–88

[1] The legend also tells that Joseph planted a thorn from Christ's crown, and this grew into a thorn tree. Such a tree was an object of pilgrimage until the sixteenth-century Reformation, when it was destroyed.

(939–946), who finally made him Abbot of Glastonbury. Here Dunstan remained for fifteen years and in that time he fully restored the life of the monastery, which had declined into a school and a loosely organised religious community without monks.

Later, Dunstan's enemies succeeded in getting him banished abroad. He was recalled by King Edgar, who first made him Bishop of Worcester, then Bishop of London as well, and then Archbishop of Canterbury. Here he remained from 959 until his death nearly thirty years later, and from here he continued to foster the revival of strict monastic life. His own reputation for holiness and learning grew – and inspired various legends. On one occasion, for instance, when the Devil appeared to tempt him, he was said to have seized that gentleman by the nose with a pair of red-hot pincers.[1]

The Church in the new Danish attacks

Dunstan, Oswald and Aethelwold, all of whom owed much to the strong support of King Edgar, died within eight years of one another. Between them, they had well and truly laid the foundations of reform. The result was that when the Danes again began to attack early in the eleventh century and succeeded so well that Swein 'Forkbeard' and his son Cnut became kings of England, the organisation of the Church was strong enough to survive this new crisis. Cnut himself became a strong supporter of the Church, which was able to remain active in missionary work and keep in fairly close contact with the Papacy.

Cnut

Revival of art in 10–11th centuries

The renewed vigour of the Church produced the second, and final, great phase of Anglo-Saxon art. With improved building methods churches became bigger, and towers became one of their special features. Outstanding work of this period may still be seen in the chancel arch of All Saints, Wittering, and in the towers of churches at Earls Barton in Northamptonshire and Clapham in Bedfordshire. At the beginning of the eleventh century Archbishop Wulfstan helped by decreeing that one-third of all church tithes[2] should be used to restore churches which had been damaged or fallen into disrepair. The last big work undertaken during the Anglo-Saxon period was Edward the Confessor's great church at Westminster, St. Peter's, consecrated nine days before the king died. The aisled nave was the longest building in England, but little of the original work survives in the present Westminster Abbey.

Church-building

Wulfstan's decree

Sculpture

Of church sculpture of the tenth to eleventh centuries there are few outstanding survivals. Among them are the sculptured columns in Chichester Cathedral, the carved angels at Bradford-on-Avon, and the fine slate tombstone decorated with a very powerful carving of a lion in St. Paul's Churchyard. There is also a notable late tenth-century sculptured cross at Gosforth, Cumberland. On the whole, what remains is not of such good quality as the surviving sculpture from the seventh and eighth centuries.

Illuminated MSS.

There are, however, still many very well-preserved illuminated

---

[1] The Devil, running away, is supposed to have burned a cleft in the Sussex Downs – hence the Devil's Dyke, near Brighton. What are claimed to be the pincers are exhibited in the priory at Mayfield, Sussex.
[2] See page 218.

manuscripts from the tenth to eleventh centuries. The main centre for the production of these, and of fine metalwork, ivory carving, and needlework, was now Winchester. Among the many splendid manuscripts produced there the Benedictional of St. Aethelwold is an outstanding example. In illumination, in metal-work, in carving and in embroidery, the artist-craftsmen of later Anglo-Saxon England revived and created traditions which were to survive the Norman Conquest and become still more glorious afterwards.

Finally, there was much progress in literature during these last two centuries of Anglo-Saxon rule – the example having been set by Alfred. The number of works which survive is not large, but they include the *Anglo-Saxon Chronicle* and several poems commemorating great events such as the battles of Brunanburh and Maldon, or the coronation of Edgar. Some of these verses are included in the Chronicle itself, as in the case of the poem on Brunanburh. There are also some lives of ninth-century saints and various collections of homilies or sermons. The best known sermon of all – 'The Sermon of the Wolf to the English' – was delivered by Archbishop Wulfstan of York around 1014, after repeated disasters had befallen the country under Aethelred the Unready. It is splendidly powerful stuff, implying that the disasters were the inevitable result of the sins of the English, and calling upon the nation to repent.

Most of this literature that has survived is written in the West Saxon dialect. This makes it difficult for us to read; for modern English owes much less to the West Saxon dialect than to that of the East Midlands, which was spoken in London. However, from what remains we can see that by the eleventh century Anglo-Saxon had become a language capable of being wrought into literature worthy of comparison with any produced in Europe at that time.

Literature:

A.S. Chronicle

Poems

Saints' lives
Sermons

The language

A late Saxon church tower *All Saints, Earls Barton, Northamptonshire. This tenth-century tower has remained largely unaltered apart from the addition of the battlements— and the clock! Towers, which served as look-out and defence points in addition to their church uses, were an important feature of late Anglo-Saxon architecture and were usually —like this one—sited at the west end of the church. With its strap-work stone ornamentation, this is one of the most decorative to have survived.*

7 Anglo-Saxon Civilisation: II Government, Law and Society

It is hard to make statements about Anglo-Saxon civilisation which are equally true for all the kingdoms for the whole 600 years from the Anglo-Saxon invasions to the Norman Conquest. All the same, it is worth while trying to pick out certain leading features of Anglo-Saxon life even if they did not apply everywhere or for the whole period.

Kingship

The broad form of government and the ranks of society, for instance, did not greatly change over most of the Anglo-Saxon age. When the Angles, the Saxons, and the Jutes are first met in England, it seems they were ruled by kings, who were doubtless their successful war-chiefs; and though one of these kings from time to time gained a supremacy, with the West Saxon rulers finally dominating all the other territories, it was not until the reign of the Danish Cnut, in the eleventh century, that the idea became fixed of a single monarch ruling the whole of England.

Upper clergy

Thegns and priests

Kings, then, stood at the peak of society. Below these ranked the chief priests – at first pagan, later the Christian bishops and other leading churchmen. Next came the king's *Gesith*, or companions – the nobles – usually known from the ninth century as *thegns*, from a word meaning 'to serve'. With the thegns were usually ranked the 'mass-thegns', or priests; and below the thegns and priests came the ordinary freemen, mostly *ceorls* (whence the word 'churl') or free peasant farmers, but including also others who owed weekly agricultural service to a lord, and were therefore not free to move as they pleased. Finally, below the various classes of freemen came the slaves. Of these there were a great many in early Anglo-Saxon England, but the influence of Christianity was against slavery, and they became fewer as time went on.

Freemen

Slaves

Evidence from codes of law

We know about these ranks of society from, among other sources, the codes or collections of law issued by various kings from the seventh century onwards. One of the common principles of Anglo-Saxon law was that, if an offence was committed, the offender must pay compensation to the injured party – which could include the king or over-lord (whose peace and good order might have been disturbed) as well as the person robbed or injured. The codes, for instance, provide penalties for unlawful killing. In cases of premeditated murder or killing a priest or one of royal blood, nothing less than death and con-fiscation of the offender's property would normally suffice; but in other cases, where the killing was done accidentally or in the heat of a quarrel,

'Wergild'

justice would usually be satisfied by the payment of the victim's *wergild* (literally, 'man-money') or official compensation figure, to the kindred of the slain and any other interested parties such as the king.

The codes mention, though not systematically, the wergilds for the various grades of society, and from this we can confirm what these grades were, and how they ranked in importance. In the laws of King Ine of Wessex, who ruled in the seventh century, the wergild of a great nobleman was 1,200 Wessex shillings, a lesser nobleman 600, and a ceorl 200. On the prices of the day, this made a ceorl worth about thirty-three oxen. These laws also mention free Welshmen, or Britons, whose wergilds varied, according to the amount of land they possessed, from 600 to 60 Wessex shillings. Stated proportions of the wergild had to be paid to the victim himself in cases less serious than killing – there was a tariff of compensations for injuries to eyes, nose, ears, etc.

At the bottom of the scale, slaves had no wergild at all, and no official kindred to support them or receive compensation. In Ine's laws, the value of a slave was reckoned at sixty Wessex shillings. If a slave was killed, this was the money due to his master from the killer or the killer's kindred; if a slave himself killed someone the slave was forfeit to the victim's kindred, or could be redeemed by his master for the sum of sixty shillings.

All these grades of society, except the slaves, had some accepted part to play in keeping law and order. The main business of government was of course the king's; but the king could not be everywhere, and the good order of the realm depended also on the smooth working of local institutions. The king himself and his retinue usually travelled a good deal, partly to keep an eye on things, partly to enjoy free hospitality – and where the king was, there was his court and his centre of government. With the king there would normally be certain leading officials, noblemen and churchmen to act as counsellors and as witnesses of his decisions, and on special occasions he would summon important thegns or bishops from distant parts. Christmas, Easter and Pentecost (Whitsun) were favoured times for such special assemblies, which became commoner as England grew more united under Alfred's successors.

From the will of the ninth-century West Saxon King Eadred, we learn that his highest Court officials included his 'dish-thegns' and his 'wardrobe-thegns'; and he also probably had 'horse-thegns'. These offices were occupied by great nobles. Many lesser nobles, without offices, were also present at Court, their main task being companionship and military support. In Cnut's reign, these became an organised military company some hundreds strong known as the 'housecarles', with special regulations of their own and courts for dealing with breaches of rules and discipline. After Cnut, the housecarles were allowed to live in their own districts, but remained men of special military training and obligations.

The king was also served at Court by many churchmen – not only by leading bishops or abbots as advisers, but also by large numbers of

Royal travel

The king's council or Witan

The leading Court officials –

– and fighting nobles

lesser clergy who were employed to draft or copy royal laws, decisions and messages. Grants of land or privileges were usually recorded in a charter, normally written in Latin. For the most part, the king's wishes were conveyed to the various regions in written form by documents or letters in English known as writs, bearing the king's seal. These probably began in the seventh century, but do not survive in large numbers from any period earlier than the tenth century.

For the enforcement of law and order the king depended on all ranks of society, each of which had some part to play. His highest officers away from Court were at first the ealdormen, who might have areas to supervise as large as one of the early kingdoms. Sometimes in the earlier days the ealdorman was in fact the former king of the area concerned. Apart from seeing that the noblemen of the region enforced the law in their own areas, the main task of the ealdorman was to summon and lead the *fyrd* or military levies when necessary, to preside over the main court or courts in his region, and to gather in the revenue for government from such sources as tolls on trade, or fines in the law courts. He was usually given big estates by the king, and had the right to hospitality for himself and his retinue throughout his province. In the north, there is evidence that his wergild could be four times that of a normal great thegn.

In Danish-ruled territory, the counterpart of the ealdorman was known as the earl. The districts ruled by earls tended to be specially created, rather than areas long established by custom as homes of separate 'peoples'. Under Cnut, much of the country came under four great earls, though there were others as well, for altogether his charters bear the names of sixteen earls. Cnut's arrangements did not last, but in general the title of ealdorman dropped out, and was replaced by that of earl; and some of the earls in late Saxon times were extremely powerful figures controlling very large areas.

Earls who supervised very large areas of the country could not take part in day-to-day administration of the laws. For this, smaller districts and less important officials were needed. Local government accordingly came to be carried out through the shires, or counties, which developed during the ninth and tenth centuries. In the south, some of these shires corresponded to the small kingdoms of earlier days, such as Kent and Sussex. Elsewhere, however, the boundaries were more artificial. By about 900, the large kingdom of Wessex was divided into shires; and by about 1000, something very close to the present-day pattern of shires had developed over the whole of England south of the Tees. In the Midlands, many shires seem to have been created round a fortified town, such as one of Alfred's 'burhs', or a Danish stronghold. In any case, the chief official of the shire was the senior steward or reeve of the king's estates in the area – the shire-reeve whose title became shortened to 'sheriff'. It became the sheriff's duty to take on much of the work formerly done by ealdormen, such as presiding over the twice-yearly shire court, raising and leading the fyrd, and collecting royal revenue.

Charters and writs

Officials in the regions:

Ealdormen –

– and later, Earls

Shires –

– and sheriffs

The shire was the most important, but not the only, unit of government. Within each shire there were by the end of the tenth century
smaller districts known as 'hundreds' (or in the Danish areas 'wapentakes'). These varied greatly in size, but many of them in the Midlands
appear to have been based on areas regarded for taxation purposes as
containing a hundred 'hides' (a hide being the amount of land required
to support a free peasant and his dependants). In these hundreds and
wapentakes there was normally a monthly court, held in the open air
under the presidency of a reeve from a local royal estate. In this justice
was administered, and the requirements of the king previously made
known in the shire court were passed down to the villages. It would be
the duty of the hundred court to see that the regular royal revenues and

*Hundreds and
wapentakes*

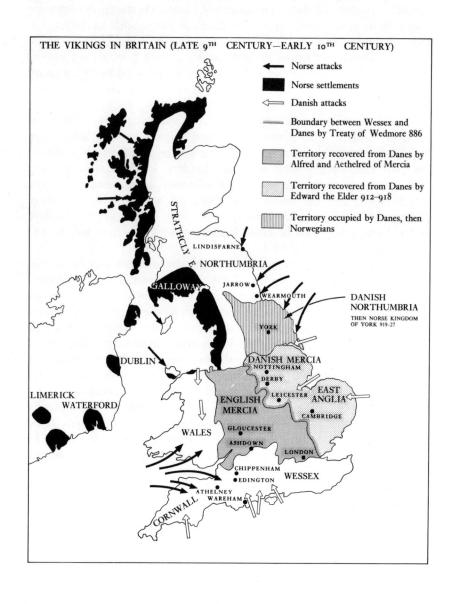

THE VIKINGS IN BRITAIN (LATE 9TH CENTURY—EARLY 10TH CENTURY)

→ Norse attacks

■ Norse settlements

⇐ Danish attacks

— Boundary between Wessex and
Danes by Treaty of Wedmore 886

Territory recovered from Danes by
Alfred and Aethelred of Mercia

Territory recovered from Danes by
Edward the Elder 912–918

Territory occupied by Danes, then
Norwegians

STRATHCLYDE
GALLOWAY
LINDISFARNE
NORTHUMBRIA
JARROW
WEARMOUTH
DANISH
NORTHUMBRIA
THEN NORSE KINGDOM
OF YORK 919–27
YORK
DUBLIN
DANISH MERCIA
NOTTINGHAM
DERBY
LEICESTER
EAST
ANGLIA
LIMERICK
WATERFORD
ENGLISH
MERCIA
CAMBRIDGE
WALES
GLOUCESTER
ASHDOWN
LONDON
CHIPPENHAM
EDINGTON
WESSEX
ATHELNEY
WAREHAM
CORNWALL

the exceptional taxes (such as Danegeld) were forthcoming from their hundred in the proper amounts, and that men were produced when required for the fyrd or for the making of bridges and fortifications. The hundred courts were 'popular' assemblies in the sense that the free men of the district, though they usually resented the time lost in attending, took an active part in the procedure. 'Popular' participation is also suggested by the word 'wapentake', which comes from an Old Norse word meaning a 'flourish of weapons'. (The custom in Scandinavia was for the free men to flourish their spears as a general sign of assent.)

The double role of Courts

All courts in Anglo-Saxon times, whether the king's court, the shire courts, the separate borough courts, or the hundred courts, had a double purpose. They looked after the ordinary business of government, and they were at the same time courts of justice. As the latter, the shire courts dealt mainly with important civil questions, such as the ownership of land. Most criminal cases came before the hundred or the borough courts, but minor or very clear cases – e.g. of a thief caught 'red-handed' – might also be judged in the private courts which many of the larger landholders were entitled to run, by special grant of the king.

Criminal justice

When a crime occurred it was the duty of everyone to help bring the offender to book. This might involve first helping to catch him. From very early times there was an obligation on the able-bodied to join in the local 'hue and cry' after escaping offenders: by the seventh-century laws of Wessex, if anyone suffered or witnessed a crime, he was to cry 'Out! Out!', and the whole neighbourhood was then to set off in pursuit – if possible with horses, arms, and horns. If the fugitive resisted arrest, he could be killed immediately; if he submitted, he was to be kept prisoner until trial.

The hue and cry

Trial procedure

The process of trial was a strange one by modern standards, but logical enough in a close-knit local society where religion was regarded very seriously and oaths were sacred things to be broken only at the risk of torments in Hell. Oaths were very much at the heart of the matter.

Oaths

The main proceedings began with an accuser – the victim or one of his kindred – swearing an oath in set terms accusing the defendant of the crime in question. The defendant then submitted, or swore an oath of denial, also in set terms. He was then told by the Court how many supporting oaths he would need, and of what value – for the oaths of thegns ranked as of higher value than those of ceorls; and he was normally given time to collect these fellow-swearers, or 'compurgators'. If he returned on the appointed day with his due total of oath-supporters, he was normally judged innocent; but if he was of bad reputation, or had actually been seen to commit the crime, the accuser could bring a due total of oath-supporters on the accusing side, and in that case the defendant's oaths were usually considered to be outweighed.

'Compurgation'

If the defendant could not produce his due quota of oath-supporters, or if his oaths were thought to be out-weighed, he could either suffer the penalties demanded by the law, or else attempt to clear himself by submitting to the 'judgment of God'. This was what is usually known as 'the ordeal'. In general, cases were settled by oaths based on local knowledge and reputation, with the ordeal in the background if the defendant could not clear himself by the oaths of his supporters.

The ordeal

For laymen, the ordeal itself was by one of God's elements – water or fire – which in practice meant by cold water, by hot water, or by hot iron. For clergy, the ordeal was by the eating of consecrated bread; if they could swallow this without choking, they were innocent. In the normal cold-water ordeal, the defendant was tied by hands and feet to a rope, and thrown into water which had been blessed by a priest and asked to accept the innocent and reject the guilty. If the defendant sank, he was innocent; if he floated, guilty. In either case he was hauled out by the rope. In the hot-water ordeal the defendant plunged his hand (or for more serious cases, arm) into a vessel of boiling water to pick out a stone. His hand was tied up with bandages, which were removed three days later. If the scalds were healing cleanly, he was innocent; if they were festering, guilty. Similarly in the ordeal by hot iron, the defendant had to snatch up a piece of red hot iron weighing a pound (or three pounds in more serious cases) and carry it for nine feet before casting it down. The healing-festering test was then applied, as for the hot water ordeal.

Types of ordeal

Trial by ordeal normally took place in church or nearby, and was conducted by the clergy with great solemnity. The defendant was in the care of the clergy for three days beforehand, and he and all witnesses fasted before the ceremony. In an age when faith was very real, it was not quite so stupid or barbarous a procedure as it appears to us now. As an institution it was world-wide in its different forms, and age-old. In England it certainly lasted a long time; for the Anglo-Saxons had trials by ordeal long before they were converted to Christianity, and such trials ceased to be general only in the thirteenth century.[1]

These details of court procedure should make it clear that a man's safety depended very much on the readiness of others to vouch for his honesty. In the early Anglo-Saxon centuries, it was a man's kindred who were expected to support him, and to help answer for his good behaviour. If a man should be sentenced, for instance, to 'work out his crime' in servitude to his victim or victim's family, it would be open to the offender's kindred to redeem him from servitude within twelve months by a money payment. Almost the worst thing that could happen to a man was that he should be disowned by his kindred, in which case he became an outlaw, to be killed and his possessions claimed by anyone who chose.

The role of kindred

By the tenth century, however, it seems that this reliance on kindred was no longer working well. Either the kindred disowned their erring

Replacement of kindred groups by tithing groups

---

[1] Trial by ordeal was abolished by a papal Council in 1215. Even then, 'ordeal by battle'–single combat between accuser and accused or their champions, which was introduced by the Normans, remained a common practice for another two centuries, and was legally abolished only in 1818.

member and refused to pay his fines, or else they developed into powerful groups who fostered criminals. Other arrangements were therefore made. To clear himself of a charge, a man had to be supported not by his kindred, but by men of equal station to himself; and it no longer fell to the kindred to produce a wrong-doer in court, but to groups known as 'tithings'. Each tithing was a group of ten men, with a senior 'tithingman' in charge, and the group had joint responsibility for the behaviour of its members – i.e. it had to produce them when necessary in court, and could be fined if it failed to do so. Cnut seems to have made this system general within the hundreds and wapentakes.

The laws of Cnut

The laws of Cnut are much the fullest of the pre-Norman Conquest codes of laws to have come down to us. For the most part they repeat earlier codes, and like them, they range from subject to subject. They show the system of hundred courts, tithings, hue and cry, oaths, wergilds, ordeals, and the rest in full working order; and they also allow for minor differences in law as between Wessex and Mercia, and rather greater differences as between those two areas and the rest of England – the Danelaw. They also show much concern for the Christian faith and the Church. The punishments laid down for offences, however, were not notable for a spirit of Christian mercy. An offender convicted of theft by the ordeal might indeed atone on the first occasion by paying compensation. On the second occasion, however, there was to be 'no other compensation, if he is convicted, but that his hands, or feet, or both, in proportion to the deed, are to be cut off'. And if, however, he has committed still further crimes, 'his eyes are to be put out and his nose and ears and upper lip cut off, or his scalp removed'.

Some penalties

'Thus', concludes this law piously, 'one can punish and at the same time preserve the soul'.

MAIN KINGS OF WESSEX AND OF ENGLAND, 871–1066

871–99   ALFRED
899–925   Alfred's son EDWARD THE ELDER
925–37   Edward the Elder's son ATHELSTAN
959–75   Athelstan's nephew EDGAR
978–1016   Edgar's son AETHELRED THE UNREADY
1014   The Danish invader, SWEIN
1016–35   Swein's son CNUT
1042–1066   Aethelred's son EDWARD THE CONFESSOR
1066   Edward the Confessor's brother-in-law, HAROLD II

8 Anglo-Saxon Civilisation: III Everyday Life

From the sixth to the eleventh centuries, the main royal tasks did not greatly change, even though a number of small kingdoms gave place to a single monarchy. A tenth-century king of England like Athelstan had far greater responsibilities than a seventh-century king of Kent, far more links with other countries, and rather more splendour and formality about his court; but the general pattern of their lives was quite similar. A king, of no matter how petty a kingdom, kept considerable state. He spent his time in business, such as making decisions, granting charters, receiving missions and hearing appeals and other cases; and he also spent it in travelling to his various estates, hunting, attending divine service, and leading his armies in war. A good many of his leisure hours at Court he spent in his hall, or palace, feasting with his companions. If he was like Alfred – but few kings were – he also found time for reading, writing and study.

The life of kings

There are few remains of Anglo-Saxon royal residences still in existence, but what there are confirm that the life of a tenth-century king had much in common with that of his seventh-century forerunner. For the seventh century, the main archaeological evidence is that at Yeavering in Northumberland, where the site of a royal township of the Northumbrian kings has been identified. Though the wooden buildings have disappeared the post-holes survive, and from these it is possible to reconstruct the nature of the township.[1] It seems to have included, apart from a fort and a temple, a royal hall built of squared timber posts, with the roof supported in part by buttresses outside. Post-holes inside the hall show that it was divided lengthwise into a large central area and two flanking aisles, and that at one end there was a separate section – which may have included the bower, or royal sleeping quarters. Not far from the hall were separate wooden buildings which may have been the houses of the chief officials, and there is also a terrace, with a suggestion of tiered seats, which may have been used for specially large meetings of the king's council.

A royal residence at Yeavering

Within the hall the king would make known his decisions and, when the evening settled in, eat and drink with his nobles by torchlight or

Night in the hall

[1] The timber posts having been burnt or rotted away, the holes became filled with earth. The pattern of the holes can be seen from the air, since crops grew differently in them from in the surrounding earth. Air photography has thus enabled us to trace the pattern of the vanished buildings.

candlelight. Minstrels' songs and tales told by the companions were favourite diversions. When the time came for sleep, the king and his immediate family would retire to the separate apartments, while the main company of nobles bedded down on the side benches on pallets of straw or similar rough mattresses. There is a description of this sort of thing in 'Beowulf':

They cleared the bench boards, it was spread with beds and bolsters. They set war-bucklers at their head, the shining shield-wood. There on the bench, above each noble, was exposed the helmet, prominent in war, the ringed mail-coat, the proud shield-shaft. It was their practice to be ready for the fray at home or in the field.

Royal halls at Cheddar

Of later royal halls of the Saxon period there is evidence at Cheddar, Somerset. In Alfred's time it seems there was a large wooden hall with doors in the middle of its ninety-foot long sides. Other wooden buildings, including a detached bower, stood nearby. During the following century, however, a stone chapel was built on the site of this hall, and a new timber hall replaced the earlier one. It had entrances at the ends, and aisles. Separate adjacent buildings included a second bower, a corn-mill, and a latrine with cess-pit. It is clear that there was a ditch, and a fence round the site, but there is no sign of all the other buildings, for servants and stores, which must have existed. By the tenth century there must also have been two-storied wooden halls. On occasion these collapsed, to judge from the incident recorded in the Anglo-Saxon Chronicle for the year 978.

Two-storied halls

In this year all the chief counsellors of the English people fell from an upper storey at Calne, except that Archbishop Dunstan alone remained standing on a beam. . . .

All told, it does not seem from the fragments of evidence available that an Anglo-Saxon royal residence of the tenth or eleventh century was much more advanced than one of the seventh century. Certainly both provided little of the luxury enjoyed by Cogidubnus, the first-century king in Roman Britain, if he was the owner of the huge palace at Fishbourne recently excavated. One thing, however, will have been common to all royal residences from the earliest times. The king's household was supposed to enjoy a specially sacred kind of peace. To commit a crime, to draw a weapon in anger, to brawl – these were offences punishable by much greater penalties in the king's immediate neighbourhood than elsewhere.

The King's Peace

The thegn's life

The senior thegns who were the king's chief officials, and others who were his companions and bodyguard, shared the king's leisure hours and, allowing for their lower station and lesser duties, lived much the same kind of life. Their supreme duty was loyalty to their lord the king. Elsewhere, away from the royal residence, thegns who were not royal officials spent most of their time in looking after their estates. For these they often paid a rent in food: one of King Ine's laws states that the correct payment each year for ten hides should be '10 vats of honey, 300 loaves, 12 "ambers" of Welsh ale, 30 ambers of clear ale, 2 full-grown cows or 10 wethers, 10 geese, 20 hens, 10 cheeses, 1 amber full of butter, 5 salmon, 20 pounds of fodder and 100 eels'. As time went on, such food rents were often translated into cash and paid in silver pennies. The thegn's main obligation to the king or to a senior thegn, however, was to serve him in war, usually with a company of followers. Thegns and their families accordingly devoted much time to mastering the use of the fighting axe, the sword, the spear, the shield and other weapons, and to perfecting their horsemanship. Their favourite pastime of hunting was doubly useful in that venison and boar could be eaten, while the exercise kept the hunter in good trim for fighting.

The importance of loyalty

The supreme importance of loyalty to a lord, whether that lord was the king, a senior thegn, or some lesser noble, is shown by the fact that in Alfred's and in Athelstan's laws treachery to a lord was punishable by death. Archbishop Wulfstan described treachery to a lord as 'the greatest of all treachery in the world'. The perfect model of the behaviour of a vassal is given in the famous poem on the battle of Maldon (991); after the death of the aged ealdorman Brihtnoth in this fight against the Danes, all his 'companions' except a few cowards 'desired

A tenth-century palace *This drawing by Alan Sorell reconstructs the probable appearance of the hall and other buildings which made up Athelstan's palace at Cheddar.*

one of two things, to lose their lives or to avenge the one they loved'. Loyalty, however, was meant to be a two-way business. The king or overlord was also supposed to support his vassal in various ways, such as providing him with arms, helping him in courts of law, or granting him land for faithful service.

Thegns did not lower themselves by doing ordinary work. Their main business lay in supervising estates, helping to govern, fighting, or practising warlike skills. Everyday work in the countryside was the task of free peasants and farmers (the ceorls) and the large number of unfree men beneath them – the 'Welsh' (or Britons), the prisoners of war, the convicted criminals and others who made up the slave population. The ceorls themselves varied greatly in wealth and status. The larger farmers, with perhaps 600 or more acres, might be reaching the point where they could become thegns; the smallest, with perhaps only three or four acres, might be extremely poor and greatly restricted in their freedom by service obligations. In any case many ceorls, as time went on and the Danish invasions persisted, tended to become less free: for in a period of turmoil it was good sense to become the 'man' of someone powerful – to 'commend' oneself to some local landowner who would become one's lord, and would supply protection in return for services rendered. And according to the nature of these services, so the freedom of the ceorl might vary. If the services were a money rent, or a food rent, or were military, or were rendered direct to the king or were given only at special seasons such as harvest-time, there was no regular restriction on freedom; but if they consisted of working on the the lord's land for one or more days a week throughout the year, then the lord was most unlikely to agree to the departure of the ceorl concerned and the status of such a ceorl bordered on serfdom. He was in effect 'tied to the land', and could not repudiate the lord–man relationship, as a more free ceorl could.

Below the various classes of freemen were the slaves, but even these had some rights. They were regarded as being entitled to certain minimum rations, and King Alfred decreed that they should have the four Wednesdays in Lent to sell anything they had been given during the year, or had managed to earn in their leisure moments. Their lot gradually improved, and their number lessened, as time went on. It was regarded as a charitable and Christian thing for a master to free his slaves – a ceremony usually performed either before an altar or at a cross-roads.

Ceorls of varying kinds and slaves together made up the labour force for agriculture, the prime occupation. They lived for the most part in villages and outlying hamlets, but also to some extent in isolated farmsteads. To judge from later evidence the villages, consisting mainly of thatched wooden huts with possibly a church, a smithy and a lord's hall, were sometimes built to no particular plan, but frequently were either of the 'village green' or the 'village street' type. In the former, the huts were clustered round a square of green – a lay-out which

The ceorls

'Commendation'

Slaves

Agriculture

Villages

enabled the village beasts to be corralled on the green at nightfall for protection against wild animals. Both 'green' and 'street' types tended to be linked with 'open-field' farming. Isolated farmsteads and formless villages usually went with a district of separate enclosed farms.

Open-field farming was found particularly in the Midlands, the east and the south of England. The typical pattern, which appeared fairly early in the Anglo-Saxon period, was for the arable or plough land of the village to be in the form of two or three large fields, which were divided into strips. Ceorls held differing numbers of strips, according to what they had acquired or inherited; and some of the strips would probably belong to the local thegn, and be worked by the villagers. These large fields were probably fenced, and one of them stood fallow each year to allow the soil to recover. Within the field or fields actually cultivated, a grain crop would normally be grown – wheat, barley, oats or rye; and since there were no divisions between the strips, the same crop was grown throughout the field. Much of the heavier work of cultivation, such as the first clearing, or the ploughing and harrowing, was done as a joint effort by neighbours who pooled their plough oxen to form a team; but the strips were individually owned and so was the produce grown on them. Similarly, the villagers usually held a permanent share, or had a different share allotted each year, in whatever field or fields were set aside as the village hay-meadow.

The fact that decisions had to be taken from time to time which affected the whole village community, such as what crop should be sown in what field at which season, means that there must have been some organisation for discussing these problems. This was probably a village folk-moot, meeting under the presidency of the thegn's reeve.

Of wasteland or woodland, suitable for fuel gathering and the keeping of cattle or pigs, there was at first plenty. If it were scarce, or became so, a ceorl's rights in it tended to be in accordance with the number of strips he held in the arable fields.

As there were as yet no root crops, it was impossible to keep a large number of cattle through the winter. Many of them were accordingly killed off at Martinmas, in November, and the carcases were salted down for winter eating. The scarcity of fresh beef, mutton and pork during the winter caused great importance to be attached, by the rich who could afford them, to spices which would disguise the taste of salt meat.

Though by far the greater part of the population lived in villages, hamlets and isolated dwellings, Anglo-Saxon England was not without towns. These were normally at natural centres of communication, such as where important road, valley or water routes met. Some of them occupied the site, or part of the site, of the Roman towns; others first came into existence as fortified burhs or as Danish strongpoints, while still others, like Southampton, grew up from their use as ports. In any case the main function of a town, apart from providing defence for the inhabitants and those in the country nearby, was to serve as a market-centre – a place where goods were exchanged.

Open-field farming

Strips

The hay-meadow

The waste

Cattle

Towns

Trade

Some of these goods were made by craftsmen in the town, but most probably came from the country outside. Certain goods – luxury articles such as jewels, furs, silks, wines and glassware – were also imported from the Continent; the Sutton Hoo burial ship contained articles from Egypt and other distant places, though whether it was in the course of trade, or of plunder, or of present-giving that these reached England is not known. On the reverse side, common English exports included wool, leather, tin, silver, fine metalwork and embroidery. Of the native articles sold in towns, most would be to do with livestock, food, drink or clothing, despite the fact that most people grew their own food and made their own wearing apparel. Of the articles taken round the countryside, salt and salted fish, pitch, iron tools and weapons, and pottery were perhaps the most important.

The size of the towns

In the early days at least, it is clear that people living in a town often held rights over town fields outside the walls; and though most townsmen let out these rights, some of them worked on the land as if they had been dwellers in a village. This became less common as towns multiplied and grew bigger. How big they did become in Anglo-Saxon times is uncertain. London, at first the capital of the East Saxons, was undoubtedly the most important throughout – Bede refers to it early in the seventh century as 'a mart of many nations coming to it by land and sea'. By the eleventh century it may have had some 12,000 inhabitants. York was next biggest, perhaps with 8,000, and Winchester was also one of the larger towns. Norwich and Lincoln were somewhat smaller with possibly 5,000 people each. All told, there were over seventy towns in England by this date, and in most of them the burgesses held their property at fixed rents from the king, and considered themselves exceptionally free. With regard to the buildings in them, the halls of great nobles from the ninth century onwards and the numerous churches – by the eleventh century there were about twenty in Norwich – were usually constructed of stone, but the ordinary houses were of timber. Collapses and fires were frequent: by one law, a man in whose house a fire started might find himself paying compensation to neighbours whose property had suffered ill effects.

Buildings

Women

Women in Anglo-Saxon England seem to have enjoyed a higher status than they did in later medieval times. Their main work was of course domestic, which could involve a big task of supervision in a large household, especially as there was bread-baking, ale-brewing, spinning, weaving and clothes-making all to be done in the home. But women were by no means the chattels of their menfolk. They could hold and dispose of land independently of their husbands, appear as suitors or oath-helpers in law courts, make donations of their property and free their slaves. The widow of Brihtnoth, for instance – the ealdorman whose great fight against the Danes is celebrated in the poem on the battle of Maldon – possessed thirty-six different estates, most of which had not come from her husband but from her own family.

Women's property rights

From the Scriptures, and especially from the writings of St. Paul, the Church derived the idea that women were inferior beings to men, that wives should obey their husbands and that marriage was a sacred bond for ever. These views conflicted in many ways with older German and Anglo-Saxon notions, and it was not until the Norman Conquest that the extreme Church teachings in these matters became fully accepted. Meanwhile, kings in Anglo-Saxon England issued laws which sound unexpectedly modern to our ears: such as that a woman whose husband had been condemned to penal servitude should be free to re-marry after one year, or that a wife who left her husband, taking the children, should be entitled to one half of the husband's goods.

That women, in Anglo-Saxon as in other times, were capable of becoming notable scholars or filling high positions, is shown by the many abbesses, such as Abbess Hild at Whitby in the seventh century, who presided over great religious houses. Such women, however, were the exceptions. For the great majority domestic tasks and work in the fields nearby made up almost the whole of life.

Little is known for certain about the upbringing of children in Anglo-Saxon times. They certainly had to obey their elders and were beaten if they did not. From a very early age they were expected to help in the home, the workshop or the fields; and only those who were exceptionally bright, and fortunate, received any formal education. This of course was given in monasteries or similar places: the only road to education, even if the boy did not eventually become a monk or priest, lay through the Church.

Something must be said of the life of those who dwelt in these monasteries – the monks themselves, the boys 'oblated' or given to God who might or might not become monks or parish priests, and the lay brethren. The last-named, who had not taken religious orders but lived in the monastery, became during the later Anglo-Saxon period the main labour force for the heavier tasks on the domestic side, in building, and in working the monastery fields and gardens.

Most of the monasteries in Anglo-Saxon England tried to follow the Rule of St. Benedict, so the life of the monks was divided into worship in church, private prayer or reading, and work. The day usually began around 2 a.m., when the monks rose and descended to the choir of their church for the first service, Matins. Shortly afterwards the boys, who shared the same dormitory as the monks, also arrived, and in darkness apart from the candles on the lectern the service proceeded, the monks singing and chanting texts they had learnt by heart. This service was soon succeeded by another, Lauds, and then, when dawn had broken, by a third, known as Prime, since it was the first service in daylight. After this the monks might read in the cloister or covered passages until around 8 a.m., when they retired to wash and prepare themselves for the day proper. Two more services followed, and then the morn-ing meeting in the chapter house, at which the monks, under the presidency of the abbot, discussed both personal problems and monastic business. During this time the children and elderly monks outside were

Children

The monastic life

The lay brethren

The monks

The earlier part of the day

allowed to breakfast – as a rule on bread and beer, taken standing up.
After this there was a period of two hours or so during the morning
before 12.30 p.m., and this was devoted to work. Since the lay brethren
usually performed the heavier duties, this consisted for the most part
of tasks like teaching, learning, practising music, gardening, copying,
bonding or illuminating manuscripts, or producing things of beauty for
church use in wood, stone, metal or ivory.

The main meal

At 12.30 there was another round of services, including a sung High
Mass, and during the last of these the monks who were to serve the
dinner, or main meal, and who were to read aloud during it, consumed
a snack in the refectory. Then followed the dinner at about 2 p.m.,
usually consisting of vegetarian dishes such as eggs and cheese, with
large quantities of bread and vegetables, followed when possible by
fruit. On occasion, fish or poultry were eaten, but not ordinary meat;
beer and water were the normal drinks. In winter, this dinner was for
long the only sit-down meal of the day, but in the tenth century it
became common to follow throughout the year the summer practice,
which permitted a second lighter sit-down meal at 5 or 6 p.m. On feast
days no work was done, there were more services, well lit by candles,
and more elaborate food, including wine to drink. On fast days, and
during Lent, the monks starved until the only meal of the day, taken
around 5.30 p.m.

The later part of the day

Dinner over, there was a second period for reading until about
5 p.m., when there was the service of Vespers. This was followed by
the second and lighter meal of the day, or else by beer and bread or
cakes – a snack known as a collation, since it was served during the
public reading in the church of the *Collationes* of St. Benedict, a collection of sacred texts. Finally came Compline, the last service of the
day, and at about 7 p.m. the community trooped off to bed. Throughout
the day, the ringing of bells announced the services; and throughout the
day, except during the morning period of work, the monks avoided all
unnecessary conversation.

Other monastic tasks

From the large amount of time spent in services, it would not be
possible to guess that the monasteries were not only the schools and the
art studios of their time, but also the hospitals, the public assistance
offices, and the hotels. Food was given to the local poor, some of whom
were also received as residents within the monastery; sick pilgrims were
nursed until they could resume their journey; travellers were entertained, and for two nights at least usually free of charge. All told, the
monasteries of Anglo-Saxon England, especially after their reform by
Dunstan and others in the tenth century, carried out a number of
highly useful tasks. In contrast to the violence, brutality and uncertainties of life outside, they were havens of peace, culture and charity.

9 The Twilight of the Anglo-Saxon Monarchy

The rule of Edgar the Peaceable was followed by two unhappy reigns. When Edgar died suddenly in 975 at the age of thirty-two, he left two sons, the children of different mothers. The elder boy, Edward, who was in his 'teens, became king; but a group among the leading thegns supported his ten-year-old half-brother, Aelthred. Three years later, some of Aethelred's retainers stabbed King Edward to death as he rode into Corfe to visit their young master.

Aethelred, who then became king as Aethelred II, was probably not a party to this crime, but he benefited from it, and this was not forgotten. Within a few years there were reports of miracles at Edward's tomb at Shaftesbury, and Aethelred had to proclaim the murdered king a martyr. All this gave a bad start to Aethelred's reign, and helped to destroy confidence in him.

Despite this, Aethelred was to reign for nearly thirty-eight years. He is known to history as Aethelred 'the Unready', which fits his record well; though the nickname as first given – 'Unraed' – did not mean 'unready' but 'without counsel', or 'evil counsel'. (This was a play on Aethelred's own name, which meant 'noble counsel'.) Most of his troubles were caused by the renewal of the Viking raids, which began again as early as 980. From 990 on they were led by outstanding leaders such as Olaf Tryggvasan, who became King of Norway, and his rival Swein 'Forkbeard', King of Denmark.

Gradually, as with the Anglo-Saxons 500 years earlier, the character of these attacks changed. No longer did the invaders come in shiploads merely seeking booty. They came in large hosts looking for a place of settlement, and their marches took them far and wide across England. They fought many battles, one of the most famous being that of Maldon described in the well-known poem (see pages 71 and 74). It told how Brihtnoth, ealdorman of Essex, cut off a group of the raiders in their island base in the Blackwater estuary. It took only three of Brihtnoth's men, holding the causeway to the mainland, to stop the enemy escaping, and at last the Vikings asked to be allowed across to the mainland to fight on equal terms. Brihtnoth chivalrously agreed, but in the battle that followed he met his death and some of his followers deserted. Victory was now certain for the Vikings, but the remaining English vowed to avenge their fallen leader and sold their lives dearly.

Aethelred had no proper plan to deal with the Viking attacks. The

Edward 'the Martyr', 975–9

Aethelred II 'the Unready', 979–1016

Renewed Viking attacks

Battle of Maldon, 991

Aethelred's helplessness

Stem post of Viking ship *The Vikings delighted in fearsome carvings intended to strike terror into opponents. This post (now in the British Museum) formed part of a Viking ship, the remains of which were discovered in the bed of the River Scheldt. It probably dates from the eighth century.*

advisers whom he employed were often untrustworthy, and their methods of defence haphazard. The Anglo-Saxon Chronicle is very scathing on this point:

When the enemy were to the east, then was our army kept in the north. Then all the counsellors were summoned to the king to advise him how this land ought to be defended, but even though some decision was taken it stood not, even for a month, and at last there was not a leader who was willing to assemble an army, but each fled as best he could.

Danegeld

Unable to defeat the invaders, Aethelred had to buy them off, and as early as 991 he imposed the tax known as the Danegeld. Very large sums were collected – big hoards of English money of this period have been found in Scandinavia – and the Vikings were bribed to leave; but they were soon back again and asking for more. On occasion, Aethelred took groups of them into his service and paid them to fight against further attacks. In 1002, however, he committed an appalling act of treachery against these men. According to the Anglo-Saxon Chronicle, on St. Brice's Day – November 13 – of that year, hearing rumours of a Danish plot against him, Aethelred ordered a massacre of all the Danish men in the kingdom. Among those who perished were many in his own service and a sister of Swein, held as a hostage. The Danes did not forgive this shameful deed. Swein led further expeditions to England

St. Brice's Day Massacre, 1002

in the next few years, and exacted large sums; and in 1012 Danish troops murdered the Archbishop of Canterbury when he refused to pay a ransom. Finally, in 1013, Swein led across a great force with the intention of conquering all England.

Swein's invasion, 1013

Against this new threat, Aethelred could do no more than before. The Danish parts of the country immediately acknowledged Swein as king, and within a few months he had forced the rest to submit including finally London. At the end of the year Aethelred fled to Normandy, the home of his Queen, Emma. No sooner was the Danish triumph complete, however, than Swein died. Aethelred was then able to return – under a promise to rule better! For a while he held off Cnut, Swein's son, but the war was going against him in 1016 when he died and his long and inglorious reign ended.

On Aethelred's death an assembly of citizens and thegns in London acknowledged as king his son Edmund 'Ironside', a skilful and resolute fighter. Another assembly, however, including bishops and abbots, met at Southampton and recognised Cnut, who seemed bound to win. A great struggle followed, and finally Cnut and Edmund agreed to divide the kingdom between them, Cnut ruling to the north of the Thames and Edmund to the south. But in the same year Edmund died and Cnut was recognised as king over all England.

Edmund 'Ironside' v. Cnut

Cnut king, 1016–35

For a few years England now became part of a great Scandinavian empire. In 1019 Cnut succeeded his brother as king of Denmark and later he won his way by force and bribery to the throne of Norway, whose possessions stretched from Greenland through the Orkneys and Shetlands to the Hebrides and the Isle of Man.

Cnut set out to make his position secure in England. He sent Edmund's two baby sons into exile, and took as his second and official wife Aethelred's widow, the Norman princess Emma. Her two sons by Aethelred she left behind to be brought up in Normandy. For purposes of military control, Cnut divided England into 'earldoms'. 'Earl' is a word of Danish origin, and those given the title supervised regions which varied widely in extent, but often consisted of a group of shires. For many of the most important earldoms Cnut chose Danes, but Englishmen also obtained positions of great power. This period saw the rapid rise of Godwin, Earl of Wessex, and of the rival family of Leofric, Earl of Mercia.

To win the support of the English, Cnut proclaimed in a council that he would abide by the laws of his predecessors, especially those of Edgar, and that he would govern by the advice of the bishops. Broadly speaking, he kept to these promises. The great code of laws that he finally issued was based on English examples, and he always took care to remain on good terms with the Church. He made, for instance, many gifts to monasteries and founded the great monastery at Bury St. Edmunds.[1]

Cnut and the Church

[1] So-called in honour of King Edmund, reputedly martyred by the Danes in the earlier invasion of 870. See page 38.

Cnut's forces

As mentioned earlier, Cnut had a picked bodyguard of trained fighting men called the 'housecarles'. They were rather like a crack regiment of troops, with special privileges and a special position. He also maintained a fleet, but as soon as possible he sent most of this and the invasion host back to Norway, probably to save expense and taxation. It is clear that Cnut felt secure on the English throne, for he was not afraid to leave England for fairly long periods. He led no less than four military expeditions into Scandinavia, and in 1027 he made a pilgrimage to Rome. During this last journey he took care to conclude treaties safeguarding English traders and pilgrims.

When Cnut died in 1035, however, his empire broke up. Legend tells us that his courtiers thought him to be so powerful that even the sea

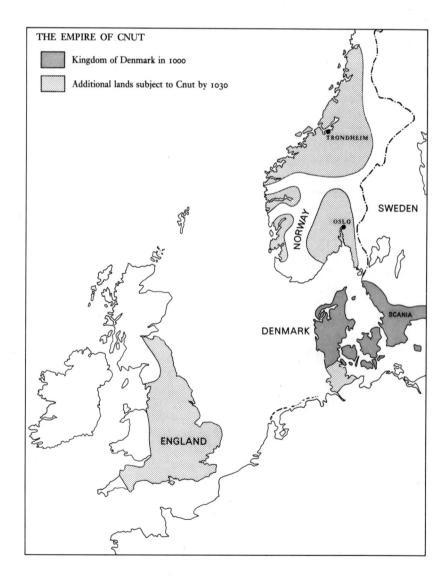

THE EMPIRE OF CNUT

Kingdom of Denmark in 1000

Additional lands subject to Cnut by 1030

TRONDHEIM

SWEDEN

NORWAY

OSLO

SCANIA

DENMARK

ENGLAND

would obey him;[1] but forgetting this exaggeration we can think of him as a strong ruler, energetic and ruthless, who managed to check for a while the slow decay of the Old English monarchy. His power did not survive him, for it was largely based on his own character, and there were few links of sympathy between England, Denmark and Norway. He left to his successors in England much the same problems as had faced him when he became king.

Between 1035 and 1042 England was ruled in turn by Cnut's sons Harold I and Harthacnut. These were troubled times, when the succession to the throne was disputed; and in 1042, on the death of Harthacnut, the West Saxon line of kings was restored in the person of Edward, whose reputation for piety later gave him the nickname of the 'Confessor'. His father was Aethelred the Unready, his mother the Norman princess Emma, and he had spent his life up to 1041 at the court of the Duke of Normandy. Here he had been brought up by monks, learning to speak French, making Normans his real friends, and growing accustomed to Norman ways of life. It was not surprising, then, that his reign saw the growth of Norman and French influence in England. One Norman, Robert of Jumièges, soon became Bishop of London. Norman barons were given estates in England, and the wine merchants of Rouen had a wharf of their own at the mouth of the Wall brook in London. Edward, whose interests lay mainly in hunting, in culture, and in church matters, and whose most lasting achievement was the foundation of Westminster Abbey, also invited Norman chaplains to his court. It would be wrong to exaggerate the numbers of Normans who came to live in England during Edward's reign, but undoubtedly the favour that was shown by the king to the Normans and other French was resented by the leading English nobles.

Of these, the most prominent was Godwin, Earl of Wessex. He controlled either directly or through his sons huge areas of the country, and in 1045 the king married his daughter, Edith. But in 1051 Godwin refused to obey an order of Edward's to punish Dover for an affront to a visiting foreign prince, and he and his sons threatened Edward with armed resistance. This gave Edward the chance to get rid of an over-mighty subject: Godwin and his family were forced into exile. At the same time the king put away his queen, Godwin's daughter. Able at last to carry out his own wishes, Edward now received the Duke of Normandy, to whom he probably promised the succession, and appointed Robert of Jumièges to be Archbishop of Canterbury. These moves caused ill-feeling, on which the exiled Godwin was able to trade. In 1052 he returned with his son Harold, bringing enough forces to make the king accept him. Godwin and his sons regained their estates, Queen Edith was restored to Court, and Archbishop Robert was deposed. For the rest of Edward's reign the Norman influence was lessened, and the leading figures in the country were Godwin, who died

Harold I and Harthacnut

Edward the Confessor, 1042–66

Norman influence

Godwin, Earl of Wessex

Harold Godwinson

---

[1] The story of Cnut vainly commanding the waves to retreat, to rebuke his courtiers for their flattery of him, first appears in a twelfth-century chronicle.

in 1053, and his son Harold, who succeeded his father as head of the family.

Godwin's other sons, Harold's brothers, also lorded it over vast lands. Very soon, Tostig controlled Northumbria, Gyrth East Anglia, and Leofwine the area around London, while Harold adopted his father's title of earl of Wessex. The king eventually surrendered much of the task of government to him. Moreover, as Harold dominated the scene and always played his cards cleverly with Edward, the childless king on his deathbed finally named Harold as his successor. This proved acceptable to the English, for Harold was a much respected warrior who had fought two successful campaigns against the Welsh king Griffith ap Llewellyn. It was Harold, too, who had helped to pacify Northumbria after a rebellion in 1065 – a rebellion which expelled the grasping Tostig and left Northumbria with a new earl in the person of Morcar, brother of Edwin earl of Mercia.

Tostig's expulsion
from Northumbria

So it was with the consent of the Witenagemot or Council, gathered from the leading thegns and churchmen within reach of London, that Harold was crowned king in Westminster Abbey on the day after Edward the Confessor died. The last of the kings of the Wessex line was buried in the Abbey which he had founded, the monastery to the west of London City which we call Westminster, and here his tomb can still be seen.

Harold II, King 1066

The reign of Harold II, son of Godwin, lasted for only nine months. During this time he had to prepare for and meet no less than three attempts to invade his realm and overthrow him. The leader of the first was Tostig, his brother, who resented his loss of the earldom of Northumbria. In the second Tostig was again a leader, allied this time with the famous Scandinavian warrior Harold Hardrada, king of Norway. Both these attempts Harold managed to defeat. The leader of the third was William, duke of Normandy.

Normandy:
Duke William

As the name Normandy suggests, it was an area – in north-west France – in which the 'Northmen' or Vikings had settled. The Normans before long merged with the local population and began to lose sight of their links with Scandinavia. Instead they tried to win neighbouring territories in France, such as Maine and Brittany, while ambitious Norman nobles also managed to set up kingdoms elsewhere in Sicily and Southern Italy. The ruler or Duke of Normandy drew great strength not only from the hardy character of his people, but also from the wide extent of Norman commerce.

William, the illegitimate son of the Norman Duke Robert, the Magnificent, nicknamed Robert the Devil, had succeeded his father in 1045 when the latter died on crusade. William was then no more than eight years of age and only extreme toughness, determination and military skill finally brought him through the dangers of his youth and into undisputed control of his Duchy. One of his companions in his early years at the Norman Court was the refugee son of Aethelred, Edward, later known to English history as the Confessor. There is little reason to doubt the story that in 1051, during the absence of Godwin in exile, William visited Edward in England and was recognised by him as his heir. It does not seem that this promise meant much to Edward, but it featured, together with his kinship to Edward, in William's claim to the throne in 1066. The Normans also maintained that Edward's recognition of William was confirmed when the English king sent Harold on a mission to Normandy. This, if it was so intended, probably occurred in 1064, when Harold seems to have been shipwrecked in Ponthieu, and held by the local ruler until William secured his release. During the course of Harold's stay in Normandy, according to this Norman version of events, Harold had campaigned with William in Brittany, and had sworn on the sacred relics of Bayeux that he would

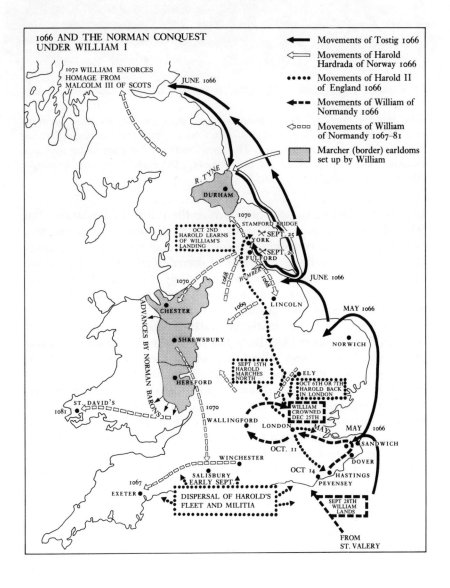

1066 AND THE NORMAN CONQUEST UNDER WILLIAM I

Movements of Tostig 1066
Movements of Harold Hardrada of Norway 1066
Movements of Harold II of England 1066
Movements of William of Normandy 1066
Movements of William of Normandy 1067–81
Marcher (border) earldoms set up by William

The Bayeux tapestry: preparations for the invasion *For no other event in medieval British history is there a pictorial record to compare with the Bayeux tapestry for the Norman Conquest. This scene shows the Normans felling trees and building boats in preparation for the invasion. Above and below are decorative friezes of beasts, real and mythical.*

William's claim to England

become William's man and help him to the throne of England. Thus when Harold accepted the crown himself in 1066, William at once branded him as an oath-breaker. For this and other reasons, including the fact that the Godwins had forced Edward to appoint an Archbishop of Canterbury – Stigand – disapproved of by the pope, William was able to secure the support of the pope for his enterprise, which sailed with a papal banner and blessing.

The account in the Bayeux tapestry

Some years after the battle of Hastings there was produced for William's half-brother Odo, Bishop of Bayeux in Normandy, a remarkable work of embroidery telling the story of these years between 1064 and 1066. It was done in wool on a linen ground, but who designed it and who worked it are unknown. This unique piece of needlework, which we know as the Bayeux Tapestry, is in the form of a narrow extended strip, 20 inches tall by 230 feet long, and it may be seen at Bayeux, where it has been preserved since Norman times. It shows, among many other scenes, Harold's visit to William, the oath-taking, the death of Edward the Confessor, the crowning of Harold, the building of an invasion fleet by William, the crossing of the expedition and its arrival at Pevensey, and finally the battle itself, and Harold's defeat and death at Hastings. For no other occurrence in English medieval history is there anything like so detailed a pictorial account dating from the period itself. In these clear, vigorous scenes we can really feel that we

The Bayeux tapestry: the death of Harold *The centre panel shows Harold being cut down by a horseman. Perhaps the man on the left of the horse, apparently holding an arrow or possibly pulling it from his face, is also Harold. In the frieze below, scenes of stripping the dead.*

have the essence of the events leading up to the Conquest, as seen by the Normans.

Harold knew that his possession of the English throne would not be left unchallenged. In the evening skies of April and May, 1066, there glowed a comet,[1] which seemed to men to foreshadow great happenings. In September, Tostig landed at the mouth of the Humber with a large force in alliance with Harold Hardrada, who claimed the throne as the heir of the empire of Cnut. They quickly defeated the local English forces commanded by Earls Edwin and Morcar at the battle of Fulford, just south of York. Five days later, on 25 September 1066, Harold came upon them and overwhelmed them at the battle of Stamford Bridge. Harold had been waiting and watching in the south against William's landing, but at the end of the first week in September he had been obliged to dismiss the fyrd. He heard about Tostig's and Hardrada's invasion in mid-September, and within a fortnight had marched his way to the north. Such was his victory that although 300 ships brought the invasion army to England, only twenty-four were needed to carry away the survivors – who did not include Tostig and Harold Hardrada, both slain on the field of battle.

William meanwhile had built up his army in Normandy with

Invasion by Harold Hardrada and Tostig, Sept. 1066

Fulford

Stamford Bridge (25 Sept.)

William's preparations

[1] Now known as Halley's comet, from the astronomer Halley's study of it in the seventeenth–eighteenth century.

volunteers from many parts of France. They were attracted by the promise of lands and booty, and by the blessing which the pope had given to the expedition. William had built or otherwise acquired some hundreds of ships to carry his men and their horses across the Channel, and he had collected provisions and the basic parts of three wooden castles. All he wanted was a favourable wind, and for a month he awaited this on the Normandy coast. Not until 27 September did the wind turn southerly. The date was now far advanced for a successful crossing and invasion; but the expedition nevertheless set forth that evening. William's own ship, the *Mora*, carried a special lantern on its mast to guide the rest of the fleet; in the night it outsailed the heavily laden transports, but they made contact again in the morning. At 9 a.m.

Norman landing at Pevensey, 28 Sept. 1066

on Thursday, 28 September, three days after the battle of Stamford Bridge, the Norman expedition disembarked unopposed at Pevensey, in Sussex.

Harold II hastens south

Within three days or so the news of this landing was brought to Harold in Yorkshire. At once he set out with his fittest troops to march south. He reached London with amazing speed, remained there for six days issuing urgent orders, and by 13 October, only eighteen days after the battle of Stamford Bridge, was in Sussex confronting the invader.

Battle of Hastings, 14 Oct. 1066

Harold took up his position on a ridge where the village of Battle now stands, not far from Hastings. Here, on 14 October, the fight was joined. The English king had perhaps 6,000 men – a mixture of his fine but weary professional forces and some ill-trained and half-armed peasants, hastily assembled – while William's army consisted of about 4,000 well-trained and well-equipped knights, besides some companies of archers. The struggle lasted all day. For hour after hour it went on, with all the attacks of the Norman cavalry and the fire of the archers failing to dislodge the English from the top of the ridge. Twice the Normans pretended to flee and then turned and cut down their pursuers; but the shield wall of the English remained firm, and Harold's banner of the golden dragon still waved proudly aloft. But as the afternoon drew on, and the Norman archers had the advantage of the sun behind them, and shot high into the sky, the deadly hail of arrows did its work. Harold fell – pierced, so tradition has it, through the eye. With his brothers Gyrth and Leofwine already fallen, the spirit of the English army was broken, and in the dusk it melted away. The Normans, in the phrase found so often in the Anglo-Saxon Chronicle, 'had possession of the field of battle'.

On the site of his victory William vowed to build a great abbey. His enemy Harold he left to be buried unceremoniously on the sea-shore. Ten weeks later William occupied London, and on 25 December 1066 was crowned king in Westminster Abbey. The days of the Anglo-Saxon kings were over. The Anglo-Saxon people and countryside had new masters, and a new epoch in English history had begun.

William crowned, 25 Dec. 1066

10 The Conqueror and the Conquest

After the death of Harold there was no native leader capable of organising united resistance to the invaders, and no force capable of defeating them. William's final success was largely a matter of time. To encourage the Anglo-Saxons to submit quickly, he used his well-tried weapon of terror. Advancing on London by a roundabout route, he left behind him a trail of burning villages – and continued to do so right up to the outskirts of the city, even after the leading men of the kingdom had met him at Berkhampstead and offered him the crown.

William's coronation in Westminster Abbey came only three months after his landing at Pevensey. He was careful to have himself crowned by the Archbishop of York rather than by the controversial Stigand. One of the incidents showed that the victors of Hastings did not as yet feel very secure. When the archbishop asked those present whether they would accept William as their king – a formal appeal which was a normal part of the coronation procedure – the shout of assent was mistaken by William's guards outside for the beginning of a riot. They promptly set fire to some wooden houses adjoining the Abbey, to drive out any rioters; and at this, many of the congregation rushed outside to see what was happening. William, with the calmness and resolution that were such striking features of his character, carried on with the service unmoved.

William's coronation

But though by Christmas 1066 William was generally recognised as king of England, and had already confiscated the vast estates of the Godwin family and other leading opponents, he had not actually marched his army very far north of the Thames, or much westward of Hampshire. When he returned to Normandy in February 1067, he was relying heavily on the cooperation of his new English subjects. Once in his native Duchy again he showed no desire to re-cross the Channel until nine months later, when news came of a revolt in England. Its causes were probably the Conqueror's absence, and the harshness of the new Norman officials and landholders. At all events, by December 1067 William was back in England to deal with trouble; and trouble there was in plenty for several years to come.

William in Normandy

Revolt in England: William's return, Dec. 1067

The first outbreak was largely confined to Dover, where there was strong feeling against William's half-brother and deputy, Bishop Odo of Bayeux. A few months later, in 1068, revolt broke out in the south-west. Here the storm centre was Exeter, which harboured Harold's mother

Revolt in Exeter and south-west, 1068

and his three illegitimate sons. William besieged the city, had a hostage blinded in full view of the defenders to impress them with the folly of resistance, and after eighteen days induced the rebels to submit. He then marched into Cornwall, took it over, and granted much of it to his half-brother Robert of Mortain. By now he was making use of English troops. It was English forces in the south-west who twice defeated invasions by Harold's sons from their new refuge in Ireland.

The West was scarcely subdued when a far more serious threat faced William. In the summer of 1068 some of the leading Englishmen broke with the king. The Aetheling Edgar, grandson of Edmund Ironside and former claimant to the throne, fled to Scotland, where King Malcolm Canmore – Malcolm III – later married Edgar's sister, Margaret. The great earls Edwin and Morcar also fled from William's court and they reached York, where they sought help from Wales. William quickly marched north against York and occupied it, only for another revolt to flare up around Durham. This too William crushed, after fierce fighting.

Revolt in the North, 1068–9

William's troubles, however, were far from over. In the autumn of 1069, on the invitation of English leaders and exiles, King Swein of Denmark, nephew of the great Cnut, claimed the throne. He sent over three of his sons and a force of some 240 ships. The Danes landed at the mouth of the Humber, where they were among people of Danish descent. A joint move on York with English rebels followed, and the Norman defenders of York were overwhelmed. Again William hastened to the scene, and finally retook York itself. He kept his Christmas feast there, then set off again in pursuit of rebels as far north as the Tees, and across the Pennines to Chester and Shrewsbury.

The Danes join the rebels, 1069

As movements in the depth of winter across difficult country, William's marches in the North were no mean feats. But they are best remembered for the devastation they inflicted. A twelfth-century chronicler, Orderic Vital, who was an admirer of William, wrote:

'The harrying of the North'

Never had William shown so great a cruelty. He gave way shamefully to this vice, and did not trouble to restrain his resentment, striking down innocent and guilty alike with an equal fury. In the anger which carried him away, he caused to be assembled crops, herds and flocks, food and utensils of every kind, and burned them all. In this manner all the sources of life north of the Humber were destroyed. There followed in England a famine so serious and widespread . . . that more than 100,000[1] individuals of all ages and both sexes perished.

This 'harrying of the North', as it was called, was meant by William to deny food and shelter to the rebels and to warn other areas of the dangers of revolt. The destruction was worst in Yorkshire, but also bad in Staffordshire, Derbyshire, Cheshire and Shropshire. For many years Yorkshire lay desolate, and it was not until the twelfth century,

[1] Medieval statistics were usually based on guesses and hearsay, and should rarely be taken literally.

when the Cistercian monks built their great abbeys in the dales and developed their great sheep-farming industry, that prosperity returned to some of the stricken areas.

The Danes had meanwhile retired to their ships at the mouth of the Humber. They also helped to fortify the Isle of Ely, until William induced Swein, probably by a gift of money, to withdraw his troops. This left the leadership of resistance at Ely to a Lincolnshire thegn, Hereward 'the Wake', who in the spring of 1071 was joined by Earl Morcar. In this area, the Normans were under great difficulties, for until a start was made to the drainage of the Fens in the seventeenth century, the whole district was one of swamp and marsh, the haunt of wild fowl of all kinds. It was a region in which the few paths to the occasional islands of solid ground were known only to the native Fen dwellers. For months the Norman army was unable to stamp out the revolt, but eventually a deserter from Hereward's forces – or possibly some monks, in return for a guarantee of their own safety – guided the Normans across the Fens. Ely, which was the centre of resistance, was captured, and Morcar taken prisoner; Hereward himself managed to escape to the coast and exile. Soon afterwards on this ground there was to be built one of the noblest of English cathedrals. Dominating the surrounding flat land, it stands as a record of the Norman victory over the last of the purely English revolts.

Resistance at Ely

After the fall of Ely in 1071, William's next task was to invade Scotland. Malcolm offered no serious resistance. He agreed to withdraw his recognition of the Aetheling, and did homage for his kingdom to William. A further expedition to Scotland in 1080, under William's son Robert, was needed to hold Malcolm to these terms.

William invades Scotland, 1072

Meanwhile in 1075 there had occurred another revolt in England. It was largely the work of two of the great Norman earls, and in defeating it William's officials enjoyed a good deal of English support. Following one victory, the royal forces under Bishop Odo and others are said to have cut off the right foot of every prisoner taken. Later William ordered the execution of the last English earl, Waltheof of Northumberland, who had taken no part in the conspiracy but had known of it.

Revolt by Norman earls, 1075

All told, William had to spend the better part of nine years in dealing, between longish intervals in Normandy, with repeated outbreaks in England. These risings finally destroyed the native English thegnhood, who had already suffered severe losses at the battles of Fulford, Stamford Bridge and Hastings. So William was able to hold down England with a fairly small army. Probably he had brought from Normandy no more than 5,000 men – but among these were some of the best-equipped and most experienced knights in Europe.

Destruction of English thegnhood

Everywhere, to help gain and keep control, William built castles. At first these usually consisted of a wooden tower on a mound protected by earthworks and moats; later he often built in stone, though stone castles cost much more and took longer to erect. From these castles William's forces or those of his vassals – his subordinates who held land from him

Castles

and had sworn allegiance – could dominate the surrounding town or countryside and in them, if things grew difficult, the garrison could hold out until help arrived from some other Norman strong-point. The number of castles built in William's reign is not known, but it was very large. It included those of Hastings, London, Nottingham, York (two), Huntingdon, Cambridge, Lincoln, Chester, Warwick and Shrewsbury, not to mention several along the South Coast and the Welsh border.[1]

The 'Marches'

The defence of the Welsh and Scottish frontier areas, usually known as the Welsh and Scottish 'marches', was a special problem. William tackled it by creating great 'marcher' earldoms in which the earls had powers – e.g. of raising taxes and armies – which elsewhere were reserved to the king. These earldoms he granted to some of his most trusted followers. To his half-brother Odo – whom he later imprisoned – he gave the earldom of Kent with the task of guarding against cross-Channel invasion. The Welsh border was to be protected by three 'marcher' earls whose centres were at Chester, Shrewsbury, and Hereford. These great feudal earldoms were to cause William's successors many difficulties, but they also supplied the driving-force for the Norman advance into Wales. The northern frontier was more difficult to keep stable. One of the main bulwarks against invasion was the great bishopric of Durham, and in 1081 a castle was built on the Tyne at the place we now call Newcastle.

Within these frontiers the country was organised largely on what is called a feudal basis, from the fact that it depended on services given in return for grants of land (an estate granted on such conditions was called a feud, feudum, fee, or fief). As we have seen (see p. 48) there had developed in England before the Norman Conquest practices which were akin to later feudalism. In some ways, however, the Normans imposed a new pattern. The novelty arose because William transferred so much land from English to Norman hands. This made it clear that the king originated the grants of land, and it also enabled the conditions of the grant to be stated clearly. The main condition, so far as big grants of land were concerned, became a military one – the landholder had to provide so many knights for the king's service, according to the amount of land granted. The same thing usually applied at the next stage down the scale, if those who held land directly from the king ('tenants-in-chief') granted part of it to others; they usually insisted on military service by a given number of knights in return. The Normans were constantly fighting, and they had learned to organise themselves in this way so as to be sure of raising forces. Later, the military side of feudalism became less important; but the lord-vassal relationship lasted because it provided a way of keeping order in local affairs at a time when there was no police force or strong central authority, and when there was often little contact between one part of the country and the next.

Norman feudalism and military service

[1] From them all, five stone keeps survive – Bramber, Pevensey, Rochester, Colchester and the White Tower in the Tower of London.

Feudalism gave to each man a lord to whom he was united by ties of personal loyalty, and to whom he gave certain recognised services. In return he expected from the lord protection and justice. At the head of all was – in England – the king. On him depended the whole structure, for if his hold slackened, his great tenants-in-chief often became over-powerful and challenged his authority.

The local strength of feudalism

Below the king in the social scale were the great barons, the tenants-in-chief who had fiefs in many parts of the country – for in England William had conquered or confiscated the land piecemeal and had granted it out to his followers in the same way. Below the tenants-in-chief were their tenants, often lesser barons, while below them were the free and semi-free peasantry of various kinds, who made up nine-tenths of the population. These peasants, whether known as freemen, villeins, sokemen, bordars or cottars[1] all held land, in varying quantities; but most of them could not leave the district without their lord's consent. Below the free and semi-free peasantry were the slaves, about one-tenth of the population, who were without land and had very few rights of any kind. Every substantial landholder in England now held his land as a fief, that is by a grant on conditions from his immediate lord, and the tenants-in-chief held estates direct from the king.[2]

The grades of Society

The relationship between a man and his lord was symbolised by the ceremony of doing homage and swearing fealty. The man knelt bare-headed before his lord, and placing his hands between his lord's hands swore an oath in terms like these: 'I will become your liege-man for life and limb and earthly regard: and I will be faithful and true to you through life and in death: so God help me.' So he made himself vassal to his lord, and for the land that he held of him he had to perform the services which were attached to the land. If he were lower down in the feudal scale and held no land, he performed the services which were expected of him in return for receiving the lord's protection.

Feudal customs

Homage

The Normans recognised in general the right of the eldest son to succeed to his father's lands; but this right was not automatic. Before the heir could succeed he had to make to his lord a payment called a relief. If the heir was not of an age to hold land or was a girl not of an age to marry, the lord would take back the lands for as long as was necessary and would hold them and the children in wardship. During this period, the lord usually managed to do well for himself out of the estate in his care. In addition, a tenant had to make payments to his lord either in money or in kind to help him on certain occasions. These came to be when the lord's eldest son was knighted, when the lord's eldest daughter got married (for the first time), and when the lord him-self, having been captured in battle, had to be ransomed. These pay-ments were called aids'. Feudal lords also made profits from the courts

Reliefs

Wardship

Aids

Feudal courts

[1] For these terms, see page 101.

[2] There was nothing to stop a tenant-in-chief, however, also holding land from people other than the king – e.g. lesser tenants. Feudalism was a complicated jungle of re-lationships rather than a clear-cut 'system'.

which they were normally allowed to hold, and in which they dealt with cases concerning the internal order of their own estates. Sometimes the 'justice' they meted out was very brutal and oppressive. Fines could be heavy and punishments very severe.

William's laws

William claimed to rule as the legal successor to Edward the Confessor, and he promised to uphold Edward's laws. There is a document from the Norman period listing the statutes or laws made by William, but it probably records his practices rather than actual laws. Its most important features include the guarantee to preserve Edward's laws, some rules governing relations between Englishmen and Frenchmen – e.g. that a Frenchman could not insist, in case of a dispute with an Englishman, on the Norman custom of ordeal by combat – and some strong assertions of the king's rights in hunting. The document also implies that William abolished the death penalty and substituted mutilation. Certainly only one important offender – Earl Waltheof – is known to have been executed. Probably William held more great men captive than the Anglo-Saxon kings had done – his castles were well fitted for the job – while the lesser men were mutilated to save the expense of imprisonment. Also, they often died afterwards from the wound or blood-poisoning. William may well have thought that mutilation was more terrible than death, but two of the admiring chroniclers of this period record this practice as proof of the king's merciful nature and high regard for human life. The 'statute' on the subject reads: 'I forbid that any man be executed, or hanged for any offences, but let his eyes be gouged out and his testicles cut off'.

William and the Anglo-Saxon institutions

Court

Sheriff

Council

Although by the end of his reign William had replaced the Anglo-Saxon ruling class by Normans, he still retained many Anglo-Saxon institutions. The shire and hundred courts, for example, continued to function and to administer English common law. The shire-reeve lived on under the Norman kings and their successors to become one of the most important medieval figures, the sheriff, the king's chief officer in local government. A counterpart of the Witan also continued. Three times a year, at certain places, William held meetings of his 'magnum concilium' or great Council, to which he summoned whom he pleased. On these occasions he received important visitors, took decisions or made judgments with or without the advice of his councillors, and ceremonially 'wore his crown'. At Easter this meeting was at Winchester, at Whitsuntide at Westminster, and at Christmas at Gloucester. By these regular journeys, William helped to keep control of all the land south of Trent, and to ensure that his authority would never be defied by any over-powerful baron.

Domesday Survey, 1085
The Salisbury Oath, 1086

In the last years of his life, William took two important new steps. In 1085 he ordered a detailed enquiry to be made into the state of his kingdom – the 'Domesday Survey' as it came to be known.[1] The following year at Salisbury he demanded that all tenants, as well as all tenants-in-chief, should swear an oath of loyalty to himself personally.

[1] It is described in the next chapter.

In this way he hoped to form a direct link with the lower levels of the feudal structure, and so prevent lower tenants from following their lord if the latter took up arms against the king.

A year later, in 1087, William died in Normandy of an injury. He had captured Mantes from the forces of the French king, and ordered it to be set on fire. As he rode through the ruins his horse stumbled on a hot ember, and the saddle-pommel penetrated William's extensive stomach.

William was a harsh man, whose chief recreation was hunting. 'He loved the stags' complained the writer in the Anglo-Saxon Chronicle, 'as if he were their father.' His passion for hunting brought him much unpopularity, even with the Church he so carefully protected; for not only did he claim the right to hunt over all other men's property, but he also set aside huge areas as royal forest, whether or not it was actual forest-land, and in these he claimed exclusive hunting rights, and laid down a special system of law and penalties to protect the game and covert. On royal forest men could be mutilated for taking a hare. How far he was prepared to go to ensure his sport is shown by his creation of the New Forest, in Hampshire, at the cost of destroying some sixty villages.

The pictures of William left by contemporary or somewhat later writers tend to agree. He is described in his final years as tall, very stout, with a balding head at the front, and a formidable, commanding air that brooked no contradiction. A faithful husband to his wife Matilda, he was a genuinely pious man, a benefactor to churches and the founder of abbeys at Battle and Caen: in the chronicler's words, 'though stern beyond measure to those who opposed his will, he was kind to those poor men who loved God'. Anxious to see the Church working at its best, he gave good support to the great Lanfranc, who was head of the abbey at Bec in Normandy, and who became Archbishop of Canterbury after Stigand had served his turn and been deposed in 1070.

William was a remarkable soldier, a man of iron determination, and a sensible ruler of a relentless but not utterly ferocious character. Though he swept away the great English landowners, he did not sweep away English institutions; but rather, as has been said, 'William's monarchy was Edward's run at full power.' The English monk who maintained the Anglo-Saxon Chronicle at Peterborough wrote: 'He was a very stern and violent man, so that no-one dared to do any thing against his will. . . . In his time people suffered much oppression and many injuries. . . . All men had to follow his will entirely if they wished to live or keep their land.' This verdict from one of the conquered race can be accepted. At the same time William's achievement in holding Normandy and winning England, and in giving sane and successful government to both, entitle him to be ranked among the great statesman-kings of the Middle Ages.

William's character:

his passion for hunting

his piety

his severity, determination and ability

11 Domesday Book and the Medieval Manor

The Survey ordered

At Christmas, 1085, William held his usual midwinter Great Council at Gloucester. There he decided that a detailed survey should be made of his kingdom. The Anglo-Saxon Chronicle records:

The King had much thought and very deep discussion with his council about this country – how it was occupied or with what sort of peoples. Then he sent his men all over England into every shire and had them find out how many hundred hides there were in the shire or what land the King himself had and cattle within the land, or what dues he ought to have in twelve months from the shire. Also he caused to be written . . . what or how much each man had who was a holder of land in England, in land or in cattle, and how much it were worth. So very narrowly he caused it to be searched out that there was not a single hide or a yard of land nor even – it is shame to tell though it seemed to him no shame to do – an ox, nor a cow, nor a swine was left that was not set down in his writing. . . .

Domesday

It is this survey that we know as the Domesday Inquest or Inquiry, and from it came the record which from the twelfth century onwards has been called the Domesday Book. Its name is proof of its importance. Reference to Domesday Book could often settle disputes about the ownership of land, and for long it was regarded as the final judgment on these matters, like that of the day of Doom.

Great and Little Domesday

Domesday Book today is kept in the Public Record Office Museum. It contains information of a kind which no other country possesses in such quantity for so early a date. It consists of two volumes. One, called the Great Domesday, covers all the shires of England apart from the four northern counties, three eastern counties and part of Lancashire, although it contains no survey of London, Winchester or Bristol. This volume is apparently in final form and is written in a uniform hand. It contains information extracted and re-arranged from the original more detailed returns. The other volume, the Little Domesday, consists of detailed returns in different handwritings for the three eastern counties of Norfolk, Suffolk and Essex.

The inquiry procedure

To collect the information the king seems to have sent out groups of commissioners, officials, and clerks to travel on circuits throughout the country. The number of circuits is uncertain – perhaps seven, or nine – but each group covered a number of counties. According to one chronicler, Bishop Robert of Hereford, the inquiry was made very carefully, for he writes: 'A second group of officials followed after the first,

An extract from Domesday Book *This extract from the larger or 'written up' volume relates to smaller tenants in Bedfordshire.*

men not familiar with the part of the country to which they were sent, so that this second group could check the returns of the first, and might set things in order for the king.' In each shire the commissioners summoned to the shire court a jury of men, both English and Norman, who gave information on oath about the divisions of the shire – the hundred and the vill. Whether the commissioners then travelled to each hundred court is uncertain, but either there or in the shire court they met not only the main local landlords but also representatives of each vill in the form of its priest, its reeve, and six villagers. It also seems likely that the great landholders were required to provide, in advance of the commissioners' arrival, details of their holdings and claims, as a starting point for the investigations.

We know what sort of questions the commissioners asked, for the monks of Ely wrote them down in a document called the 'Ely Inquest'. This is what they were:

Information sought by commissioners

Then what the manor was called, and who held it in the time of King Edward; who holds it now; of how many hides does it consist; how many ploughteams are there on the demesne; how many men; how many villeins; how many cottars; how many slaves; how many free men; how many sokemen; how much woodland; how much meadow; how much pasture; how many mills; how many fishponds; how much has been added or taken away; how much it was worth in 1066, how much it is worth now; how much land each freeman or sokeman holds on it? All this three times over; that is to say, for the time when Edward was king, when King William gave it, and now; and if more can be got from it than is in fact being obtained.

It says much for the control that William had imposed on the country that so detailed a survey could in fact be carried through. Its purpose has been much debated, for Domesday Book is not really a record of services due. It is a record of landholding, and of the actual and the possible future value of land. The survey could thus be used to settle disputed points of title, to give the king a picture of the possessions of

Suggested purposes

his great men, and to see what each estate might bear in the way of taxation. Most, but not all, historians have considered this last to be its main object.

Great Domesday – the final form

The information collected in each shire was sent to various centres throughout the country, where it was re-arranged by the royal clerks so as to group the facts under the names of the principal holders of land, the tenants-in-chief. Mesne tenants – those who held not directly from the king but from a tenant-in-chief – appear under the entry for the latter but are not always fully listed. For each shire, the information is presented in almost a standard form. First are listed the chief boroughs in the shire, then the lands of the king, then the tenants-in-chief. These appear in the following order: churchmen, lay tenants-in-chief from earls downwards, English thegns (if any), and women (if any). After this comes the detailed information about the lands of each of these tenants-in-chief. The returns for East Anglia – the Little Domesday – were never put into this final form. When the returns were all sifted and brought together, they gave to William – or rather to his successors, for he probably saw only the first fruits of his enquiry – a mine of information about the resources of his kingdom such as was possessed by no other ruler at that time.

The Domesday Survey was not a census: the king was not trying to find out how many people lived in England. It has been worked out that the population at the end of the eleventh century may have been around $1\frac{1}{2}$ million; but Domesday mentions only 283,242 names, mainly those of the heads of families. Few clergy except the great clerical landholders, and few women and no children, appear in it. What Domesday does show us very clearly is the extent to which the Norman invaders had taken over the countryside. Something like 1,500 foreigners had received land as fiefs since 1066, including about 300 as tenants-in-chief. The royal demesne covered about one-fifth of the cultivated area of the country, church lands just over a quarter, and nearly a half was held by the greater lay tenants-in-chief. Englishmen held only a very small part, about one-twentieth. The English peasant farmers continued to work the land and retain their traditional rights, but the English landholders above them had almost disappeared. In the twenty years between 1066 and 1086, power and wealth, based on land, had been transferred solidly into Norman hands.

Landholding as revealed in Domesday Book

In the eleventh and twelfth centuries there were few towns of much size. At the Conquest, something like twenty seem to have had populations of over 1,000 people, but probably only Lincoln, Norwich, York and London had more than 5,000. London, with perhaps 20,000, was quite exceptional. The great majority of Englishmen lived in villages, and spent their lives working on the land or in the occupations connected with agriculture. They seldom moved away from the district in which they were born, although there might be marriages between people from different villages; they travelled very little, if at all; they grew food for their own needs. The world beyond they hardly en-

Towns still small

A country of village dwellers

countered, except when a group of officials came round on the king's business, or a pedlar or travelling minstrel brought them news, often untrue or exaggerated, from outside. It was the life of the village or the doings of their feudal overlord which filled their minds and gave their work its purpose.

It is not the village, however, but the manor – a lord's holding worked as a unit – which appears as the main feature of rural England in Domesday Book. To some extent this pattern which the Domesday clerks have left for us is much simpler than what in fact existed. Not until the thirteenth century did the manorial system develop any clear and regular shape, or did the status of 'freeman' or 'serf' take on clear legal meaning. In the Norman period there were great differences in different parts of the country. The degree of freedom, for instance, enjoyed by the peasant cultivators in the south was normally less than that enjoyed by their counterparts in the former Danelaw and the north.

The manor

The French word 'manoir' originally meant little more than 'residence', but gradually the English word 'manor' took on a definite legal meaning. A manor was a working unit usually centred on the lord's 'demesne' or home farm. All the tenants were bound to the lord, his free tenants paying him rent for their land and service at busy seasons, his less free tenants or serfs doing weekly labour service and paying him other dues, and all attending regularly his court of justice or 'hall-moot' for the regulation of manorial affairs. It would be wrong to think that a village was always within one manor. Frequently, but not usually, part of a village was in one manor, and part in another, with the result that neighbours could be tenants of different lords.

The greatest landholders, as we have seen, were by 1086 all foreigners. The total estates of such men were known as their 'honours', and they were often very widely separated. William himself, for example, had land in every Domesday county except Cheshire, Shropshire and Middlesex. An extreme instance was the Count of Mortain, who held

The widespread estates of the tenants-in-chief

Windmill *From a sixteenth-century manuscript in the Bodleian Library. The windmill is of the post-mill type, in which the mill-building could be revolved on the posts to make the sails face the wind.*

Braunton Great Field *At Braunton in Devonshire there is a great field which has remained to the present day largely unenclosed. The different colours indicate different crops and the narrower bands of colour correspond to some of the old medieval strips. The bands are different in size because some of the strips have been consolidated. An example of very early enclosure (fourteenth century) may be seen in the hedged strip at bottom left of the photo.*

797 manors in twenty different counties. This spreading of estates was not deliberate on William's part: William rewarded his followers with land as he confiscated it during the course of his reign, and the Norman barons often took over estates which were already scattered. But the fact that a baron's estates were seldom in one region alone meant that he had little chance of becoming strong enough to escape the king's control, and this helped towards unity and better government.

A big landholder could deal with his estates in various ways. He could run them himself through a bailiff, he could grant them out to a feudal sub-tenant, or he could rent them out to a 'farmer' for a regular rent or 'farm'. Much land was rented for money and some for payments in kind. When land was granted out on condition of service, it was not necessarily the tenant himself who performed this: often he paid other men to do the required tasks.

Killing the Christmas hog *From the St Albans Psalter (twelfth century).*

The pattern of farming

The Norman Conquest, though it put the English countryside under foreign landholders, made little if any difference to the pattern of English farming. What really influenced this was the character of the land and the quality of the soil. The light soils of the southern downlands supported a different type of agriculture from the heavier soils of the Midland counties; and much of the country was still either heavily wooded – and here the special Forest Law usually applied – or undrained. Farming was largely what is called subsistence farming: that is, people grew food simply for their own needs, as was possible before the days of large towns. There were times when other demands were made on the farmers, however: for example, in 1171, 3,000 loads of corn were sent across to Ireland for the campaign of that year; 1,900 chickens were bought in Kent for the coronation of 1189; the carcases of 2,217 pigs were shipped to Rouen in 1203 for the use of the army in

Subsistence farming

Normandy. But generally speaking, each manor grew the food for its own requirements, and this type of agriculture remained normal throughout the Middle Ages.

Over most of the country apart from the north and west, land was worked on the open field system. This was based on either two or three fields, but two-field farming gradually disappeared. The three fields, which normally surrounded the village and any separate demesne land, were divided into strips of which each peasant farmer held a certain number in each field. The average holding amounted to about thirty acres. An entire field was worked in the same way: it was ploughed at the same time, sown at the same time, and harvested at the same time. Oxen had to be pooled to provide plough teams, and the times at which

The open field system

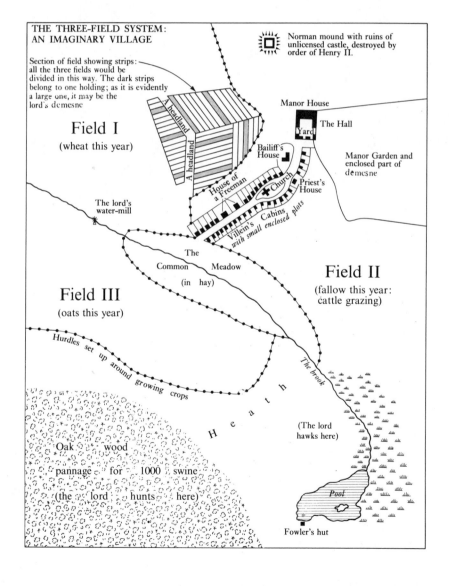

THE THREE-FIELD SYSTEM:
AN IMAGINARY VILLAGE

Norman mound with ruins of unlicensed castle, destroyed by order of Henry II.

Section of field showing strips: all the three fields would be divided in this way. The dark strips belong to one holding; as it is evidently a large one, it may be the lord's demesne

Field I

(wheat this year)

A Headland

A headland

Manor House

The Hall

Yard

Bailiff's House

Manor Garden and enclosed part of demesne

House of a Freeman

Church

Priest's House

The lord's water-mill

Villein's Cabins with small enclosed plots

The Common Meadow

(in hay)

Field II

(fallow this year: cattle grazing)

Field III

(oats this year)

Hurdles set up around growing crops

H e a t h

The brook

(The lord hawks here)

Oak wood pannage for 1000 swine

(the lord hunts here)

Pool

Fowler's hut

the different activities were carried out were decided in the manor court. One of the fields might perhaps be sown in the autumn with wheat or rye; another might be sown in spring with wheat or barley, or oats with vetches, beans or peas; and the third field might rest or lie 'fallow'. In each field, the crops followed a three-year sequence, e.g. wheat first year, barley second year, fallow third year: the most exhausting crop normally being taken in the year after the field had lain fallow. The yield was not normally great. There was little manure to put goodness back into the soil, there was no selection of seed, and 'broadcast' sowing – scattering by the hand – was a very wasteful method.

The keeping of livestock took second place in early medieval agriculture, although a man's wealth was often assessed by the number of beasts that he owned: our word 'chattel' is derived from the word 'cattle'. There was little grazing ground: perhaps some round the homestead, and a limited right of grazing on the common or waste land, or for pigs in the woods. Sometimes there was a hay meadow, the crop of which was divided in accordance with the size of holdings in the open fields. Also, after the harvest the reaped fields were thrown open for grazing. But for many of these rights the peasant farmers had to pay a due to their manorial lord, just as they had to use the manorial mill for grinding their flour, or the manorial oven for baking their bread – and pay for doing so. Sheep were the animals of most use, for from them could be obtained wool for clothing, skin for parchment, milk for cheese, and meat for food. There are records of some very large flocks. The Bishop of Winchester, for example, had a flock of 1,764 on one of his Wiltshire manors in the early thirteenth century, and the Cistercian monks were to build up enormous flocks on their great abbey estates.

Livestock

Apart from the lord of the manor and the outright slaves – a class which diminished after the Conquest and almost disappeared by A.D. 1200 – all those who worked on the manorial land were tenants. They had different degrees of freedom: in Domesday Book, the classes which appear most frequently, apart from the outright slaves *(servi* and *ancillae)*, are freemen *(liberi homines)*; socmen or sokemen *(socmanni)*, villeins *(villani)*; bordars *(bordarii)* and cottars *(cotarii)*. Of these, the freemen and socmen (freemen with obligation to attend the lord's court of justice for service on so many days in the year) had the fewest obligations, the villeins (literally 'countrymen'), bordars and cottars (cottagers) a good deal more. The chief dividing line was whether one or more day's work had to be given on the lord's demesne each week throughout the year. Freemen and socmen were normally not obliged to provide this and were therefore considered 'free'; while villeins, bordars, and cottars normally had this obligation, and so became classed as 'serfs', bound to the manor, from which they could not depart without the lord's permission. This status was to some extent a matter of tradition; there were villeins who held more land than many freemen.

The freeman would generally pay a money rent to his lord for his

The status of the tenants

– freemen and socmen
– villeins, bordars and cottars

The tenant's obligations

A fourteenth-century overseer *This picture, from a manuscript in the British Museum, shows a reeve supervising labourers in a field as they reap with sickles.*

holding, and he would render certain services at peak seasons, such as harvest time. The obligations laid on the other tenants were much heavier. By the end of the twelfth century two tests were emerging to decide a man's status. If the nature of his service was uncertain and if he paid 'merchet', that is, a fine to his lord when his (the villein's) daughter married, then he was considered to be unfree. In theory he could own no property and he could be given away by his lord if the lord granted away the land on which he worked; many grants of this sort were made by lords to monasteries and abbeys. The villein would have to give to his lord a regular, weekly labour service, generally three days; bordars or cottars with smaller holdings would give less service and so were often available as labourers for hire or for such trades as cowman, shepherd, smith or carpenter. The villein would also have to help his lord at the busiest times such as ploughing or harvest, and he would have to pay seasonal dues such as poultry at Christmas or eggs at Easter. He would have to hand over his best beast to the lord as a kind of death duty – the second best beast went to the parson – and he would have to pay charges for the use of mill and oven.

The freeing of serfs   It was difficult, although not impossible, for a serf to become free. His lord could grant him his freedom; or he could buy it – although as he was not supposed to own property or money outright, the purchase would have to be done through a third party. He could also gain his freedom by taking holy orders – of which there were grades lower than priest – but for this again he would need his lord's permission. Later in the Middle Ages, the serf could gain his freedom by escaping to a chartered borough for a year and a day. If he ran away from his manor and was recaptured, however, he could be cruelly punished. In effect the unfree or semi-free villein was wholly tied to his manor, and was

Woman milking cow *From a Bestiary of the early thirteenth century in the Bodleian Library. The pail is of wood and has a stave handle.*

bound to his lord's will. Yet the line between 'free' and 'unfree' was not really clearly drawn, for there were often mixed marriages, and the records of the courts are filled with cases in which men tried to establish their status.

A great baron would usually have a steward for the general supervision of all his manors. On each manor there would be a bailiff, who was responsible for its general organisation, and a reeve who would see to the day-to-day arrangement of work. The reeve was nearly always a villein, elected by his fellow villeins. It was not a popular post to hold, for he had to see that their services were performed properly.

The organisation of the manor

Disputes were settled in the manorial court or 'hall moot', but such courts had in theory no power to try more than a very limited range of criminal charges. The manor was not a part of the main legal system. Law and order in the village was maintained by the 'frank-pledge' system whereby all unfree men over twelve years of age were enrolled in groups which were responsible for the good behaviour of their members. It was also still the duty of the village to raise the 'hue and cry' in pursuit of criminals. In justice, as in much else, the Conqueror continued many of the existing arrangements.

Justice

Dressed in homespun cloth, eating the food produced by himself, his life tied to the regular pattern of the farming year, the peasant farmer is one of the commonest figures of the Middle Ages. For worship he went to the parish church, where a man like himself was often the parson, and at the church festivals and at times such as when the harvest was gathered in, he had his feasts and his merry-making. But life in general for him and his fellows must have been hard and comfortless; and the Norman Conquest, by giving him in so many cases a harsh, vigorous and foreign overlord, did little to improve his lot.

January – drinking by the fire.

February – digging in the fields.

March – pruning vines.

April – carrying flowering branch.

May – hawking.

June – mowing the hay.

July – cutting the corn with a sickle.

August – threshing with a flail.

September – picking grapes.

October – sowing winter corn.

November – gathering acorns to feed the pigs.

December – pig-killing.

The months of the year *The changing occupations as shown in a fourteenth-century calendar belonging to Trinity College, Cambridge.*

1. Aquarius, the water carrier.

2. Pisces, the fishes.

3. Aries, the ram.

4. Taurus, the bull.

5. Gemini, the twins.

6. Cancer, the crab.

7. Leo, the lion.

8. Virgo, the virgin.

9. Libra, the balance.

10. Scorpio, the scorpion.

11. Sagittarius, the archer.

12. Capricorn, the goat.

The signs of the Zodiac *In the Middle Ages men's fate was widely believed to be influenced by the stars. The name Zodiac was given to a belt in the sky through which the sun and other planets appeared to pass in the course of the year, and it was divided into twelve equal parts. Each part or sign took its name from the constellation or group of stars considered to be predominant in that period.*

12 The Conqueror's Successors

The Conqueror's
wishes

William I left to his successors an authority that was greatly respected –
and feared. His final wishes were that Normandy should go, despite
their previous quarrels, to his eldest son Robert, nicknamed Curthose
because of his short legs. Brave and attractive, Robert was also headstrong and a spendthrift. England was to go to William's second son,
William, nicknamed Rufus because of his red complexion. William's
third son, Henry, was promised merely a sum of money. He was off to get
it from the royal treasury at Winchester almost before the breath was
out of his father's body.

William II (Rufus),
1087–1100

Rufus was a man with many of the qualities of his father, including
the courage and vigour, but with none of the respect for religion. He
thought of himself mainly as a Norman, and spent much of his time and
energy trying to seize the Duchy from Robert. Relations between them
consisted of quarrels and fighting varied by periods of reconciliation.
Finally in 1096 Robert, wishing to go on the great Crusade for the
recovery of Jerusalem from the Moslems, pawned Normandy to William
in return for a large loan.

Ranulf Flambard

In England, government continued along the lines laid down by the
Conqueror. Rufus's chief servant was his chaplain Ranulf Flambard,
who became much hated for his skill in raising revenue for the king. In
1096, for example, a Danegeld, a tax started by the Anglo-Saxon kings
to buy off the Danes but later exacted for other purposes, was imposed
at the rate of 4s a hide to raise the sum needed for Robert's lands in
Normandy. Flambard also exploited very fully the king's feudal rights,
and in general he provided the warlike Rufus with the cash to wage his
campaigns and reward his boon companions. By way of return, William
later made Flambard Bishop of Durham, where he pressed on vigorously
with the building of the great cathedral.

Revolts against
William

Wales

William seems to have aimed to increase royal control over distant
parts. In doing so he met much opposition from his barons. He had to
put down two major revolts, and was also involved in struggles in Wales
and Scotland. In Wales, the Norman marcher earls advanced steadily
into the three main Welsh kingdoms of Deheubarth (South Wales),
Powys (eastern North Wales) and Gwynedd (North Wales), only for
princes in the two northern kingdoms to strike back. Twice Rufus
invaded the country and by the end of the reign the Normans had a
secure hold in South Wales but not elsewhere. In Scotland, he forced

Scotland

Malcolm III, who had at first supported Robert and invaded North-umbria, to do homage to him; and soon afterwards he built a castle at Carlisle to guard the west coast route into England. In 1093 Malcolm and his son and heir were killed in further hostilities, and Malcolm's brother Donald seized the crown; but William soon took up the cause of Malcolm's younger sons and placed them in turn upon the throne. For some time afterwards the Scottish monarchy, with its power based on Lothian, was rather like a Norman marcher earldom – subordinate, but free from close control and determined to be as independent as possible.

One of Rufus's main quarrels was with the Archbishop of Canterbury, and this lasted throughout his reign. William the Conqueror, who kept a keen and fairly pious eye on matters connected with the Church, had remained on good terms with Lanfranc, the Italian from Normandy

The Church under William I and II

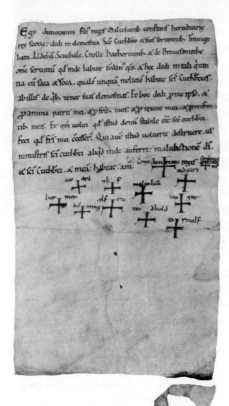

An early Scottish charter *This is the earliest surviving Scottish charter. By it, Duncan II in 1094 granted lands in East Lothian to the monks of Durham.*

whom he had appointed to Canterbury in 1070. Lanfranc had enjoyed William's support in carrying out church reforms: the supremacy of Canterbury over York was clearly established, the centres of dioceses were moved in some cases to new towns, attempts were made to establish the rule that clergy should not marry, discipline within the monasteries was made stricter, and in 1095 William ordered the setting-up of separate church courts.[1] All this accorded with reforming ideas on the Continent, and could be done because William and Lanfranc trusted one another.

William I, however, was never prepared to allow the pope to exercise authority in England without his consent. Still less was the irreligious William Rufus, and during his reign this led to a serious dispute. Lanfranc died in 1089, but not until 1093 did William appoint a successor. He seems to have done so then only because he became suddenly ill, and thought he was about to die. His choice was Anselm, a saintly scholar from Bec who, knowing Rufus's blasphemous habits and violent nature, accepted the office very unwillingly. On the Continent there was at this time a dispute over who should be pope; and Anselm, in Normandy, had already recognised the claimant who established himself as Urban II. William had not taken sides; and when he recovered from his illness he was aggrieved that Anselm stood by Urban II, and would not leave the king a choice in the matter. After a number of quarrels Anselm in 1097 went voluntarily into exile, and he did not return until after William's death. During his absence the king, characteristically, took many of the revenues of the diocese of Canterbury for his own use.

On 2 August 1100 William was with a hunting party in the New Forest when he was killed, apparently by accident, by an arrow said to have been shot by one of his companions, Walter Tirel – though Tirel always denied that the shot was his. The monastic chroniclers saw in this untimely death God's judgment on an impious man. William had not married, and had no children. Within three days of his death, his brother Henry had seized the royal treasury at Winchester and had himself crowned by the Bishop of London, despite the fact that the elder brother Robert, not yet home from crusade, was seemingly William's heir. Henry claimed that his right was the stronger, since unlike Robert he had been born when his father, the Conqueror, was actually king. The speed of his actions has persuaded some historians that he may not have been wholly unprepared for Rufus's sudden end.

Though he shared their taste for war and hunting, Henry I was a craftier man than his father and brothers. He had all the cruel severity of the Conqueror. Before he was king he once personally threw a rebel in Normandy, a leading citizen of Rouen, from a high castle to death on the stones below; and in 1124–5 he had all the official moneyers in England mutilated, without closely investigating their individual guilt,

William II's quarrel with Anselm

Anselm in exile

Death of Rufus

Prompt action by Henry

Henry I, 1100–1135

---

[1] Previously church cases had been heard, with the church authorities assisting, in the ordinary shire courts.

because there was too much bad coin in circulation. On another occasion, he ordered two of his granddaughters whom he was holding as hostages to be blinded, in retaliation for a similar act performed on hostages by their father. However, to the unpleasant qualities of cruelty, greed and lust – he acknowledged some twenty illegitimate children – he added great gifts as a ruler. During his thirty-five years on the English throne there was no big rebellion, once he had dealt with Robert's supporters; before very long he easily outwitted Robert himself, and added Normandy to his possessions; and the peace and good order of the realm were such that in the following reign chroniclers looked back to it as to a golden age. Two of the nicknames by which posterity knows him testify to different aspects of his reputation. 'The Lion of Justice', a term used soon after his death, bears witness to his concern for order and his development of the judicial system. 'Beauclerc', a fourteenth century term, referred to his encouragement of learning – he endowed many monasteries – and mistakenly assumed that he could write.

Henry's earliest acts as king were very shrewd. He at once issued a charter – his 'coronation' charter – promising good government according to the laws of Edward the Confessor and William the Conqueror. At the same time he imprisoned the unpopular Ranulf Flambard and recalled Anselm from exile. He also made a marriage designed at once to appeal to his English subjects and to secure a hold over Scotland; for he married the daughter of Malcolm III of Scotland and his wife Margaret, who became widely revered as a saint and who was the sister of Edgar Aetheling. The young lady bore an Anglo-Saxon name, Eadgyth, but this was a little too much for Henry and as his queen she became known as Matilda.

Within a few weeks of Henry's accession Robert returned from crusade and took over his old inheritance of Normandy. A struggle quickly broke out between the two brothers. In the course of this Robert invaded England, the quarrel was patched up, and then Henry invaded Normandy. Finally, Henry defeated and captured Robert at the battle of Tinchebrai in Normandy. From then on, his hold over both England and Normandy was secure. It was fairly typical of him that he kept his brother a prisoner until Robert's death twenty-eight years later.

Henry fought much against Louis VI of France and others, but he also tried hard to increase his power by diplomacy. In 1114 he secured a marriage for his daughter Matilda, then thirteen years of age, to the ruler of the Holy Roman Empire, the Emperor Henry V. Unfortunately his hopes of building up a great family inheritance received a severe blow in 1120 when his only legitimate son, William, was drowned in the wreck of the *White Ship* on passage from Normandy. With the intention of fathering further sons, Henry promptly married again – his wife had conveniently died a year or so beforehand – but he was disappointed in this hope. However, in 1125 the Emperor Henry V died, and Henry was soon able to summon Matilda back from Germany and induce his

Struggle with Robert

Tinchebrai, 1106 – Henry controls Normandy

Marriage of Matilda to Emperor

Matilda, Henry's heiress

leading bishops and barons, and King David of the Scots, to acknowledge her as the next in line to the English throne.

Since a female ruler in the Middle Ages was an open invitation to baronial plotting and disorder, Henry also quickly chose for Matilda another husband. He made a pact with an old enemy, the Count of Anjou, and forced on his reluctant daughter, who as a former Empress thought the marriage much beneath her, the hand of Anjou's heir, the sixteen-year old Geoffrey Plantagenet. This bade fair to create a very large inheritance – England, Normandy and Anjou – for Henry's eventual descendants. Matilda and Geoffrey in due course produced sons, the elder of whom, Henry, was later to become Henry II of

Marriage of Matilda and Geoffrey Plantagenet of Anjou

Dunfermline Abbey *The nave shown here is a fine example of Norman church architecture, with its rounded arches, massive columns, and chevron (zig-zag) and similar decorations. The abbey was built in the first half of the twelfth century, and was designed as the burial place for Scottish kings.*

Rochester Castle *An impressive surviving example of the Norman stone keep. It was built in the reign of Henry I, and probably replaced an earlier and less formidable castle.*

England. Nevertheless, the match brought grief to Henry I, for he quarrelled with his son-in-law and died in 1135 while campaigning against him in France. It was not, however, the hardships of war but an over-heavy meal of lampreys which is said to have killed him.

Advances in government

The reign of Henry I saw several improvements in government and administration. It was said by a writer at the time that Henry 'raised men from the dust to serve him', and he certainly employed many very able officials. Chief amongst them was Roger, Bishop of Salisbury, who was known as the Justiciar, or chief Justiciar, and who sometimes acted as Henry's deputy when the king was abroad, even issuing writs in his own name.

The Exchequer

It was in Roger's time that the Exchequer seems to have originated. Twice a year, at Easter and Michaelmas, the sheriffs were summoned to the king's court to pay in the money that they had collected from their shires: few of them could read or write and so a special system was devised for the conduct of the business. Receipts were given in the form of a tally, that is a notched stick, each notch representing a certain amount of money. The stick was split down the middle, producing identical or 'tallying' halves, and the Treasury kept one half, the sheriff the other. Each shire contribution was also written up by the Treasury clerks on what was called a 'pipe' – two sheepskins sewn end to end; and on the October visit each sheriff had to account, before the barons of the Exchequer, presided over by the king or Justiciar, for all the money collected during the year. For this purpose a chequered cloth (called the 'scaccarium', from which we derive our word 'Exchequer') and counters were used, and each sum of money was represented by a counter or square. When all the shire accounts were approved and recorded on pipes, the pipes for the year were placed together and rolled up, to form the Great Roll, or pipe-roll, of the Exchequer. From the closing years of Henry's reign these pipe-rolls are still in existence.

Money payments in place of service

Henry's reign also saw the first beginnings of the break-up of the Norman feudal system. Duties which under William I and II had normally been obligatory, such as knight-service and castle-guard, became more frequently replaced or 'commuted' by money payments. The king also sent officials out from his household to try cases in the shires.

'Justices in eyre'

'Justices-in-eyre' (eyre = tour) they were called, and by their journeys they gradually ensured that a common law was enforced throughout the regions they visited.

The king's household

The king himself spent much of his time travelling, and wherever he went his court and household went with him. Although there were many royal castles and manors in different parts of the country, there were no fixed royal residences; when the king moved, his servants had to load all his furnishings and clothes and plate and baggage of all kinds on to pack-horses and journey with him. By travelling about he could see for himself conditions in different parts of the country and also could ensure that the burden of feeding the royal household did not fall upon one area, or manor, all the time. There is a document dating from the early part of the next reign – the Constitutio Domus Regis – which explains how the king's household worked, what were the tasks of its various officials such as the Chancellor (in charge of the chapel and the clerks), the Steward (in charge of food) and the Butler (in charge of drink) and how much they were paid. As the king's business grew so he required more officials to carry it on for him and the household became larger. Those officials who were closest to the king, like the Chamberlain, who looked after his private apartments, tended to grow very important and to become responsible for great matters of state.

Henry I and the Church

The monasteries

Henry's reign was a great age for the monasteries. The existing houses flourished, important chronicles were written by monks like William of Malmesbury and Simeon of Durham, and the arts of illumination and carving again reached great heights. Moreover, several new orders established houses in England. Of these orders the Austin canons were specially favoured by the king, but the most important were undoubtedly the Cistercians, so-called from their parent house at Citeaux, in Burgundy. Their first English monastery was set up at Waverley, in Surrey, in 1128; and today the ruins of three great Cistercian abbeys established in Henry's reign – Tintern, Rievaulx and Fountains – still testify to the scale and vigour of this great monastic movement.

Investitures dispute with Anselm

But though the king was keen on fostering this development, it did

Wrestlers *From a twelfth-century manuscript belonging to Corpus Christi College, Cambridge.*

Jousting *From the lid of a fourteenth-century ivory casket (French). Jousting was a favourite sport with the nobility and knighthood, both privately and in tournaments. It was introduced from France in the eleventh century and retained its hold until the seventeenth century.*

not take long for a dispute to spring up between him and Archbishop Anselm. This was over what were called 'investitures' – the investing of the upper clergy with their symbols of office, such as the ring and the staff in the case of a bishop. This matter did not affect Henry and Anselm alone. Throughout Christendom, rulers and the Church were arguing about it, for the Church under papal leadership was now trying to take over, or take back, from rulers certain rights which it thought the Church alone should exercise. The real essence of the dispute was – who should choose the bishop or abbot? Should the lay ruler have this power, or should the Church authorities select the man? The dispute, however, was waged largely about the outward symbol of this power of choice, i.e., who was to invest the new bishop with his ring and staff? Should he receive them from the hands of the king (as was the custom in England) or should he have them from the archbishop (as the popes had begun to insist)?

Anselm, obeying papal orders, refused to recognise a large number of bishops whom Rufus had invested during Anselm's exile, and denied that Henry had the right to make fresh investitures. The king's problem was that in a feudal society the bishops were normally great landowners, that is, they were lords of the lands belonging to their diocese, which might be very extensive. They were also very often, like Bishop Roger of Salisbury, the king's chief government officials. On both these grounds, the king wanted to choose men acceptable to himself, and to have some control over them. Equally, however, the bishops and abbots were great officials of the Church, and the pope and the archbishop felt that the Church should play the main part both in selecting them and in investing them with their signs of office.

Henry I and Anselm were not on bad terms personally, and the pope was anxious to see Anselm back in England, and in charge of the Church there. After a few years, they reached a compromise, and this formed the basis of the relations between Church and Crown in England for the rest of the Middle Ages. Something like it was already operating in France, and it was later widely applied elsewhere. The agreement worked out as follows. The bishop or abbot was in theory elected freely by the priests or monks of the cathedral or abbey; but in practice the king normally informed them of his choice when he gave them the 'congé d'élire', or right to elect. In other words, the king gave them the right to elect the person of whom he approved. Once elected, the bishop or abbot did homage to the king for his lands, and was then invested by the archbishop with the insignia of office before taking up his appointment. In this way the king preserved the essence of the matter, the power to choose whom he wanted; but the Church gained in prestige by exercising the outward show of authority.

Death of Henry, 1135

The thirty-five years of peaceful growth in England under Henry I ended abruptly with his death. Henry's chosen successor was his daughter Matilda, the wife of Geoffrey, now Count of Anjou; and this meant that Geoffrey would become king, and would expect in practice to govern. Many of the leading barons, however, despite their promise to Henry, were not prepared to accept the rule of a woman, and others disliked the connection with Anjou. Led by Matilda's cousin, Stephen of Blois, a favourite nephew of Henry's and one of the greatest landholders in England, they challenged Matilda's right to the throne.

Stephen seizes Crown

Stephen, a popular man and a fine soldier, acted swiftly – before Matilda and Geoffrey could arrive from France. He crossed the Channel from Normandy, and through the influence of his brother, who was Bishop of Winchester, secured the Treasury there and the backing of the Archbishop of Canterbury. With the support of London following, he was able to have himself crowned at Westminster before Matilda's party was properly organised. Stephen was now legally king and the pope recognised him. To complete his triumph, the barons in Normandy accepted him as duke.

Reign of Stephen, 1135–54

For two years Stephen had no great difficulties. Then trouble began. Dissatisfied with their rewards in England or Normandy, a number of barons began to take up the cause of Matilda. In 1138 Geoffrey invaded Normandy and Matilda captured Dover, and Stephen was kept busy besieging rebellious barons in their castles. To make matters worse, King David of Scots invaded the North. He met defeat by the Archbishop of York and others at the 'Battle of the Standard' in Yorkshire; but by the end of the year Stephen had lost his hold on Northumberland and the west. After this an intermittent civil war raged for most of the reign. The fortunes of this swayed back and forth. Matilda was captured only for the chivalrous Stephen to release her. Then Stephen was defeated and captured, and Matilda was able to act as queen – though not to secure coronation. Her arrogant behaviour gave offence, and Stephen's supporters were soon able to defeat hers and capture her illegitimate brother, Earl Robert of Gloucester. An exchange of prisoners – Robert for Stephen – resulted, and the war soon broke out again. Meanwhile, Geoffrey conquered Normandy. Not till 1148 did Stephen, who persisted in his task with great courage and determination, restore real order in England, and even then some districts held out till the end of the reign.

Though not as chaotic throughout as has often been depicted, the reign of Stephen was a lawless age, marked by much violence and cruelty. In general the system of government created by the Norman kings still functioned, but in places over certain periods it broke down, mainly through the actions of greedy local barons. Of these, the most notorious was Geoffrey de Mandeville, sheriff of London and Middlesex, Constable of the Tower, and Earl of Essex. In his key position he tried to swing the fortunes of the contestants by more than once changing sides, as also did Stephen's brother the Bishop of Winchester. In many of the areas which escaped from Stephen's control unlicensed castles were built, armed bands of men roamed the countryside, and the system of justice collapsed. Inevitably, too, Stephen and Matilda tried to buy support for themselves by gifts of land and titles, and this tended to weaken the authority of both. The Church, too, began to ignore royal control in a way which the earlier Norman kings would not have tolerated.

Eventually, in 1153, the elder son of Matilda and Geoffrey, Henry of Anjou, negotiated a settlement. An able and restless youth, whom Geoffrey had installed as Duke of Normandy, he had already twice invaded England on his parents' behalf – the first time as a boy of fourteen. The terms of the treaty were that Stephen should be recognised as king, but that Henry would be his heir, Stephen's own son having died. This agreement was not tested for long, for in the following year, 1154, Stephen himself died and Henry of Anjou came to the throne as Henry II.

Stephen was the last of the Norman kings. Their main achievements had been to impose a full military feudal system upon England, to make improvements in the system of government, and to support the Church in its strivings for reform.

Government under Stephen

Agreement, 1153 – Matilda's son Henry to succeed

Death of Stephen, 1154

13 Henry II and the King's Justice

Henry II, 1154—89

Henry of Anjou was exactly the type of king needed to restore order after the civil war under Stephen. Twenty-one years of age, he had great strength of character, and he was full of violent energy – so much so, that a legend arose of his descent from the Devil! Several chroniclers have left good descriptions of him. Gerald of Wales, for example, described him in this way:

His strength –

Henry II, King of England, was a man of reddish, freckled complexion with a large round head, grey eyes which glowed fiercely and grew bloodshot in anger, a fiery countenance and a harsh cracked voice. His neck was somewhat thrust forward from his shoulders, his chest was broad and square, his arms strong and powerful. His frame was stocky with a pronounced tendency to corpulence, due rather to nature than to indulgence, which he tempered by exercise.

Henry was careless of his appearance, and his clothes were generally of the plainest. He introduced to England the short cloak which was popular at this time in France, and hence he was often known as Henry

– and restlessness

Curtmantle. He seldom remained still and was hardly ever seen to sit down, except for meals or on a horse. These were days when the royal court was continually on the move – the porter of the king's bed was a recognised official – and Henry was a tireless traveller. His fellow-monarch in France is said to have remarked of him: 'Now in Ireland, now in England, now in Normandy, he must fly rather than travel by horse or ship'.

Like so many medieval kings, Henry was a keen huntsman. He spent countless hours in the chase, flew his hawks as he travelled about the

A man of action

countryside, and insisted that the forest laws were strictly enforced. But this did not mean that he neglected the business of state, or had no intellectual interests. Also, although he was a brave and competent soldier, he did not enjoy war for its own sake as did many men of his time, including his own son Richard. His ideal seems to have been to follow the example of his grandfather, Henry I: to leave a great inheritance, to patronise learning, and to maintain law and order firmly.

The Angevin Empire

Henry II was one of the most important rulers of his day, for his possessions – usually known as the Angevin Empire – stretched from Scotland to the Pyrenees. He had acquired most of his Continental lands before he became king of England. Normandy he had inherited from his mother Matilda; Anjou, Maine, and Touraine from his father

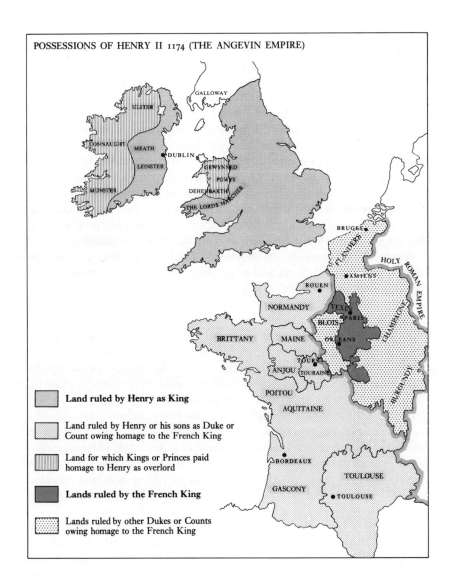

POSSESSIONS OF HENRY II 1174 (THE ANGEVIN EMPIRE)

Land ruled by Henry as King

Land ruled by Henry or his sons as Duke or Count owing homage to the French King

Land for which Kings or Princes paid homage to Henry as overlord

Lands ruled by the French King

Lands ruled by other Dukes or Counts owing homage to the French King

Geoffrey; and Aquitaine, Poitou, and Auvergne from his wife Eleanor – a brilliant and strong-minded woman who had earlier been the wife of Louis VII, king of France. Many of these provinces were rich and prosperous, and Henry spent less than half of his reign in England. Nevertheless he considered England specially important, for it was the only territory which gave him the title of king. For all his Continental lands he was in theory the vassal of the king of France; and many of the wars that he fought were against his feudal overlords, Louis VII and his successor Philip Augustus.

Henry aimed to round off his Continental possessions and by 1173 he was himself the feudal overlord of Brittany, the Vexin, and Toulouse. The Angevin Empire was united only in its allegiance to Henry II. In

Henry king only in England

each province he placed a chief official or justiciar, who was responsible for governing on behalf of the king; and he also tried the experiment of giving his sons authority over certain territories. Richard, for example, governed Aquitaine for over sixteen years.

The extent of Henry's influence

It was not only in France that Henry's influence was felt. His daughters married the rulers of Saxony, Castile, and Sicily; his cousins ruled in Champagne and Flanders; the Emperor Frederick Barbarossa was for many years his ally. To Henry's court came ambassadors from several monarchs, including the Eastern Emperor at Constantinople. But as his reign drew on, he found it more and more difficult to keep his possessions intact. He become estranged from his wife, quarrelled

Decline in his last years

with most of his sons, and finally lost Auvergne to an alliance of Richard and the unscrupulous young king of France, Philip Augustus.

When Henry came to the throne of England his first task was to make himself secure there, and to prevent any further outbreak of civil war. He expelled unpopular officials who had come into the country during Stephen's reign, destroyed unauthorised or 'adulterine' baronial castles, and took back – if necessary by force – royal castles and crown lands which had been given away. In carrying out these measures Henry was seldom vindictive; his sole object was to establish his own control as quickly and as effectively as possible. So successful was he that order was quickly restored and the country remained peaceful until 1173, when his own sons led a baronial outbreak.

Development of government under Henry II

In the Middle Ages in England we can trace the slow growth of a national system of government, of taxation, of law, and of courts in which that law was administered. Henry II's reign saw some very important steps forward in this direction. Neither in his nor in later reigns, however, were these advances easy, for they involved repeated struggles between the kings and the feudal barons, who disliked giving up what they thought were their customary and proper powers.

As we have seen, those officials who attended to the king's needs at court and travelled around the countryside with him also became responsible for the government of the country. As business grew more complicated, however, it became more and more difficult for the great officers of State, the Chancellor, for example, to travel with all the documents needed. Very slowly these departments broke away from the court, and settled down in offices of their own. This process started early, with the Treasury. Originally the king's money and valuables had been carried around with him in great chests; but by the reign of Edward the Confessor some part was being held in a royal Treasury at Winchester. Though the Norman kings still kept hoards of gold in their bedrooms and local reserves in various castles, this Treasury became increasingly important, until finally in the twelfth century it was moved to Westminster to link up with the Exchequer.

Growth of separate Government offices – e.g. the Treasury

Revenue

We have already seen how the Exchequer came into being and how it functioned (see p. 111). In general the officials of Henry II seem to have worked an existing financial system, but there were certain innovations.

In place of military service from his barons, the king levied scutage – shield-money – much more frequently than had been done under the Normans. He also introduced a new system of direct taxation. Direct taxes, including the Danegeld, had so far been levied almost entirely on landed property; but Henry, to raise money for the relief of the Holy Land, also ordered a tax on moveable property. At first the rate was small, and the valuation of the property was left to the conscience of the owner. In 1188 Henry went much further. He imposed a direct tax of a tenth of the value of rents and moveables – the so-called Saladin tithe (tenth), exacted to recover Jerusalem from the victorious Moslem leader. This time there were arrangements for local enquiry if the owner's valuation seemed too low!

Direct taxation on moveables

After the Conquest, the sheriffs were for many centuries the most important local officials. They were responsible for gathering and paying in revenue, raising and commanding local military forces, and presiding over the shire court. They were very powerful and often made a great profit for themselves – which is why they usually paid the king a large sum for the position. They were frequently oppressive and unscrupulous. Under Stephen the barons had largely recovered these positions from the men of humbler birth favoured by Henry I; and during one period when Henry II was abroad they took such advantage of their opportunities that a great outcry against them greeted the king on his return. He called for an investigation into their conduct and that of many other officials and landholders – the so-called Inquest of Sheriffs – dismissed most of the sheriffs, and filled the vacancies mainly with trained officials from his own household. This, like many of his other actions, helped to bring the country more closely under royal control.

The sheriffs

Inquest of Sheriffs, 1170

But it was in the administration of law that Henry II introduced the most important changes. He claimed that he was not creating anything new but was merely giving proper order to an existing system. What he tried to do was to extend the Anglo-Saxon idea of the King's Peace to cover the whole country, instead of only special places such as the royal domains and the highways, so that a single form of justice – the King's Justice – could be available to all free men. In doing this he came up against opposition from the barons (who had courts of their own), but won much popular support.

Henry II and the law

The legal changes were introduced in a series of statements of law called Assizes, from the fact that they were framed at sittings (French 'asseoir' = to sit) of the King's Court, the two most important being the Assize of Clarendon (1166) and the Assize of Northampton (1176). The biggest change was in the greater use of juries. The jury, or sworn group of men (French 'jurer' = to swear), did not then give the verdict, as a modern jury does; but it became a main part of the legal process. Under the Norman kings, juries had been sometimes used, as in the Domesday Inquest, to supply sworn information; and they had also been used in the past in the Danelaw to 'present', or accuse, criminals – to bring them before the courts. What Henry II did was to make the use of the jury much more regular, both in criminal and in civil (non-criminal) cases. He laid down that juries should swear on oath before the sheriff or travelling justices whether in their locality there was anyone suspected of murder, robbery, or arson. For these offences the judge was not to allow the accused to clear himself by compurgation, but was to send him to the ordeal. This use of the jury to 'present' offenders for trial was rigorously enforced as part of a drive to round up the many criminals then at large.

The jury of presentment

Henry, however, also extended a similar use of juries to civil cases. In questions of land ownership, for instance, a defendant was allowed under Henry to decline trial by battle, and to choose instead a form of trial by jury, in which the twelve local knights who knew most about the case were called to state the facts. If they disagreed, others were added, until twelve were found of the same opinion. This process, later known as the Grand Assize, then decided the case. For using it payment had to be made to the king, who thus found in the jury a way not only of improving justice but also of increasing his revenue.

Juries in civil cases

The Grand Assize (for land ownership)

So popular did this kind of legal process become, that a series of royal writs was developed for use in the different types of case of disputed possession. There was one, for instance, in cases concerning the right to appoint to a clerical living; another in cases of disputed inheritance; and a third in cases of eviction of a landholder. In each type of case the aggrieved person could buy a writ from the king which directed the sheriff to summon a jury and ascertain from them the facts about recent possession. Such writs prevented the barons' own courts from dealing with the case, and marked an important step forward in the extension of royal justice.

Royal writs giving right to jury inquiry

Side by side with the use of the jury, Henry II developed a practice already begun under his Norman predecessors, that of sending justices from the royal court to hear cases throughout the country. These justices-in-eyre – the travelling or itinerant justices – were despatched far more frequently under Henry than before, but even so they could not deal speedily with all the cases that accumulated, and that Henry was increasingly reserving for the royal courts. Eventually he was forced to leave a group of justices in session at Westminster to deal with the flow of cases; and from this group we can perhaps trace the origin of our present Courts of King's Bench and Common Pleas, just as we can trace the origin of our present Assize Courts to the travelling justices.

Itinerant justices

Justices at Westminster

Just as Henry in the Assize of Clarendon claimed merely to be giving a clear statement of the existing law concerning the main criminal offences, so in the Constitutions of Clarendon of 1164 he claimed only to be stating the existing law concerning the Church and clerical offences. Here, however, Henry's action led to the most serious quarrel of his reign.

Henry II and the Church

On becoming king in 1154, Henry had chosen as his Chancellor a priest, Thomas à Becket, who had been trained in the household of the Archbishop of Canterbury. Becket and the king, being both young men

Thomas à Becket, Archbishop of Canterbury, 1162

The whale *From a twelfth-century Bestiary, or Book of Beasts, in the Bodleian Library, Oxford. The boat gives some idea of a vessel of the time.*

The scribe *A self-portrait by the monk Eadwine in the psalter which he wrote out at Canterbury in the twelfth century. (Trinity College, Cambridge.)*

of great energy and ability, became close friends and for eight or nine years worked together in harmony. When the old archbishop died in 1162, Henry quite naturally chose Becket to succeed him; for he needed someone at the head of the Church in England who would not try to carry out policies contrary to his own.

Becket seems to have been something of an unconscious actor. As the king's Chancellor, he had been gay, a great lover of feasting and hunting, and obedient to the king's wishes; but when appointed to Canterbury he at once resolved to be an outstanding Archbishop. He cast aside worldly habits, and lived frugally and with great self-abasement – to the extent of wearing a hair shirt next to his skin and periodically whipping himself. He also enthusiastically supported the claims of the Church and of the pope in matters of dispute with the king, such as the extent of the power of the separate church courts established by William I.

The growing crisis between the king and the archbishop came to a head over the question of 'criminous clerks' – clergy who had committed crimes. By established custom, which was to continue for many centuries, anyone in holy orders – which meant not only priests but

Becket as archbishop

Disputes with king

'Criminous clerks'

those in lesser orders like deacons, and in practice almost everybody professionally connected with the Church – could claim 'benefit of clergy' if charged with a crime. This meant that they could be tried only before one of the separate Church courts – which inflicted punishments much milder than those of the ordinary shire courts. Moreover any criminal, lay or clerical, fleeing from arrest could claim sanctuary in a church or churchyard – a privilege in most places subject to a time limit which was frequently overstayed. Henry intended to reduce these gaps in the royal legal system, partly because they enabled criminals to escape lightly, and partly because he was losing the income which he might have obtained in such cases from fines and confiscations. He looked to Becket to help him in this policy.

When Becket on the contrary showed signs of supporting the more extreme claims of the Church, Henry resolved to force the issue. In the so-called Constitutions issued at Clarendon in 1164, he put forth a statement of what he claimed were the accepted customs concerning Church and State. Among these were two which Becket was specially loth to accept. One concerned 'criminous clerks'. The Constitutions stated that when the church courts had dealt with the crime by depriving the criminal of his holy orders, the Church should no longer protect him. This meant that the sheriff could then apply the penalties, such as confiscation of goods, which an ordinary layman would have suffered. In Becket's opinion, this was punishing the clerk twice for the same offence. The other provision to which he objected forbade any appeal from the Church courts to go to Rome without the king's consent. At Clarendon the king forced Becket to accept these customs, only for the archbishop to withdraw his agreement later. The king then summoned him to Northampton, and ordered his trial on several charges.

Becket flees abroad

Becket refused as a priest to accept the royal jurisdiction, appealed to the pope and stormed from the Court. That night he escaped in disguise from Northampton, and later made his way across the Channel to a refuge in France.

During the next five years there were many attempts to bring the king and the archbishop together, and even two meetings between them. The negotiations, however, always broke down at some point. In 1170 a fresh issue was added to the quarrel. In that year Henry decided that his eldest surviving son, Prince Henry, should be crowned in order to avoid disputes about the succession. It was the recognised right of the

Coronation of Prince Henry, 1170

Archbishop of Canterbury to conduct all coronation services, but as Becket was in exile Henry ordered the Archbishop of York to perform the ceremony, which he did with six other bishops. This was a violation of Canterbury's rights which much milder archbishops than Becket would have resisted. Surprisingly enough, however, a meeting between the king and the archbishop held in France shortly afterwards resulted in a reconciliation – without any discussion of the disputes between them! Becket agreed to return to England, and did so towards the end of 1170. But the peace was short-lived. Just before he embarked,

Becket suspended all the bishops who had taken part in the coronation service and excommunicated those of London and Salisbury. When some of the bishops concerned, including the Archbishop of York, went to Normandy to complain to Henry of this, the king exploded with rage against the Archbishop. 'Is there no-one', he said, 'who will rid me of this turbulent priest?' Four of his knights took him at his word. They at once left for England and made for Canterbury, where they sought out Becket and killed him in his own cathedral.

The horror of this deed shocked Christendom – including Henry himself, who had vainly sent a servant after the knights to restrain them.

Becket suspends Coronation bishops – returns to England

Murder of Becket, 1171

The murder of St Thomas à Becket *A thirteenth-century carving in ivory.*

Within next to no time, miracles were reported from Becket's tomb, and within little more than two years the pope canonised him as St. Thomas of Canterbury. The cult of St. Thomas soon spread throughout Europe, and his shrine became and remained until the sixteenth century the principal object of pilgrimage in England.

The cult of St. Thomas of Canterbury

There were also other consequences of the murder. The pope placed Henry's continental lands for a time under the dreaded penalty of interdict – churches were closed and services within them forbidden – and Henry had to promise reparation. He then went off with an expedition to Ireland until things quietened down. In 1172 he agreed the terms of reconciliation with the pope, and submitted to a public penance. In the course of this he walked barefoot through the streets of Canterbury and allowed himself to be whipped by a number of bishops and monks. Over the matters originally in dispute, he had to give way on one big point: appeals from the church courts to Rome went on without royal permission. But in the trial of 'criminous clerks' the State still acted for the most part as Henry had laid down, except that clergy deprived of their orders were not normally liable to the death penalty. As to the degree of control which the king continued to exercise over the appointments to bishoprics and abbacies, this may be seen from a writ which he sent to the monks of Winchester: 'I order you to hold a free election but, nevertheless, I forbid you to elect anyone except Richard my clerk, the archdeacon of Poitiers'.

Henry reconciled with pope, 1172

Henry's control of the British Isles was never seriously threatened. Wales he left under the rule of the native princes provided they recognised his overlordship; one of them, Owain of Gwynedd, twice beat back an English invasion. In Ireland, Henry's expedition of 1171 compelled the Irish native princes to accept his authority, and at the Council of Cashel of 1172 the Church in Ireland was brought more into line with the Church in England and with Rome. In Scotland, William 'the Lion' tried to assert his independence, and during the revolt of Henry's sons he invaded Northern England. He was defeated, captured and compelled to agree to the Treaty of Falaise in 1174, by which he accepted Scotland back as a fief from Henry.

Henry's control of Britain

Wales

Ireland

Scotland

This rebellion of Henry's sons in 1173–74 was the most serious movement against him. Young Henry, Richard, and Geoffrey, resenting their father's reluctance to give them territory to rule, were all involved, and they were supported by Eleanor and by Louis VII of France. But Henry's energy and the lack of concerted action by the rebels enabled him to overcome this threat; and not until the end of his reign, despite a threatened uprising in 1183, did he have to fight again to maintain his throne. Here again most of his sons – even his favourite John, the youngest – were against him. This time, with the help of the young Philip Augustus, they were successful, and Henry's reign ended on a note of failure. Nevertheless his eldest surviving son and successor, Richard, inherited the Angevin Empire almost intact. Not until some fifteen years later, when John lost Normandy, did it begin to fall apart.

His sons' rebellions: 1173–4 and 1188–9

14 Islam, the Crusades and Richard I

Around the year 570 there was born in Mecca, on the western side of the Arabian peninsula, the prophet Mohammed. The city of his birth was a centre not only of trade but of worship; for in Mecca was the Ka'ba, the sanctuary devoted to the god Allah, to whose shrine came travellers from all over Arabia.

Mohammed, born c. 570

Mecca

Mohammed's first important employment was with camel caravans on the desert trading routes. Later he married his employer, a wealthy widow several years his senior. When he was about forty, he began to have visions and to preach ideas which clashed with those accepted in Mecca. He attacked Arabian tribal gods other than Allah, of whom he claimed to be the inspired Prophet; and he made so great an impression that his utterances were remembered and later written down to form the sacred book of the Koran ('recitation'). Eventually opposition to him among the leaders of the city grew so great that some of them determined to take his life. Learning of his danger, in 622 Mohammed fled from Mecca with a few companions to an oasis thenceforth known as Medina.

This flight of Mohammed is famous in history under the Arabic name of the *Hijra* or *Hegira*, and 622 is taken as the foundation date of Islam ('submission to God'), the religion of Mohammed and the body of believers which accepts his teachings.[1] The next ten years Mohammed spent in winning followers, organising the new faith, and spreading it at the point of the sword over much of Arabia. Before his death in 632 he had captured Mecca and made it the centre of Islam.

The Hegira, 622

Mohammed's conquests

Throughout the Moslem world, five times a day there sounds the cry of the muezzin, or public-crier: 'There is no God but Allah, and Mohammed is his prophet.' At this call, devout Moslems bow themselves on the ground in the direction of Mecca, and pray. For prayer, the recital of the creed given above, almsgiving, fasting during the sacred month of Ramadan, and pilgrimage to Mecca at least once in a lifetime, together make up the 'Five Pillars of Islam'. But some have urged that there is a sixth pillar, that of the *Jehad* or Holy War, the carrying of the Faith by force throughout the world. Mohammed himself had ended by overrunning most of Arabia; the Caliphs ('successors') who followed him made far wider conquests.

'The Pillars of Islam'

The Jehad

---

[1] From the same verb which gives the word Islam comes also the word for an adherent of this faith – Muslim or Moslem.

The spread of Islam was indeed astonishing. Within half a century of Mohammed's death, under generals such as the Caliph Omar, Arab armies had captured Mesopotamia and overthrown the Persian Empire. They had also stripped the Eastern Roman or Byzantine Empire of great provinces such as Syria, Palestine and Egypt, and had struck at its heart by raiding Constantinople itself. They had begun, too, to reach into northern India and to move along the North African coast. Another half-century and Arab power had stretched westward along the Mediterranean to Spain and southern France. Here, however, in western Europe, the onrush of the Arabs – generally known in the West

as Saracens – at last slackened. After a check by Charles Martel, the grandfather of Charlemagne, at Tours in 732, they fell back to the Pyrenees.

Within the Moslem empire a brilliant civilisation developed. Under a caliph such as the famous Haroun-al-Raschid at Baghdad, learning flourished and many great scholars extended the knowledge of the ancient world. But in some ways the Mohammedan state was always

weak. Rival families competed for the caliphate, rival parts of the empire fought each other, and rival sects began to destroy the unity of the Moslem faith. These quarrels opened the way for outside enemies. From the tenth century onwards Arab rule over the eastern part of the Moslem Empire was disputed by a new race of invaders from Central Asia, the Seljuk Turks. Already Mohammedans, these Seljuks, who

took their name from a Turkish royal family, during the following century gained control of Persia, Mesopotamia, Syria and Palestine.

Protected by the sea and the mountains of Anatolia (Asia Minor), the Eastern Roman Empire had by now maintained itself for four centuries against Islam. It had surrendered provinces, but during the tenth century had recovered much lost ground. The arrival of the Seljuks put an end to this recovery. They struck deep into Anatolia and Armenia, and in a decisive battle at Manzikert, in Armenia, their great leader

Alp-Arslan defeated and captured the Emperor. After this the Seljuks went on to occupy much of Anatolia and to set up a kingdom there known as Rum. The Eastern Roman Empire was now in mortal danger,

and soon a new Emperor, Alexius Comnenus, was appealing for help to the West. Alexius was hoping for forces to use under his own command. What he got instead was the First Crusade.

The difference was the work of the Papacy. In the same year as Manzikert, the Seljuks captured Jerusalem. The previous Moslem rulers – the city had fallen to the Arabs as far back as A.D. 637 – had become accustomed to dealing with the local Christian communities, but under the Seljuks these were treated more harshly, and Christian pilgrimages from the West to Jerusalem became more difficult. The constant fighting in Syria, too, between the Seljuks and the Eastern Roman Empire made such pilgrimages doubly dangerous. Help from

the West had been contemplated before, but now after Alexius's appeal Pope Urban II took action. At Clermont, in France, he preached the

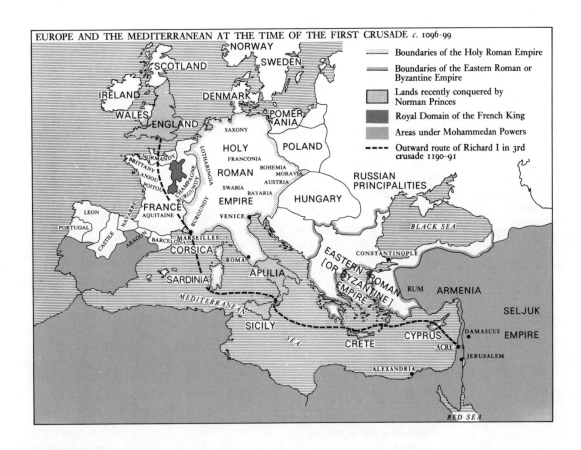

need for a great Crusade – a war of the Christian Cross against the Mohammedan Crescent. In such a war, Christian forces from the West would help the Eastern Roman Empire to recover lost lands, but above all they would fight to free Jerusalem and the other Christian holy places of Palestine from the rule of the infidel.

Urban promised a full indulgence, or remission of some of the penalty for sins, to those who joined the Crusade. 'God has ordained a tournament between Heaven and Hell and sends to all His friends who wish to defend Him, that they fail Him not', went a song, sung by those who went on the Second Crusade. Ordinary pilgrimage was pleasing to God; but a pilgrimage under arms to recover the Holy Land would be the most acceptable of all. So thousands flocked to answer the pope's call; and armies, together with large groups of non-combatants, came together under Bishop Adhemar of Le Puy, named by Urban as leader of the whole enterprise, and under a number of princes and counts from France and neighbouring lands. But before the armies of the princes could set out, a fiery priest from Amiens, Peter the Hermit, had preached the Crusade among the poor of France and the Rhineland, and persuaded thousands to follow him. Other wandering preachers had similar success, and five great contingents of common folk – the

The People's Crusade

The First Crusade,
1096–9

People's Crusade – left for the East. Three of these five groups did not even reach the general meeting-place, Constantinople. The other two, including Peter's, managed to cross into Asia Minor, only to perish swiftly at the hands of the Seljuks.[1]

The Crusade of the Princes, however, actually succeeded in its objects. Its various parts set out from western Europe in 1096, reached Constantinople, and in cooperation with the Emperor Alexius crossed into Asia Minor. Here they helped to wrest large areas from the Seljuks and restore them to the Emperor's rule. As the crusading armies pene-trated further south, however, divisions arose, for the selfish interests of the princes emerged. Several of them strove to seize land and create new states for themselves. First one founded a principality for himself around Edessa, then another hung on to Antioch when it was wrested from the Turks after a year-long siege. More than once the armies of the princes fought each other. However, in Godfrey of Bouillon (Bologne), Duke of Lorraine, there was at least one pious and selfless leader. Reluc-tantly joined by Count Raymond of Toulouse, he pressed on towards Jerusalem; and in July 1099, after a month's siege, the city fell. A letter to the pope, written after the capture in the names of Godfrey and the 'whole army of God', informed His Holiness:

The princes seize
territory

Edessa and Antioch

Capture of Jerusalem,
1099

> If you desire to know what was done with the enemy who were found there, know that in Solomon's Porch and in his Temple our men rode in the blood of the Saracens up to the knees of their horses.

That night the bloodstained victors gathered at the Holy Sepulchre, 'weeping for excess of joy'.

With Jerusalem taken, the conquest of Palestine was soon completed and Godfrey ruled over the new state. This became a kingdom – usually known as the Latin kingdom of Jerusalem – when his brother Baldwin succeeded him in 1100.

The Latin Kingdom of
Jerusalem

Meanwhile Raymond had set up a principality of his own round Tripoli, in the Lebanon south of Antioch. This, like the establishment of the other states, offended Alexius, who thought that all the liberated territory should come under his overlordship. Quarrels also sprang up between the Emperor and the great Italian trading cities of Pisa, Genoa and Venice, whose fleets and supplies had made the crusade possible. These cities were mainly interested in extending their trade, which often meant intruding into areas regarded by the merchants of Constantinople as their own preserve.

Italian trading
interests

For some years, the western princes hung on successfully to their new territories, which they organised on a feudal pattern. They built huge castles, like the almost impregnable Krak des Chevaliers; and two great military orders were founded on monastic lines to provide defence for Jerusalem and protection for pilgrims – the Knights Hospitallers and the Knights Templars.[2] But many of the Crusaders went home once

Organisation of
Crusader States

---

[1] Peter himself reappeared in Constantinople before the fighting, and survived.
[2] So-called from the Hospital of St. John in Jerusalem and the Temple of Solomon.

Jerusalem was captured, and those who remained often quarrelled bitterly amongst themselves. The Crusaders were always in a minority in their new lands, and their control did not spread far inland from the coastal plain. For some time, with the Seljuks in decline, their enemies to the east were weak and divided; but in the 1130s a new strong Moslem ruler arose – Zengi of Mosul on the Tigris. In 1144 he attacked and captured the most northerly Crusader state, Edessa.

Fall of Edessa, 1144

A crusader castle *The ruins of Krak des Chevaliers, in Syria, built by the Knights Hospitallers early in the twelfth century. Note the similarity of the general 'concentric' design to that of Harlech and Beaumaris, which were built much later. Krak was never taken, despite constant fighting, until the Knights had to abandon it in 1271.*

The fall of Edessa struck Christendom with horror. The second great Crusade, ardently preached by one of the noblest of medieval figures, St. Bernard of Clairvaux, was soon organised in response. Its leaders were the foremost monarchs of Europe, the Emperor Conrad III and Louis VII of France. It proved a total failure, its commanders quarrelling and its armies wasting away in Asia Minor. It broke up in confusion after a short and unsuccessful siege of Damascus.

Second Crusade, 1147

So Edessa was not recovered; and forty years later, in 1187, the Latin
kingdom of Jerusalem itself collapsed. Its conqueror was a warrior of the
Zengi family who had patiently succeeded in winning Egypt as well as
most of Northern Syria, and had restored a long-lost unity to the
Moslem ranks. His name was Saladin. With Jerusalem exposed to his
forces on two sides, he proclaimed a holy war for the extermination of
the Christian states. Under a blazing July sun he defeated the Crusader
army at Hattin, and Jerusalem was once again in Moslem hands.

Only the northern Christian territories round Tripoli and Antioch
now survived. Once more western Europe armed itself for a Crusade –
the third. At Mainz in Germany a Diet, or meeting of the heads of the
various states of the Holy Roman Empire, decided on a Crusade under
the Emperor, Frederick Barbarossa; and in western Europe Henry II
of England and Philip Augustus of France made peace and agreed to
lead a joint expedition. Henry's son Richard also took the vow. Henry
died without fulfilling his pledge, but as soon as Richard succeeded
him he threw his great energies into preparing an army.

Richard has gone down to history as 'Coeur de Lion', the Lion-heart,
the nickname given to him soon after his death. To men of his time, he
seemed the very ideal of Christian knighthood. Tall, strong, handsome,
and with red-blond hair, he was outstandingly brave and skilful at
arms, but also a great lover of music and poetry. His greatest pleasure
was to lead his army into battle, and he spent most of his reign at war.
The idea of a Crusade suited him perfectly, since it gave him both an
inspiration and an outlet for his natural instincts. But although a great
soldier he was no statesman, and his high-handed actions brought him
many enemies. Except as a source of money, he cared little for the
country of which he was king.

Richard was in England for only two short periods, amounting to
less than a year, during the whole of his reign. Having had himself
crowned, very magnificently and expensively, he made peace with his
father's supporters and started to raise money. He re-imposed the
Saladin tithe on all those who were not going on Crusade, and sold
numerous offices to the highest bidder. He is reported to have said that
he would sell London if he could find a purchaser. At length he was
ready. With his territories well organised, he met his army and sailed in
hired vessels from Marseilles in the late summer of 1190

Richard's voyage through the Mediterranean took him to Sicily,
where he stormed the city of Messina. It had refused to supply his army.
Thence he sailed to Cyprus, where he attacked the ruler – a rebel against
the Eastern Emperor – occupied the island, and got married. From
Cyprus, in June 1191, he joined the other crusading armies outside the
Moslem-occupied port of Acre, on the Palestinian coast. Of the three
kings who had set out from Europe, only Richard and Philip Augustus
reached this point; the third, the elderly Barbarossa, lost his life crossing
a river in Asia Minor.

Acre had been captured by Saladin in 1189 and was now being

besieged by the Christian king, Guy de Lusignan, whom Saladin had driven out from Jerusalem. On his arrival, Richard took command of the siege – which had gone on for nearly two years – and inspired new life in the Crusaders. Within a month the city had fallen. But the Crusaders were disunited and short of supplies, and Richard and Philip Augustus were soon quarrelling bitterly. Before the end of 1191 the French king returned home, leaving Richard in undisputed command. Under his leadership, the Crusaders recaptured Jaffa and advanced to

Capture of Acre, 1191

Richard I watching a massacre of Moslems at Acre *This scene, from a manuscript in the Bibliotheque Nationale, Paris, is presented in terms of a French rather than a Syrian town. The massacre was real enough, however. After taking Acre, the Christian commanders had about 2700 prisoners slaughtered on the ground that Saladin (who had perpetrated a similar act earlier) was delaying in carrying out an agreement.*

within sight of Jerusalem; but it was beyond their strength to drive the Moslems from the city. Frustrated, Richard opened negotiations with Saladin, who agreed that a coastal strip should be left temporarily in Christian hands and that Christian pilgrims should be allowed to visit Jerusalem. In October 1192, Richard left the Holy Land and headed home. The Crusade of the Kings, though it had won territory and concessions, had failed in its main object of retaking Jerusalem.

As a movement, the Crusades continued until the fifteenth century; but the motives that inspired Pope Urban in the eleventh century had by then largely disappeared. The Fourth Crusade, for example, was intended to recover Jerusalem but in fact spent its energies in attacking the Eastern Roman Empire and seizing Constantinople. This diversion, which resulted in a 'Latin' Empire based on Constantinople until the Byzantine line expelled the intruders in 1261, arose from three main causes. One was the desire to have a friendly ruler in Constantinople who would give real help to the Crusaders. Another was the fact that the division between the Roman and the Greek or Byzantine halves of the Christian Church, which had first arisen during the barbarian invasions of the fifth and sixth centuries, had hardened into a final break during the eleventh century. This made the pope at the time of the Fourth Crusade, Innocent III, eager to restore the unity of the Church and prepared to overlook the use of force. The main drive behind the attack on Constantinople, however, came from the city state of Venice, on whose fleets, equipment and money the Crusaders depended, and whose traders were eager to break in on monopolies held by Byzantine merchants.

This episode was the turning point in the Crusades. The idea of recovering Jerusalem lingered for centuries, but never again inspired movements on the scale of the first three Crusades. Louis IX of France – St. Louis – in the thirteenth century was moved by religious devotion to attempt two crusades, but his efforts ran largely against the spirit

of his age. The Crusades by this time were all too often excuses for land-grabbing and other selfish aims. In fact, in many ways the Crusades as a whole were a blot on western Christian history. Their effects, however, were considerable, and extended far beyond the setting up of short-lived western feudal states in Syria and Palestine. Among other things, the Crusades helped to expand trade with the east, to increase the influence of the Papacy, and to relieve Europe of many restless barons and warriors. The Crusades also to some extent brought Western Europe more into touch with the learning, notably in medicine

and mathematics, that had been preserved and developed in the Islamic empire. Any benefit of this kind, however, was small by comparison with the knowledge of Arab learning that was gained by the West in more peaceful contacts with Moslems in Spain and Sicily.

Richard had an adventurous journey back from the Holy Land. Pirates, storms and shipwrecks were only some of the hazards that he faced. Eventually he landed on the cost of Istria – in present-day

Yugoslavia – and made his way to the neighbourhood of Vienna. There he fell into the hands of Duke Leopold of Austria, with whom he had unfortunately quarrelled on Crusade; the Duke made him a prisoner and handed him over to his overlord, the Emperor Henry VI. During Richard's captivity Philip Augustus tried to capture his lands in France, and Richard's brother John tried to seize control in England. Eventually Richard and the Emperor came to an agreement. Richard's ransom was fixed at the enormous sum for the time of 150,000 marks of silver; then having sworn to become the Emperor's vassal, and paid over the first instalment of the ransom – which was raised with great skill by his officials at home – he set off back to England in 1194. This was bad news for John, who received from Philip Augustus the friendly warning: 'Look to yourself, the devil is loosed.' The castellan of St. Michael's Mount, one of John's supporters, was so frightened to learn of Richard's return that he fell down dead when he heard the news. *Richard ransomed*

By that time, however, the king's officials had frustrated John's schemes. For the time being, Richard stripped John of all his possessions; but the king's return did not mean that he took any greater interest in England than before. He stayed for only a few weeks – just long enough to regain control and go through a second ceremony of coronation. Then he crossed to France, to spend his last five years in almost continuous war against Philip Augustus, who was trying to absorb Normandy. In 1199 he met death from an arrow wound, suffered while he was besieging the castle of a rebellious vassal. *Disgrace of John* *Richard's death, 1199*

It says much for the strength of the system of government developed under Henry II that it continued to work fairly well throughout Richard's reign and that the bulk of his ransom could be collected without much difficulty. His mother Eleanor was a staunch supporter and he was well served by his chief officials. One of the two bishops he left in charge in 1189, William Longchamp, Bishop of Ely, became very important and held the offices of Justiciar, Chancellor and Papal Legate. Longchamp's enemies banded against him and he was deposed in 1191, to be restored on the king's return three years later. *Richard's officials*

For the rest of Richard's reign, however, the chief official was not the Chancellor but Hubert Walter, who became Archbishop of Canterbury and Justiciar in 1193 and Papal Legate two years later. He was a very great administrator, trained in the methods of Henry II's household, and he further developed the institutions of his old master. Enquiries were carried out into the workings of justice, new methods in which can be traced the germs of the system of Justices of the Peace were tried out, and the Exchequer administration was improved. Richard's reign in fact showed something new and very important. It showed that the system of government which had been built up was by now strong enough to work effectively, over a period of several years, even in the absence of the king.

15 The King and the Barons

1 John and Magna Carta

John, finally recommended by the dying Richard as his successor, was the last of Henry II's sons. He was a fairly typical member of that family of whom St. Bernard said: 'From the Devil they came, to the Devil they will go.' Only 5 ft. 5 in. tall, he was cruel, treacherous, cunning, and violent-tempered; but he was also energetic, capable, tough, often generous – and a lover of reading! The main chronicles dealing with his reign were written by monks soon after his death, and are strongly critical of him: they stress his laziness, his greed, his cruelty and his rages. One of these writers, Matthew Paris of St. Albans, describes how John in a temper would start to 'gnash his teeth and roll his staring eyes in fury. Then he would pick up sticks and straws and gnaw them like a lunatic and sometimes he would cast them away half-chewed'.

The public records of the reign, however, leave a rather different impression. It is evident from these that, whatever John's other failings, he was a very hard-working man who took a great interest in his work as a ruler. It is worth remembering, too, the great difficulties he had to face. He had some extremely able enemies, such as Philip Augustus of France and Pope Innocent III; his family's hold over their French lands had long been weakening; and he needed greater revenue in order

to offset a fall in the value of money. Also the English barons, accustomed to the long absences of Henry II and Richard, resented the more intense activity of a king who spent by far the greater part of his reign in England.

John kept his throne not so much by military prowess – one of his nicknames was 'Softsword' – as by persistence, by ruthlessness, and by the outwitting of his enemies. He was keenly anxious that the royal system of justice should work well – it was to his financial advantage that it should – and that the king's peace should be maintained. 'Our peace', he once said, 'should be inviolably preserved, even if it were only granted to a dog.' But although he could make men fear him, he could rarely make them respect or trust him: it was hard to respect a king who enjoyed seeing brutal physical punishments, or to trust one who had sudden mad fits of energy and rage. John travelled widely across the country, appearing in parts rarely visited by previous monarchs, and seldom spending more than three days in any one place. Yet all the time the royal administration ran smoothly. Despite the disasters of his reign there was no major rebellion against his rule until the great baronial uprising of 1214–15.

It was during John's reign that the Angevin Empire broke up. He encountered trouble in France from the moment of his accession. His right to succeed Richard was at once challenged by various barons there; for his elder brother Geoffrey had left as his heir a boy who at John's accession was about thirteen years of age – Arthur, Prince of Brittany. Naturally Philip Augustus seized this opportunity to extend the authority of the French crown; he gave his support to Arthur and in 1202 invaded Normandy. In the war which followed John captured

War with Philip Augustus, 1202

Persecutions under King John
Drawings by the chronicler and artist Matthew Paris, of St Albans Abbey, in a manuscript at Corpus Christi College, Cambridge.

Arthur; who soon afterwards disappeared. He was probably done to death on John's orders, but it was rumoured at the time that John himself, during a fit of drunkenness, had killed his nephew with his own hands.

In any case, the crime did little to benefit John. Even the great fortress of Chateau Gaillard ('Saucy Castle') which Richard had built to control the lower Seine, fell into Philip's hands, and by 1204 Normandy, Brittany, Maine, Anjou and Touraine were all under the French king's control. Of the Angevin Empire in France, only Poitou and Aquitaine now remained to the English king.

The separation of England and Normandy probably brought benefit to England. Very few barons managed to retain land in both places; and those who chose to live in England tended to become Englishmen in thought and action. To John and his English contemporaries, however, the defeat was bitter and the blow to prestige very great. The king therefore bent all his energies towards recovering Normandy and revenging himself on Philip Augustus. For the next nine years he strove to raise money, to equip armies and a fleet, and to build up alliances with his nephew the Emperor Otto IV in Germany and with the Count of Flanders. To obtain money he stretched his feudal powers to the limit – and in doing so, violently offended many of the English barons.

At length he had an army in Poitou ready to attack Philip from the south while a much larger force under the Emperor and the Count, including an English contingent, struck at Philip in the east. The movements, however, failed to coincide. At Bouvines, in Flanders, Philip met and defeated the Emperor's attack, and the coalition which John had built up fell to pieces. All his hopes of recovering his lost possessions were now dead. And at home John had to face the wrath of his affronted barons.

In England the first five years of John's reign had been peaceful. But 1205 brought crisis; for in that year, in addition to the loss of the last castles in Normandy, occurred the death of two of John's most influential supporters – his mother, Eleanor of Aquitaine, and the Archbishop of Canterbury, Hubert Walter. The latter's death revived the problem of finding an archbishop acceptable at once to the pope, the king, and the monks of Canterbury. In this case Pope Innocent set aside two choices made by the monks – the first of their own free will, the second when bullied by the king – and persuaded a delegation of them to elect Stephen Langton.

Langton was a cardinal and a famous teacher in the University of Paris, well fitted to be the archbishop. This did not matter to John. Enraged by the pope's action, he refused to allow Langton to enter the kingdom, and defied all Innocent's threats. After a year the pope then placed England under an interdict. The exact terms of this are uncertain, but it seems that priests were forbidden to conduct most of the normal services, except for baptism and the administration of the

Death of Arthur

The break-up of the Angevin Empire

John's aim – recovery of lost lands

Defeat of Otto IV at Bouvines, 1214

Langton Archbishop, 1206

King John hunting *From a thirteenth-century manuscript in the British Museum. Like nearly all medieval monarchs, John was a great hunter. The extent of the royal 'forest' and the strict code of law by which it was governed was a great grievance in medieval times, and four clauses in Magna Carta aimed at cancelling recent extensions of royal forest rights. Deer, whose flesh provided good food, were the main quarry throughout the Middle Ages, fox hunting did not become important till the eighteenth century. Hawking rivalled the chase in popularity among medieval nobles; there is an order of King John's that his hawks should be fed on doves, chickens and pork.*

Last Sacrament, that such services as took place were normally held in reduced form behind locked doors or in the church porch, and that the whole English people was made to suffer for their king's actions. Yet strangely enough this produced no serious outward opposition to John at home, and the king for his part took advantage of the situation to absorb a good deal of church property. In 1209 Innocent therefore went a step further and directly excommunicated John. This was the greatest spiritual punishment that could be inflicted on any medieval Christian, placing him beyond the ministrations of the Church and rendering liable to excommunication any who helped or served him. Even this did not at once break the king. He continued to resist for nearly four years, and it was not until 1213 that he gave way.

John submitted to Innocent then, but only because of other and more pressing dangers. Taking advantage of John's plight, his old

The Interdict, 1208

John excommunicated, 1209

John submits, 1213

enemy Philip Augustus had gathered together an army to invade England – officially, to assert the pope's authority. At the same time the English baronage, upon whom John had made great demands for money and service, were at last beginning to show signs of rebellion. By a brilliant and unscrupulous move the king not only made peace with Innocent but got the pope on his side against these two dangers.

To do this he recognised Langton as archbishop and offered to do homage to Innocent III as his feudal overlord for England and Ireland, which would become Papal fiefs. The pope could not resist these terms: he accepted John as his vassal and gave him his blessing and special protection. The following year John had the nerve to take the vows of a Crusader and to ask the pope to excommunicate his opponents!

Having skilfully escaped from his quarrel with Innocent, John threw his energies once more into trying to recover his Continental possessions. His hopes, as already described, were shattered by the defeat of his allies at Bouvines in 1214. Meanwhile, opposition from the barons at home had been growing steadily. This was partly personal to John, the result of repeated levies of taxation and demands for military

service. Beneath this, however, there were deeper-rooted causes at work. Many of the barons who were not royal officials strongly resented the steady growth of royal power, for as it grew so their own decreased. The crisis of 1213–16 was thus one phase, and an acute one, in a long tug-of-war between the Crown and a large part of the baronage.

Langton, who believed in an orderly system of government working by accepted rules, tried to find a compromise between the two sides. But in November 1214 a group of the northern and eastern barons took an oath to withdraw allegiance from the king until their accustomed privileges were restored. In the spring of 1215 they assembled with their followers at Stamford and marched to London. On the other side of the Channel, the French were still threatening invasion. John felt obliged to come to terms with the opposition at home. In June he agreed

to meet the rebellious barons in a meadow by the Thames at Runnymede.

Here, on 15 June 1215, took place one of the most famous scenes in English history. The opposition's demands were contained in the 'Articles of the Barons'. The king, for whom a throne and a tent had been set up, agreed to them. Then, or on one of the following days, they received his seal, and on 19 June they were issued as a Charter.

For many years to come the Charter was regarded as an important restraint on royal power. Later monarchs repeatedly felt obliged to confirm or re-issue it. With the rise of a powerful monarchy in Yorkist and Tudor times and with the passing of feudalism, much less was made of it, but in the early seventeenth century it was brought into the forefront again by the lawyers who opposed the Stuart kings. Giving

many of its clauses a meaning they did not possess in 1215, they proclaimed its importance for the liberty of *all* Englishmen. But when the barons forced John to accept it in 1215 they were probably thinking much more of their own traditional privileges than of the population as a whole. Magna Carta was largely a baronial attempt to check royal power in the interests of the barons.

Probably because of the insistence of Stephen Langton, however, there were in fact also some clauses in Magna Carta which directly concerned wider sections of the community. These included provisions for the liberties of the Church (including free elections), and the privileges of merchants and burgesses. Of these more general clauses, number 39 has often been considered the most important:

'No free man shall be seized or imprisoned, or deprived of his property, or outlawed, or exiled, or in any other way destroyed, nor shall we (i.e. the king) move against him or send others against him, unless by the legal judgment of his equals or by the law of the land.'

It mattered little to the lawyers of the seventeenth century and to succeeding generations that the term 'freeman' was here used in a feudal sense, and that in this sense most English peasants in 1215 were not freemen. The later lawyers saw in this statement a true charter of English liberties, the right of every individual to live protected by law, and not simply at the mercy of the ruler.

After the meeting at Runnymede twenty-five barons – all opponents of John – were chosen to act as 'Guardians of the Charter', to see that it was carried out. They were not to meet regularly, but only if necessary. 'They have given me twenty-five over-kings', said John. This was a striking attempt to make the king honour his undertakings, but in 1215 it proved of little use. The pope, now on John's side, quickly released

'The Guardians of the Charter'

Seal of King John *This is one side of the seal that was placed on the Articles of the Barons – later expanded into Magna Carta – presented to John at Runnymede in 1215.*

the king from his promises; and when some of the barons maintained their opposition, Innocent told Langton to excommunicate them. The archbishop refused, was suspended from his office, and left the country.

Civil War, 1215–17

The last year of John's reign was taken up by a cruel and bitter war. The fault was not John's alone, but also that of barons who made exaggerated claims for the return of confiscated estates and then ravaged the king's manors when they did not receive satisfaction. The rebellious barons, though they controlled London, had a difficult time until they offered the crown to Prince Louis, the heir to the French throne, who had a respectable claim. In 1216 he arrived with valuable help. They also appealed for aid to Alexander II of Scotland; and Llewellyn, Prince of North Wales, took advantage of the situation to raid the border shires. John, however, showed a skill and energy which astonished his enemies. Assisted by mercenaries who left dreadful devastation behind them, John marched from his western bases into East Anglia. But advancing in the area of the Wash he lost his treasure and his crown in the quicksands of the Welland; and a short while afterwards he was struck down by an attack of dysentery, brought on, according to monastic chronicles, by over-indulgence in 'peaches, wine, and fresh cider'. In October 1216 he died at Newark – unlamented.

Death of John, 1216

Accession of Henry III

Some days later his young son, a boy aged nine, was crowned as Henry III. One of the most respected of John's followers, William the Marshal, Earl of Pembroke, agreed to act as Regent. He was supported by other great men including the Papal Legate and Hubert de Burgh, who since Magna Carta had been Justiciar. Their first act was to reissue the Great Charter.

Retirement of French, 1217

The fighting lasted until 1217, when the French army finally left the country. From dislike of the French or sympathy with the blameless boy-king, supporters gradually rallied to the Crown, and the royal army won an easy victory and much loot in the encounter mockingly called the 'Fair of Lincoln'. At sea near Sandwich, de Burgh defeated the French fleet bringing reinforcements; and with the departure of the French, the turmoil of the civil war came slowly to an end.

2 Henry III and Simon de Montfort

Minority of Henry III

William the Marshal died in 1219 and for the next twelve years the leading figure among the English royal officials was Hubert de Burgh. As Justiciar he proved capable, but also amassed titles and possessions for himself, which made him many enemies. Not the least among these was Henry III, who began to resent Hubert's control and in 1227 declared himself of full age and royal powers.

The young king, now nineteen, was not a tough, soldierly figure of the kind the barons normally admired. Instead he was impulsive, wayward, and easily scared. Though suspicious, he had a kind of innocence of mind, and the chronicler Matthew Paris writes of his

Character of Henry III

King John *In this thirteenth-century effigy in Worcester Cathedral the dead monarch's features and expression accord well with the tales of his ruthlessness and cruelty.*

'simplicity'. He was deeply interested in architecture and the arts, and was a lavish patron of them; with this went his desire to be a loyal son of the Church. He took Edward the Confessor for his patron saint and model, and though he showed little skill as a ruler, he was a good husband and father.

Hubert de Burgh's policy was to recover for the king royal lands and rights which had earlier been granted away, but also to avoid further trouble between Crown and barons. In 1225 the Government reissued

Magna Carta, with the forest clauses expanded into a separate Charter. But the Justiciar found himself increasingly clashing with the young king, who once even drew his sword upon him. Finally in 1232 Henry suddenly dismissed and imprisoned him, calling him to account for sums expended over many years.

To fill Hubert's place, the king looked to a group of foreign-born men whom he had long liked and trusted. In an age when the king really was the main source of government, it was natural that he should want to select his officials from friends about him at court. The great offices of State, such as the Chancery and the Exchequer, had developed out of the royal household; but owing to opposition among the barons the king was no longer always able to appoint to these positions men who would dutifully follow the royal line. The kings of the thirteenth century accordingly turned once again to those who were closest to them in everyday life. They made much wider use of their trusted servants in the king's Chamber and the king's Wardrobe, issuing orders from these places, franked by the king's Privy (or private) Seal. This often avoided the need to have documents franked by the Great Seal used in the Chancery.

The first of Henry III's foreign favourites were the Poitevins, men who came from Poitou. They were people such as Peter des Roches, Bishop of Winchester, who succeeded de Burgh as Justiciar, and his nephew (or son ?) Peter des Rivaux. The latter controlled several offices including the Wardrobe and the Privy Seal, and was at one time Sheriff of twenty-one counties. But their very energy and ability caused trouble with some of the barons, and after only two years Henry dismissed them. His marriage to Eleanor of Provence in 1236 then brought in further foreigners, on whom Henry showered grants of land and offices. But as he built up this new group of supporters, so opposition among the barons increased.

Another grievance, even among the clergy, was the increasing influence of the papacy in English affairs. These years were in fact a period of revival in the Church, and Innocent III and his successors stretched papal powers to the full. Henry III felt deeply conscious of a great debt to the Church. He said:

'At a time when we were orphan and minor, when our subjects were not only alienated from us, but were organised against us, it was our mother, the Roman Church, which brought this realm once more under our authority, which consecrated us King, crowned us, and placed us on the throne.'

The papacy, however, needed money, and made continuous demands upon the English and other Churches. In 1240 the rectors of Berkshire issued a manifesto denying the right of the pope to tax the English Church, and there was also much opposition to the papal practice of appointing foreigners to English livings.

In 1254 the papacy was trying to destroy the power of the strange and unorthodox Frederick II of the Holy Roman Empire. It offered

Margin notes:

de Burgh disgraced

Royal government

Chamber and Wardrobe

The Poitevins

Henry marries Eleanor of Provence, 1236

Henry III and the Papacy

Sicily for Prince Edmund? 1254

the crown of Sicily, part of Frederick's dominions, to Henry III's son Edmund; and this offer Henry accepted. He was very foolish to do so, for one of the conditions was that he should meet the costs already incurred in trying to dislodge a son of Frederick's from the island.

The king in fact soon found that he could not raise enough money by ordinary means, and he was forced to appeal to the clergy and the barons for special help. To get it, he had to promise to accept their suggested reforms in government. The critics of the king's actions had found a leader. He was Simon de Montfort, a Frenchman who had become Earl of Leicester and had married Henry's widowed sister Eleanor.

Taxes and trouble

In the past, Henry and de Montfort had been on very good terms, but they had quarrelled over de Montfort's actions as the king's representative in Gascony. Ill feeling also grew when Henry refused to give Simon's wife possession of lands which she claimed as her dowry. Eventually the dispute became fierce – 'I am more afraid of him than of all the thunder and lightning in the world', Henry once remarked. De Montfort, for his part, had come to despise the wayward king. He was a strict man with a keen eye for his own rights, but he also saw the need for some reforms in Church and State. He believed that it was the duty of the king to consult the great barons and other leaders of the community and to allow them some recognised place in government. As a man of upright character and great determination he was able to inspire others with his own beliefs, even though few could work with him for long. 'Sir Simon the Righteous', many of the common people called him. A monk at St. Albans later wrote:

Split between Henry and de Montfort

'He stood firm like an immovable pillar and neither threats, promises, gifts, nor flattery could avail to move him . . . to betray the oath which he had taken to reform the kingdom.'

The growing opposition to Henry's actions, especially to the taxes imposed for the Sicily scheme, came to a head in 1258. In the spring of that year Henry was obliged to call a Great Council. This was the kind of meeting at which his normal councillors were joined by many of the greater barons and clergy and sometimes, more recently, by some representative knights. Such a meeting was already coming to be called a 'Parliament'. This Parliament in the spring of 1258, before it would agree to any further aid for the king, demanded reforms. Henry then swore to carry out such changes as were recommended by a special committee of twenty-four, of whom half would be elected by the magnates (the earls, barons, upper clergy and other great tenants-in-chief).

Meeting of the Great Council (Parliament), April–May, 1258

At Oxford a few weeks later the Parliament assembled, and the committee was chosen. Many of the hostile barons came with their retainers on the excuse that there was danger of a Welsh invasion, and altogether the opposition was too strong for Henry. The result was that the king had to agree to a number of conditions, or provisions, intended

The Provisions of Oxford, June 1258

to control the future actions of the Government. The scheme, which included provision for three Parliaments a year, was designed above all to restrict the king's free choice of councillors.

Work of new Council

During the next few months a new regular Council, chosen by representatives of the earlier committee, achieved some notable successes. De Montfort and the Earl of Gloucester were its leading spirits: they drove out most of Henry's foreign officials, withdrew from his Sicilian entanglements, negotiated a treaty with France renouncing the lost provinces, and set up machinery for an enquiry into grievances. But harmony came to an end over the question of further reforms. After

Division among the barons

these first obvious steps the greater nobles became divided. In addition the lesser barons and the knights tended to oppose the greater nobility.

From 1261 on, civil war began to loom ahead. Henry repudiated the Provisions of Oxford, and in this was supported by the pope, who declared many of the king's opponents excommunicated. They proved strong enough, however, to make Henry promise once more to accept the Provisions; and to help him keep to his word they invited de Montfort, who was in France, to return to England. Threats and negotiations then followed, and finally both parties agreed that the

Arbitration of Louis IX—

greatly respected king of France, Louis IX – later St. Louis – should decide the issues between them. In agreeing to this, de Montfort must have thought that Henry was by now firmly pledged to observe at least the Provisions. The French king, however, in a judgment known as the

— the Mise of Amiens, 1264

Mise of Amiens, declared that the Provisions were an unjustified restriction of Henry's right to appoint his own officials. His verdict was that they were null and void.

Fighting begins, 1264

Though many of the barons now hesitated to oppose the king further, the Mise of Amiens was greatly resented by others, as well as by the lesser clergy and the authorities in London and the Cinque Ports. The clash developed into open fighting in 1264. The king's opponents, like his supporters, claimed to be fighting in Henry's name – only they stressed the need to rescue the king from false counsellors, and to observe the Provisions of Oxford. The first actions began in the Welsh Marches, where a main supporter of the king was the powerful Roger Mortimer. To despoil Mortimer's territory of Radnor, de Montfort and his sons allied with Llewellyn, the ruling prince of North Wales. This cost them the sympathy of other Marcher lords hostile to Llewellyn.

After a few weeks of minor clashes the main loyalist forces marched south and camped in and around Lewes. De Montfort's men gathered near the town and two days passed in vain negotiations. The king then renounced the allegiance and homage of the hostile barons, and formal war began. The battle which followed was a brilliant victory for de

Henry III *This fine head, expressive of Henry's many troubles, is from the gilt-bronze effigy of the king in Edward the Confessor's Chapel at Westminster Abbey. The statue dates from 1291 and is the work of William Torel.*

Montfort. Though the king's eldest son, Prince Edward, on his wing routed the contingent of Londoners, Earl Simon in the centre overwhelmed the forces of King Henry. The royalists were shattered and the king, Edward and Roger Mortimer all fell into Simon's hands.

De Montfort now went boldly ahead. He confiscated the estates of the king's supporters and virtually ran the Government, supervising a new Council. During this period he called a Parliament in 1265 to which not only the barons and bishops were summoned but also two knights from each shire and two burgesses from a number of carefully selected towns. In this he was extending what was an already developing practice: knights had been summoned before to such assemblies, but not burgesses.

In the long run, de Montfort was bound to fail. Too many of his followers, including his own sons, were lawless and undisciplined; also he took too much power into his own and his sons' hands, and for this reason lost the support of the Earl of Gloucester, who changed sides. It was Gloucester's younger brother who soon helped Prince Edward to escape from captivity and it was to attack Gloucester's lands in Glamorgan that Simon moved west. Forced to turn back, he tried to join his son at Kenilworth, and was caught at Evesham by a much larger force under Prince Edward. The royalist victory was complete. As his followers fled away through the orchards, de Montfort realised that the time had come to die, 'for God and the just cause'. He and the other leaders of the movement, fighting in a circle round their captive the king, were one by one hacked down.

It was another year or more before the last rebels were expelled from their castles, and some sort of settlement had then to be worked out. In this Prince Edward played a leading part. By the Dictum of Kenilworth (1266) most of the defeated who had had their lands confiscated were allowed to redeem them on the payment of a fine. By 1270 a sort of peace had been achieved, and Edward felt secure enough to go on Crusade. He was returning through Italy when, two years later, Henry died and he succeeded him as Edward I. It is striking evidence of the way in which the country had by then settled down, that Edward was able to spend nearly another two years travelling home.

Henry III was buried in the newly rebuilt Westminster Abbey upon which he had lavished much care and interest. On the whole it was astonishing that the king, who delighted in 'ceremonies and feasts, religious services and pilgrimages, magnificent jewels, clothes and buildings' should have managed to hand on the power of the Crown more or less intact to his son. But, in the words of a great historian, King Henry 'got through all his troubles and left England more prosperous, more united, more peaceful, more beautiful than it was when he was a child'.[1]

Lewes, 1264

De Montfort in charge

Burgesses called to Parliament, 1265

Evesham, 1265: death of de Montfort

The peace

Accession of Edward I, 1272

---

[1] Sir Maurice Powicke: 'The Thirteenth Century', O.U.P.

16 Wales, Scotland, and Edward I

1 The Anglo-Normans in Ireland and the Conquest of Wales

No single ruler reigned over the British Isles until 1603, when James VI of Scotland also became James I of England. Until that date – and indeed afterwards – a great deal of British history is concerned with the efforts of the English to dominate the Welsh, the Scots, and the Irish.

In the later Anglo-Saxon period, the various rulers in Wales and Scotland sometimes acknowledged the overlordship of the English monarch. All the same, they did what they pleased within their own kingdoms. The Norman conquest altered this in at least one region: Norman adventurers fought their way into south and south-west Wales, seized the land there, and ruled it from their castles. By setting up the great 'marcher' earldoms of Chester, Shrewsbury and Hereford, William I also threatened other parts of Wales and at the same time made it more difficult for the Welsh to break into England. Despite this, and the expeditions of William I and II against King Malcolm of Scotland, the Norman kings were much more concerned with claims and territories in France than with any in Wales, Scotland or Ireland.

The Normans in Wales

This situation began to change only when Henry III officially recognised the loss of Normandy, Maine and Anjou. From then on the English kings were much more free to deal with territories within the British Isles – as the reign of Edward I soon showed.

Effect of loss of Normandy, etc.

There had also been early attempts to secure control of Ireland. To understand these, we must recall that Ireland was a very disunited country, with many areas cut off by hills, lakes or bogs. Until Scandinavian raiders built such fortified places as Dublin, Waterford, Wexford and Cork, it had hardly any towns; and – as in the mountainous regions of Scotland and Wales – the people lived mainly in extended family groups, or clans. Christianity was a unifying force, but even this had been threatened by the Danish and Norwegian invasions of the ninth to eleventh centuries, which plunged much of Ireland into chaos.

Ireland

In such a country there was very little organisation at the top. The clans came under tribal kings – there were seven main kings as well as lesser ones – and over them all was the 'High King of Tara', whose rights were vague and usually disputed. Until the eleventh century the High King was generally a member of the O'Neill family, but then the power of this group was broken and the supremacy eventually fell into the hands of the famous Irish hero, Brian Boru. Brian himself, by that time an old man, was killed fighting against the Danes at Clontarf in 1014, and after that all semblance of unity disappeared. For many decades, Ireland was torn by the struggle for the high kingship between the O'Neills of Ulster, the O'Briens of Munster and the O'Connors of Connaught. None of this was good for the Irish Church, and in 1155 Pope Adrian IV – the only Englishman to hold the papal office – issued a bull[1] granting the overlordship of Ireland to Henry II of England and his heirs.

Henry II's overlordship, 1155

At first, Henry had too many other problems to bother much about his new overlordship.[2] In 1166 however, Dermot, King of Leinster, was driven out of his kingdom by his enemies. He presented himself before Henry II and got permission to seek help from the Anglo-Norman landholders in Wales. Among others, Richard de Clare, Earl of Pembroke, known as Strongbow, responded to Dermot's appeal; the two men arranged that in return for helping to recover Dermot's kingdom, Strongbow would be recognised as Dermot's heir and would marry his daughter. In 1169 the first Anglo-Norman contingent from Wales landed, and captured Wexford; and in 1170 Strongbow himself followed with 200 knights and 1,000 other troops. Taking Waterford and Dublin, he was soon able to restore Dermot to his full possessions. Dermot then died, and Strongbow succeeded him.

Strongbow's expedition, 1170

This quickly brought Henry II to the scene, for no English monarch would willingly allow one of his earls to become an independent ruler. It also suited Henry to be out of England for a while after the death of Becket. Henry's expedition was completely successful. He reduced Strongbow's territory to Dublin, Wexford, Waterford and the adjoining country, and got his own overlordship acknowledged not only by Strongbow but by most of the other kings and chiefs of Ireland.

Henry II in Ireland, 1171–2

The submission of the Irish chiefs was followed by that of the Irish bishops. In 1172, at the Council of Cashel, the Irish Church agreed to accept the practices of the Church in England. By degrees, more than half of the country now came under the control of the Anglo-Norman barons, who ruthlessly seized land wherever they could. Henry's settlement, however, did not endure. The barons were soon able to set themselves up as petty kings, and John paid two visits to Ireland in an attempt to curb them. On the first he was said to have behaved disgracefully, pulling the beards of the chiefs during negotiations; on the second his forces were successful, and he received the homage of many chiefs and nearly all the barons.

Expeditions of John

Edward I never visited Ireland, which presented him with no great threat, but under his son Edward II English authority became gradually confined to a number of walled towns and to the area around Dublin known as the Pale.[3] Here English laws and customs were applied and

Extent of English influence

[1] A papal order, so called from the *bulla*, or seal, with which it was franked.
[2] The title 'King of Ireland' was not taken by the kings of England until the reign of Henry VIII.

[3] So called from the wooden palings, or stakes, often used in establishing a boundary.

a Parliament met. The greater part of Ireland, however, remained either under native rulers or under the control of almost independent Norman families such as the Fitzgeralds.

The course of events in Wales in the thirteenth century was very different. We have seen how the Normans had penetrated into south Wales, and how William the Conqueror had allowed the creation of the great lordships along the border. But in doing this William bequeathed difficulties to his successors, for the Marcher barons became extremely strong and often disregarded the authority of the Crown. Practically independent in their own areas, they controlled their own system of justice and ran their own private armies. By waging repeated war into Wales, they were also able to extend their own power and possessions.

The Marcher lords

In the south the Welsh were unable to resist the Anglo-Norman pressure, but northwards it was a different story. Here the Welsh had the natural defences of their own countryside. In such regions it was easy enough for the heavily-armoured Norman knights to ride through the valleys; but the Welsh simply took to the hills where they could not follow. Like Ireland, Wales was at this time very disunited; allegiance was local and hereditary as, for example, to the Powys family in the area around Welshpool. Sometimes a local ruler managed to gain greater authority, like Rhys ap Tewdur who resisted the first Norman advance; and by the end of the twelfth century there was fairly wide agreement that supremacy among the Welsh rulers rested with the princes of Gwynedd in north-west Wales, whose power was based on Anglesey and Snowdonia. But it would be wrong to think that the Welsh had any real sense of unity, despite the words spoken by an old Welshman to Henry II:

'I am persuaded that no other race than this and no other tongue than this of Wales, happen what may, will answer in the great day of judgment for this little corner of the earth.'

During the thirteenth century some of the Welsh princes seem to have come to the view that to retain any independence the Welsh needed stronger central control. Two of the outstanding rulers of Gwynedd – Llewellyn ap Iorwerth (Llewellyn the Great) and his grandson Llewellyn ap Gwyffyd – shared this opinion. The former married King John's illegitimate daughter Joan, and later cooperated with the English barons to secure Magna Carta, which confirmed several Welsh rights. Though he acknowledged himself as a vassal of the English king, he was able, with the help of other Welsh princes, almost to wipe out English power in Wales before he died in 1240. After his death, however, jealousies among his descendants allowed the English to win back many of their losses.

Princes of Gwynedd:

Llewellyn ap Iorwerth (the Great)

Wales

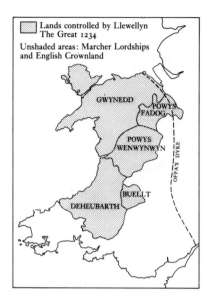

Under Llewellyn ap Gwyffyd Welsh power rose to its greatest height. He was really the first and last native Prince of Wales – a title he assumed in 1258. He became Prince of Gwynedd in 1246; but largely thanks to the quarrels between Henry III and the barons under de Montfort (with whom he allied) he was able to overrun a large part of central and southern Wales as well. Though Henry was victorious over the barons, he did not feel strong enough to tackle Llewellyn. Instead, by the treaty of Montgomery in 1267, the English king recognised Llewellyn as overlord of all the Welsh rulers and as hereditary Prince of Wales.

Llewellyn ap Gwyffyd

This agreement lasted only a short time. When Edward I succeeded Henry III, Llewellyn refused to heed a summons to do homage to the absent king. He also fell behind on some payments due to the English crown. Amid these disputes, his brother David entered into a plot against him with the prince of Powys and fled to England. All this, and the fact that Llewellyn's successes had made the Marcher lords ready to welcome royal intervention, played into Edward's hands. He detained Simon de Montfort's daughter Eleanor as she was travelling to Wales to marry Llewellyn, and in 1276 issued a final summons to the Welsh prince to come and do homage. When Llewellyn still absented himself, war quickly followed.

Edward's invasion, 1276–7

Edward had prepared for the struggle with the utmost care. Three armies operated, one from Worcester, one from western Wales, and one under Edward from Chester. Before Edward himself advanced, Llewellyn's alliances with other Welsh princes in the south had crumbled and English power was firmly re-established in the south-west. Edward thus had to deal with Llewellyn alone, and his success was complete. His fleet cut Llewellyn off from his granary in Anglesey,

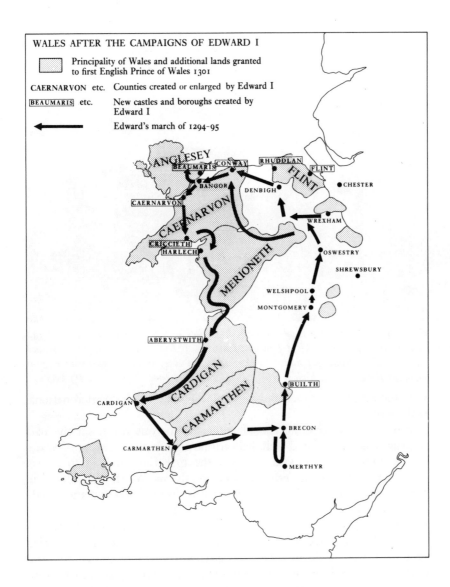

WALES AFTER THE CAMPAIGNS OF EDWARD I

Principality of Wales and additional lands granted to first English Prince of Wales 1301

CAERNARVON etc.   Counties created or enlarged by Edward I

BEAUMARIS etc.   New castles and boroughs created by Edward I

⟵   Edward's march of 1294-95

and though the Welsh prince and his troops took refuge in Snowdonia lack of food soon forced them to seek terms. By the treaty of Conway that then followed, Llewellyn lost all that he and his grandfather had won in the previous fifty years.

Having defeated Llewellyn, Edward at first showed him no great severity. He was allowed to retain his title of Prince of Wales, to rule over his much reduced territories, and to marry Eleanor de Montfort. He was also excused from certain payments due. The spread of English customs and influence, however, offended the Welsh, and in 1282 war again broke out. This time the leading spirit was David, who suddenly attacked the castle at Hawarden. The princes of southern Wales supported the rising, Llewellyn could hardly remain aloof, and

David's revolt

Harlech Castle *Harlech is one of the eight castles built by Edward I to govern and hold down Wales after his defeat of Llewellyn. It has inner and outer walls and towers and a strong gatehouse on the landward side, while its natural defences included the crag on which it was built and at that time the sea directly below.*

soon the English were faced with something like whole-hearted national resistance.

Edward's second invasion, 1282–3

Infuriated by what he considered a treacherous revolt on the part of princes he had treated well, Edward now made the crushing of Wales his first and foremost task. He was the first English king to do so. The army that he raised consisted partly of Welsh 'friendlies' in English pay, partly of mercenary troops from Gascony, and partly of one of the last appearances of the feudal levy. Though he had to act without the careful preparations of his earlier expedition, his general plan was the same as it had been in 1277: after recovering ground in the south, to drive Llewellyn's troops into the central and northern mountains, to cut them off from supplies, and to prevent them getting out again by building a chain of immensely powerful castles. His base of operations was Shrewsbury, whence he advanced into north-east Wales while other forces invaded and captured Anglesey. In December 1282, Llewellyn met his death near Builth, in central Wales, in a clash with the forces of the Mortimers. The following year David, who had been holding out in the hills, was betrayed and captured by 'men of his own tongue', and Welsh resistance came to an end. A few months later he was condemned by a parliament at Shrewsbury and sentenced to be hanged, drawn and quartered. His body was then distributed to four different parts of the country and his head sent to join Llewellyn's, already exposed on a lance at the Tower of London.

Death of Llewellyn and David

Statute of Wales, 1284

By the Statute of Wales Edward then set up a pattern of government

Beaumaris Castle *Beaumaris, on Anglesey, was the last of Edward I's great castles in Wales. It is the most perfect from the point of view of 'concentric' defence; defenders on the low outer or curtain wall and defenders on the high inner wall could fire on besiegers at the same time.*

which remained largely unchanged until the Tudors united Wales with England in the sixteenth century. Wales was regarded as falling into three divisions: the parts directly ruled by the Crown, which were made 'shire-ground' and given a county organisation complete with sheriffs, county courts and coroners; the parts controlled by Welsh rulers, which were confined to the Powys land around Welshpool and to a small southern area; and the Marcher lordships. In the areas under direct royal rule – the newly created shires of Anglesey, Caernarvon and Merioneth, and the enlarged shires of Cardigan and Carmarthen – English law was largely applied although it did not entirely sweep away local custom. In 1301 these areas became the new Principality, with Edward's young son, who had been born seven years earlier at Caernarvon, proclaimed as the first English Prince of Wales.

The Prince of Wales, 1301

Royal control

After his victories of 1282–83 Edward's hold on Wales was not seriously shaken, despite two further Welsh uprisings. From the great castles that he built at Flint, Rhuddlan, Builth, Llanbadarn, Conway, Caernarvon, Criccieth, Harlech, Beaumaris and Denbigh, royal authority was strongly maintained: they still stand as impressive symbols of Edward's policy towards Wales. Still existing, too, are the many towns which he created or enlarged, often in association with one of his castles, and to which he gave borough privileges: towns which served as centres of English influence and power. But though the native Welsh themselves now for the most part accepted the new arrangements, the Marcher lords remained something of a danger to the king, and the border lands a breeding ground for trouble.

Castles and boroughs

2 The Attempt to Conquer Scotland

One of the treasures of Westminster Abbey is the ancient Coronation Chair of the kings of England. Beneath the seat is the rough-hewn Stone of Scone, on which the kings of Scotland were crowned, and which Edward I carried off to Westminster. Its presence there, and the words on his tomb nearby 'Scotorum Malleus' ('Hammer of the Scots') are permanent reminders of Edward's long struggle in the north.

From the tenth century Scottish kings had sometimes admitted the overlordship of the king of England, but it was by no means always clear what this implied. The plainest and most extreme statement of the position came when William the Lion invaded England during the reign of Henry II and was taken prisoner. In the Treaty of Falaise of 1171, he had to acknowledge that he held Scotland as a fief of the English crown.

The Treaty of Falaise, however, did not last long. The Scots persuaded Richard I to cancel it in return for money. This and the strife in England under John and Henry III enabled Scotland's next two kings – Alexander II and Alexander III – to reign without much English interference. These kings were considered friendly to England, and both were married to English princesses. They were helped, too, by their country's growing prosperity during this period, which saw Alexander III wrest the Western Isles and the Isle of Man from Norway. Scottish monarchs, however, were never very secure on their throne. They had little control over the clans north of the Highland line, and the power and violence of the nobles gave them constant trouble.

On a stormy night in 1286 Alexander III insisted on setting out from Edinburgh to visit his young wife – Edward I's sister – at Kinghorn, on the Firth of Forth. He had crossed the Forth by ferry-boat and was riding along the cliff track when it seems that his horse slipped. In the dark his companions were unable to see what happened; but the next morning the king was found dead on the shore below, his neck broken. This was the prelude to a long period of strife. Alexander left no heir except his grand-daughter Margaret, 'the Maid of Norway', a sickly child not yet three years old – her mother, married to the king of Norway, had died in giving her birth. The regents appointed in Scotland discussed the problem and agreed that Margaret should be brought over from Norway and betrothed to the English king's heir, the young Prince Edward. This would have united the two crowns in the next English reign. During her voyage to Scotland in 1290, however, the young princess upset these plans by dying.

The field was now more open, and more than a dozen contenders laid claim to the Scottish throne. The foremost of these were two men descended from the daughters of David, brother of William the Lion. John Baliol was the grandson of the eldest daughter, while Robert Bruce, Lord of Annandale, by now eighty years old, was the son of the second daughter. Bruce was a man of gre t experience who had held important posts in both kingdoms; Baliɔl was a man with big estates but without much character, whose connections until recently had been mainly with England. Bruce had some popular feeling on his side, but by right of descent the strongest claim was Baliol's. All the claimants, and the Scottish nobility as a whole, agreed that the case should be heard and decided by Edward I, for otherwise Scotland would have dissolved into civil war.

Edward I, whose reputation for justice was high, used this situation to force his own views on the Scots. He first obtained from the claimants a clear admission that he was their overlord, and that during the vacancy he should rule the Scottish kingdom. In return, he undertook to install the new king within two months of the decision. He also promised to make no further demands, except for homage and associated rights, from the new monarch when a Scottish king died. After a year's delay, in 1292 the case was argued and Edward, following the unanimous advice of his counsellors, awarded the throne to Baliol.

As King John of Scots, Baliol soon found difficulty in controlling his nobles. They resented his dependence on Edward, who insisted as overlord on summoning Baliol to his court and hearing appeals from Scottish subjects. Eventually the Scottish nobles set up a committee to overrule Baliol, and drove away his English advisers. Edward was at this time beset by troubles, for he had to deal not only with a Welsh rebellion but also with King Philip IV ('the Fair'), of France, who had occupied Edward's province of Gascony. Amid these troubles, Edward was furious to hear that Baliol, pressed by the Scottish nobles, so far from helping him in France as he demanded, had made an alliance with Philip the Fair.[1]

Edward took rapid action. In 1296 he marched north, sacked and looted the then Scottish town of Berwick, and overran southern and central Scotland. At Montrose he deposed Baliol, who acknowledged his errors and was taken off to honourable captivity in England. Unwisely, Edward then made no effort to find another Scottish king. Instead, he left the country in the hands of English garrisons and of an English council under the Earl of Surrey. The harshness of their actions against opponents soon swelled the ranks of those who were not prepared to accept the rule of Englishmen.

So Scottish resistance was not quite broken, and from the south-west there soon came a leader of grim and ferocious purpose. Sir William Wallace, a tenant of the king's steward at Renfrew, had, if legend is correct, killed an English official and become an outlaw. Declaring himself still an adherent of John Baliol, he and his followers attacked English posts in south-west Scotland and gradually built up an army – ragged and badly equipped, but of dauntless courage. It was joined by other resisters from the north under Sir Andrew Moray,

Marginal notes:

Edward's arbitration

Baliol: king
Baliol's difficulties

– and Edward's

Franco-Scottish alliance

Edward invades Scotland, 1296

Deposition of Baliol

Scottish resistance: Wallace

[1] This was the first alliance between France and Scotland – a combination which, on and off, endured for many centuries.

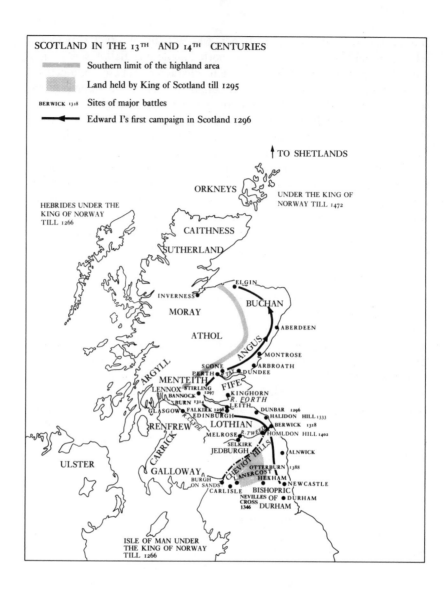

SCOTLAND IN THE 13TH AND 14TH CENTURIES

Southern limit of the highland area

Land held by King of Scotland till 1295

BERWICK 1318   Sites of major battles

Edward I's first campaign in Scotland 1296

Stirling Bridge

Edward's second invasion, 1298

Wallace at Falkirk

and by a number of Scottish nobles. So successful were Wallace's activities that the Earl of Surrey led an army north to deal with him, only for it to be set on and overwhelmed after crossing the bridge at Stirling. This triumph Wallace followed up by raiding deep into the northern English counties.

Seeing Scotland escaping from his control, Edward now abandoned a campaign against the French king and in 1298 moved north with the greatest army that had ever left England. It included many Welsh bowmen, whose value Edward had learned in Wales. Against such a force Wallace had no chance: in the grimly-fought battle of Falkirk his army was destroyed and he himself became a fugitive. For the next seven years, some of which he spent abroad looking for help, he avoided

Bruce's sword *This sword, in the possession of Sir Alec Douglas-Home, was reputedly given to Sir James Douglas in token of Bruce's last request, that Douglas should go to the Holy Land 'and thair bury my hart'.*

Seal of Robert I *The Great Seal of Robert Bruce, bearing his title Rex Scotorum. (British Museum.)*

capture, only to be betrayed in 1305 and sent for trial at Westminster. There he was declared guilty, among other crimes, of treason and murder. As a warning to others who defied Edward, he was executed with special barbarity that same day. He was dragged at the horse's tail from Westminster to the Tower, and from the Tower to Tyburn, before suffering the normal penalty for treason – hanging, disembowelling and quartering.

Execution of Wallace, 1305

Edward's victory at Falkirk in 1298 by no means ended the struggle in Scotland. The English king had to return there almost yearly before he could complete the conquest of the country. He at length achieved this in 1304, when he captured the last great resistance stronghold, Stirling Castle. He then set up a new, and, as he thought, fair and acceptable system of government. A joint committee of English lords and Scottish bishops, lords and commons drew up the scheme, and most of the official positions went to Scotsmen. Edward hoped that the problem of Scotland was now solved. But once more resistance flared up; and Edward, by now desperately ill and worn out by his life of campaigning, was again drawn north.

Edward's conquest completed, 1304

The new Scottish leader was Robert Bruce, Earl of Carrick, the grandson of Baliol's rival. He had been brought up in Edward's court, and had English as well as Scottish estates. He had changed sides more than once, but until he inherited a personal claim to the Scottish throne on his father's death in 1304, he had mainly professed allegiance to Edward. Early in 1305, having left England secretly, he met in a convent near Dumfries an old rival, the former regent John Comyn, Lord of Badenoch. The two men quarrelled – possibly because Comyn would not take part in Bruce's plans. A fight broke out, and Bruce's men finished off Comyn before the high altar. Though an outlaw after this, Bruce managed to link up with confederates, and within six weeks succeeded in having himself crowned at Scone in the presence of several lords and bishops. To support him, half Scotland soon rose in revolt against Edward's committee.

Further resistance: Robert Bruce

Bruce crowned, March 1305 (King Robert I)

Edward at Lanercost

This challenge Edward could not ignore. By now aged 67 and too infirm to march or ride, he set out north in a horse-litter, and made his headquarters at Lanercost Priory, near Carlisle. Here for some months he was too ill to take the field. Meantime the Prince of Wales and Edward's other generals campaigned in Scotland and drove Bruce

Bruce in refuge

to take refuge in the Western Isles. It was in Rathlin Island, off the coast of Ireland, that according to the well-known story Bruce lay in a hut one day watching a spider build its web, and taking heart from its persistent refusal to be beaten. In 1307 he returned to the mainland,

Bruce active again

and never again wavered in the struggle, despite the fact that the pope excommunicated him and all his followers. His success was at first mixed, and to his great grief most of his family were captured and three of his brothers executed. At this stage Edward I, having burnt his horse-litter before his troops as a sign that he would lead a new campaign personally, mounted his charger and rode towards the border at the head of a fresh army. His pain and weakness were so great that he could ride only a mile or two each day, and at Burgh-on-Sands, less than six miles from Carlisle, a further illness smote him down. A few

Death of Edward I,
1307

hours later the 'Hammer of the Scots' was dead.

Had he lived, Edward would have had hard work to keep Scotland subdued. The task was not actually impossible, because divisions among the Scottish nobility were so acute. His death, however, trans-

Withdrawal of
Edward II

formed the situation because his son and successor, Edward II, entirely lacked the pride and fierce determination of his father. As soon as he could, he left Scotland, only to fall out with his own barons at home. More than a match alike for Edward's generals and Scottish opponents, Bruce meanwhile extended his hold over his own country, and even carried out devastating raids on northern England. By 1313 only Stirling, Berwick and Bothwell of the Scottish castles remained in English hands. One by one the others – even Edinburgh – had been taken by ruse and daring.

Edward II now decided on a supreme effort. With a great host he marched north to the relief of Stirling, only to be trapped by Bruce

Bannockburn, 1314

on marshy ground near the Bannock stream just south of the castle. Hemmed in, the English could not deploy their archers properly, and the English cavalry were worsted by the Scottish spearmen. The rout was complete. Edward himself with difficulty reached Dunbar to escape by sea.

Bruce was now a national hero, recognised as King Robert I throughout Scotland. He was strong enough in the next few years to raid as far south as Lancashire and Yorkshire, and to send his brother Edward with a large force to Ireland. There, in the three years before he met

Edward Bruce in
Ireland, 1315–18

his death in battle, Edward Bruce defeated the English forces and, with the help of the Irish princes, won for himself the title of High King.

The Scottish recapture of Berwick in 1318 once more stirred Edward II into action, but Bruce readily countered this and other attempts to restore English control. He was now receiving more wholehearted support from the Scottish nobles, a number of whom – on Bruce's prompting – expressed their determination in a declaration made at Arbroath in 1320. It was sent to the pope to persuade him to lift a sentence of excommunication placed on Bruce at Edward's behest, but its terms rang very proudly and still find a responsive echo in Scottish hearts.

For as long as one hundred men shall remain alive we shall never under any circumstances submit to the domination of the English. For it is not for glory or riches or honour that we fight, but for freedom alone, which no good man will give up except with his life. . . .

In 1322 Bruce invaded England again and defeated Edward at Byland, in Yorkshire. By this time, Edward's troubles at home were so acute that he had no hope of dealing effectively with Scotland, and a truce was made. In 1328, after Edward's deposition, this was followed by a formal peace. The treaty of Northampton recognised Bruce as king, and Scotland as independent. Bruce's fight seemed to be won. The following year he died. He left his heart to Sir James Douglas, one of his most valiant supporters, to take on Crusade against the Moors.

The attempt of Edward I to unify Britain, only partly successful in his own lifetime, thus collapsed under Edward II. But this was not the end of the story. The new boy-king of England, Edward III, in whose name the Treaty of Northampton was made, was soon to grow into a proud and active warrior. He had no intention of allowing part of his inheritance to slip. Though he did not manage to destroy Scotland's independence, he several times came near to doing so. Probably only the lure of the crown of France, which he claimed in the conflict later known as the Hundred Years War, prevented him from succeeding where his father and grandfather had failed.

Declaration of Arbroath, 1320

Treaty of Northampton, 1328–
Scottish independence
Death of Bruce, 1329

Renewed threats under Edward III

The Declaration of Arbroath *This famous letter, probably inspired by Bruce or his chancellor, was sent to Pope John XXII in 1320 sealed by some fifty Scottish earls, barons and lairds. A copy was retained in Scotland, where it may be seen in the Scottish Record Office with most of the seals still attached.*

17 King, Barons, and Parliament

1 Edward I and the Growth of Parliament

When Edward I came to the throne in 1272 he was thirty-three years old and already famous. Nicknamed Longshanks on account of his height, he was fearless and energetic and dominated all about him. As a young man, his violent behaviour and friends had made him unpopular: his cavalcade swept through the countryside, seizing whatever it pleased, and on one occasion he was said to have ordered his followers to put out an eye and cut off an ear of a youth who merely crossed his path. During the struggle with de Montfort, however, he had learned greater wisdom and self-control. His religious beliefs and his legal training helped to discipline him, and by the time he became king he was a warrior admired throughout Europe for his defeat of de Montfort and his success on crusade.

As king, Edward remained an extremely warlike man; he even fought in a tournament on his way home to his coronation. His other recreations, such as hawking and stag-hunting (in which he chased the stag on horse-back with a sword) were little less violent. But though a hard man, Edward also had a sense of justice and a determination to keep his word. He was capable, too, of strong affection, and was devoted to his wife Eleanor of Castile. When she died he raised a series of crosses, the last at Charing Cross, to mark the places at which her body rested on its final journey from Lincoln to Westminster.

Edward was determined to have order after all the troubles of his father's reign. Before there could be good order there must be clear and just law, and Edward took great pains to establish his idea of this. 'We must find out what is ours and due to us, and others what is theirs and due to them', was the guiding thread of his work. But he never completely lost the violent temper of his family, and the numerous wars fought to assert his rights were expensive, with the result that as time went on he encountered increasing opposition.

Immediately after his coronation Edward set on foot a great enquiry. Its aims were to find out how far royal rights had been usurped and in what ways justice was faulty. This was the first of several similar undertakings. As a result of what he found out in these surveys, the king embarked on a course of law-making which was unmatched until Tudor times.[1] A series of statutes – a term coming to mean laws

[1] In the Middle Ages, the king was normally expected to 'declare' law (i.e. decide clearly what the law was) rather than make new laws. The latter, it was thought, were needed mainly when new kinds of wrong-doing arose.

passed in Parliament – established an ordered system which outlived the troubles of the next 150 years. These statutes, in the words of Sir Maurice Powicke, 'stand out like a range of hills in a misty landscape'. In them Edward was not for the most part trying to create anything new; his main aim was stability and the clearing up of uncertainties. His work in checking what he thought were abuses, however, had effects far beyond his intentions.

Edward's statutes are too complicated to examine here in detail, but most of them dealt with land-holding or justice. One, for instance, set up machinery for examining very closely all claims to 'franchises' or 'liberties' – special privileges which might take the form of anything from the right to hold a private law court for one's own tenants, to the right to take tolls from passing travellers. Such rights, Edward considered, should not be allowed to flourish unchecked.

Statutes dealing with justice and order

Another of Edward's statutes established a system of thrice-yearly local assizes, instead of the irregular visits of judges which had meant long delays and much injustice. In addition, there was the very famous Statute of Winchester, which among other things laid down that where a hundred failed to produce the culprit when a crime was committed within its boundaries, the inhabitants should pay a fine. Another striking feature of this law was an order that highways between market towns should be widened, and all small trees, hedges and ditches removed for 200 feet on either side, so that wayside robbers and assailants could not lie in wait under cover.

Statute of Winchester, 1285

Among the statutes dealing with land tenure, some important ones were intended to prevent the king and the great land-holders losing feudal rights, such as the 'relief' payment when a tenant's heir took over the dead man's estate. These rights were often lost to the overlord if his tenant was allowed to grant out part of his estate on feudal terms. The statute therefore laid down that no more sub-tenancies of a feudal kind should be created: henceforth grants were to be outright, or else leases for a term of years. In the same way the Statute of Mortmain ('dead hand') forbade further gifts of land to the Church, since such institutions did not die, marry, or become minors, and so were not liable to the normal feudal payments. In practice, this meant that the king's permission was now needed for any such gift – and would have to be paid for. This statute was important, for it sharply restricted the growing power and wealth of the Church in England.

Statutes dealing with land tenure

Statute of Mortmain, 1279

There can be no doubt about Edward's determination to maintain his royal powers, and at the same time to improve justice and public order. To do so he had to keep – and kept – a close eye on his own servants. Adam of Stratton, for instance, one of his clerks who made a great fortune out of corrupt administration and private money-lending, was finally severely punished by fining and imprisonment. At his fall, more than £12,600 was found in cash in his house – an enormous sum for those days. Edward also found it useful to create officials of a new kind. It was during this period that the power of the sheriff,

Edward's officials

lac de soye a vng ymage de sainct george pendãt a icelluy
Aussi se ledit colier dor auoit besoing de reparacion il pora
estre mis en la main de louurier iusques a ce quil soit
repare. Lequel colier aussi ne pourra estre enrichy de
pierres ou daultres choses reserue seß ymage qui pourra
estre garny au plaisir du cheualier. Et aussi ne pourra
estre ledit colier vendu engaige dõne ne aliene pour
necessite ou cause quelconque que ce soit

Alexander Rex
Scotor

Lewellin
princeps
wallie

which had so frequently been abused, began to wane, and that there appeared in the English countryside the figure of the guardian – later justice – of the peace.

As the king's work broadened and as his activity increased in Wales, Scotland and France, so his need for money grew. He borrowed much, first from the Jews whose power he increasingly resented and whom he expelled in 1290, and then from Italian bankers and money-lenders. But loans had to be repaid with interest, and borrowing offered only temporary relief. In his difficulties Edward turned to the 'community of the realm' as expressed in Parliament.

Edward's financial difficulties

Although 'the High Court of Parliament' as it was called had mainly judicial functions, it quickly became important as a money-granting body. From it the king could get approval for taxation and so avoid the trouble that could easily arise when officials tried to collect taxes that had not been given general consent. Edward received the approval of Parliament in 1275, for instance, for the collection of customs duties on the staple commodities, such as wool and leather, passing through the ports; this was to replace the older practice of taking a proportion of the goods themselves. In addition he turned more and more to general property taxes, either of a tenth or a fifteenth of the assessed value of a person's property. In this way the old feudal demands, e.g. for scutage in place of military service, began to disappear, and English taxation took on the form that it was to have for the next two hundred years. The extreme demands of Edward for money during the wars in the last part of his reign, however, proved to be more than his subjects would quietly accept.

The Customs –

– and property taxes

Edward has been called the creator of Parliament, but this is not correct. Assemblies very like Edward's Parliaments had been meeting throughout the thirteenth century. Between 1258 and 1272 over thirty assemblies that can be called 'Parliaments' met, but after 1272 the meetings became more regular. Edward seems to have adopted the policy of twice-yearly meetings at Easter and Michaelmas, often at Westminster but not always so. Between 1274 and 1286 Parliaments met twice nearly every year; but after 1294, when his demands for money began to cause great trouble, meetings became less frequent.

Edward and Parliament

There were no fixed numbers in these Parliaments and sometimes Edward summoned merely those who he thought could be of most use to him, the merchants or the lawyers. The separation into 'Houses' – the 'Peers' and the 'Commons' – was a very slow development, and at this time the Commons had few independent rights. From 1272 to 1289,

Edward I presides in council *This contemporary illustration shows Edward I presiding over his Great Council or Parliament (as specially enlarged meetings of the Council came to be called). Right and left of Edward, just below him, are his two greatest vassals, Alexander King of Scots and Llewellyn Prince of Wales, and the two Archbishops. Below them are the mitred clergy – the bishops and abbots – on the left, a group of barons on the right. In the centre are judges and officials on woolsacks.*

the Commons came to only one in eight Parliaments, but from 1290 to 1307 to one in three. By the time of Edward III, however, they were attending practically every Parliament and by the latter part of the fourteenth century they had their own regular meeting-place in the Chapter House at Westminster. After 1283 the lower clergy also had their own assembly called Convocation, which met usually at the same time as Parliament; but the upper clergy – the bishops and abbots – being of baronial rank, attended Parliament.

'Model' Parliament, 1295

In 1295 Edward summoned what many historians have called 'the Model Parliament'. A personal summons was sent to each archbishop, bishop, earl and baron, and each bishop was ordered to bring representative clergy with him. In addition, each shire was to elect two knights, and each borough two burgesses. Not all future Parliaments were like this, and the lower clergy gradually ceased to attend; but otherwise the assembly of 1295 was of a pattern which eventually became regular. The Commons were ordered to come 'with full power' to bind their communities, and out of this emerged the principle 'what touches all should be approved by all'.

The business discussed in Parliaments was very wide. One historian has written: 'Justice could be done in Edward I's Parliaments, statutes could be made, taxes granted, campaigns discussed, papal envoys received, constitutions for Scotland determined, and daughters married'. The main business was for long to do with justice, but the king's main reason for calling Parliaments was to secure consent to taxation. Eventually, this was to give Parliament the power to help shape policy, for it could refuse grants until its wishes were met.

Opposition to Edward I

Before the end of his reign, Edward was at odds with all the leading parts of the community. Besides pressing Parliament and the Church for very great sums of money by the standards of the time, he had also seized large quantities of goods from foreign merchants and others engaged in overseas trade. These quantities were far in excess of any to which the Crown had previously laid claim.

The first crisis came over Edward's attempt to tax the clergy. To prepare for his campaign in France in 1294, he demanded from every holder of a clerical living no less than half of the annual income. When denied, he raged so greatly in front of Convocation that the Dean of St. Paul's fell dead in fright. Despite opposition, he got most of his money, only for the pope, Boniface VIII, to issue in 1296 the bull *Clericis Laicos*, which forbade the Church to pay taxes without papal consent. A clerical assembly in 1297 thereupon refused any further aid to the king. The furious Edward promptly declared the entire clergy outlawed: anyone meeting a cleric riding along the road could confiscate his horse if he chose. The king also declared that if the clergy did not submit by Easter 1297, all their lands would be forfeit. Before such extreme pressure the Archbishop of Canterbury gave way, and nearly all the clergy paid the required taxes. In getting his money, however, Edward had aroused immense ill will.

As much offended as the merchants and the clergy were the barons, who resented not only Edward's demands for money but also the whole growth of royal authority. Since very few barons by now had estates in France, they also resented his demands for service in Gascony, and many of their leaders at first refused to go. The barons' opposition came to a head in 1297 when Edward was in Flanders. His son Edward, acting as Regent, was forced to call a Parliament, and to renounce any such taxes as those recently levied unless voted by the common consent of the realm. In addition, the regency had to 'confirm the Charters' – Magna Carta and the Forest Charter. All this Edward I had to accept: and in 1300 he had to agree to certain 'Articles in addition to the Charters' which tried to restrict the power of the royal household. Only by making all these concessions was Edward able to raise the money and the army for the conquest of Scotland.

The Confirmation of the Charters, 1297

The last word lay with Edward. Before the end of his reign he had broken the magnates' opposition by contriving that several of the great earldoms should fall into the hands of his own family. He had also weakened clerical opposition by a compact with a new pope, who released him from some of his promises. These were the successful rearguard actions of a ruthless and efficient ruler. But the power of the Church, the barons, the knights and the burgesses – the classes meeting in the new type of Parliament – was now such that, under a less able or determined king, the struggle was likely to go the other way.

Trouble for Edward II?

2 The Tragedy of Edward II

Edward I died in 1307 and was succeeded by his son Edward of Caernarvon, earlier proclaimed the first English Prince of Wales. Edward II had not been on very good terms with his father, who thought him too fond of amusement. He had no love for the company of the great lords, but instead enjoyed such pursuits as music, play-acting, rowing, swimming, racing, digging and thatching. Twenty-three years of age, he was cultured, handsome and strong, with a passion for open-air exercise; but he had little sense of the conduct expected from a king. The formidable problems he inherited from his father included a war in Scotland, an exhausted treasury, and all the grievances arising from unaccustomed taxation.

Character of Edward II (1307–27)

The conflicts which Edward I had just managed to survive came to a head in the reign of Edward II. As a result, this period is important in the history of Parliament. The great noble who became the leader of the opposition to the king's counsellors and actions was his young cousin, Thomas of Lancaster, the owner of vast estates and eventually the holder of five earldoms. Several other relatives of Edward also became critical of him: they considered that they were the king's natural advisers and they bitterly resented the power of the Household officials and Edward's reliance on his close personal friend, Piers Gaveston. The son of a respected Gascon knight, Gaveston offended the English

Thomas of Lancaster

Opposition to Piers Gaveston

barons by his arrogance, his wit, his superiority at jousting, and above all by his rapid advancement and complete dominance over the fond and admiring king.

One of Edward II's first acts on coming to the throne was to recall Gaveston, who had been his companion at court, from the exile to which Edward I had recently condemned him. The new king then infuriated the leading nobles by making Gaveston Earl of Cornwall, giving him a leading place at the coronation, allowing him to marry into the royal family, and appointing him regent during a royal visit abroad. Opposition quickly grew, and forced Edward into banishing Gaveston from the kingdom. Instead of sending him away in disgrace, however, the king appointed him to be his lieutenant in Ireland – and went down to Bristol to see him off! Within a short time Edward secured his return, but neither monarch nor favourite had learned their lesson: Edward continued to dote and Gaveston continued to show his contempt for the English lords – even to bestowing slighting nicknames on them, such as 'The Black Dog of Arden' for the Earl of Warwick. After several clashes with the returned favourite, Thomas of Lancaster and other earls forced Edward into agreeing to set up a committee of bishops and lords to institute reforms, or, as they put it, 'to ordain and establish the estate of the realm and the household according to right and reason'.

Under the terms of this agreement, the Lords Ordainers, as they were called, in 1311 drew up a series of Ordinances or decrees. These declared that 'evil counsellors' (Gaveston foremost among them) were to be 'put out and utterly removed'. The Ordinances also reaffirmed the liberties of the church, confirmed Magna Carta and the Forest Char-

Banishment and return of Gaveston, 1308–09

Reform Committee, 1310

The Ordinances, 1311

A royal 'coach' *From the fourteenth-century Luttrell Psalter – a Psalter commissioned by Sir Geoffrey Luttrell of Irnham, Lincs., and famous for its illustrations of everyday life of the time. Owing to the state of the roads in the Middle Ages, only ladies and invalids of royal rank expected to ride in wheeled vehicles:*

ter once again, and attempted to control the appointment of the chief officials. In addition, they strove to curb the growing financial independence of the royal Household: money for the latter was not to be taken directly from the tax-collectors, but must pass through the official channel, the Exchequer. The Ordinances also stressed the need for Parliamentary consent: all the chief officials were to be appointed 'by the counsel and assent of the baronage and that in Parliament'. Parliamentary consent, too, was to be obtained before the king could declare war or leave the country. We must beware, however, of thinking of 'Parliament' on modern lines. While the barons might be willing for representatives of the Commons to sit in Parliament, they obviously intended to dominate it themselves.

The role of Parliament

The Ordinances were proclaimed in public from places like St. Paul's Cross, but for the most part the king soon got round them. Gaveston left for exile in November 1311, but before Christmas was back again at the king's side. Edward loaded him with favours and made military preparations, whereupon Thomas of Lancaster and other leading nobles raised forces and captured Gaveston in Scarborough Castle. What they then did earned Edward's undying hatred. By the terms of Gaveston's surrender, he was to be tried in Parliament; but while being brought south, he was captured from his captors by 'the Black Dog of Arden'. Lancaster and two other earls then took him from Warwick Castle and had him beheaded. They claimed that they were only killing an outlaw, as the law required.

Further exile and return of Gaveston, 1311

Execution of Gaveston, 1311

This extreme action, coupled with Lancaster's ambition to set himself up above his fellow earls, offended many of the barons, and Edward was able to patch up some kind of truce with his opponents. The improve-

Improvement in Edward's position —

journeys by others were normally made on horseback. This fourteenth-century coach was really only a covered cart: strap-suspension did not come in till later. Coaches began to be more elaborately constructed in Elizabethan times, and became commonly used in the seventeenth century.

ment in his position, however, was quickly shattered by developments elsewhere. Taking advantage of the confusion in England, Robert Bruce had since 1307 steadily extended his hold over Scotland. His successes, which included raids into England, were a further cause of the contempt now widely felt for Edward's government. Too late, Edward tried to recover lost ground, only to be defeated overwhelmingly by Bruce at Bannockburn. Among those who refused to march north with him was Thomas of Lancaster.

By destroying the king's army the disaster in Scotland played into the hands of Lancaster and Edward's other opponents at home. For three or four years they were able to dominate the government. The king was made once more to promise to observe the Ordinances, and Lancaster became head of his Council. The king's critics, however, soon fell out among themselves, for many began to resent the ambition and incompetence of Lancaster. Among those who tired of Lancaster was his own wife, who had brought him much of his property: in 1317 she left him and took refuge with another earl, thereby starting a private war. The years of Lancaster's dominance also proved to be years of great general distress: all over Europe the harvests of 1315 failed through heavy rains, and from then until 1317 there was severe famine. People were reduced to eating dogs and horses, and assaults and robbery in quest of food multiplied. In 1316 the price of wheat was six or seven times what it had been two or three years before. All this, combined with the growing divisions among the king's enemies, helped to lead to the formation of a group of more moderate men, who exercised control from 1318 to 1321. At first they cooperated with Lancaster; later they were able to by-pass him.

During this period there rose to great influence another favourite, whose emergence led on to a brief period of royal triumph. He was Hugh le Despenser, the son of an experienced soldier and courtier of the same name. The elder Despenser had become Edward's chief adviser after the death of Gaveston, but his influence over Edward was soon eclipsed by that of his son, a man of great ability around Edward's own age. In 1318 he was appointed Chamberlain – an important Household position – and as his usefulness to Edward increased, so he was able to acquire greater and greater possessions. In particular, he managed to gather together large estates in South Wales.

This aroused the hatred and jealousy of the Marcher lords, who allied with the northern barons led by Thomas of Lancaster. The result was a struggle in which Lancaster and his allies were at first victorious. Edward had to agree to banish both Despensers; but he managed to gather forces and quickly struck back. Seeking out his chief opponent, he marched north and defeated Lancaster at Boroughbridge, in Yorkshire. A few days later he took his long-delayed revenge for the death of Gaveston. In one of Lancaster's own castles at Pontefract, the defeated earl was given a rough trial, then led to execution outside.

In the four years that followed, the recalled Despensers tried to make the government work well without surrendering any of the king's power. The Ordinances were cancelled – on the ground that they had not been approved by the Commons! – and it seemed that Edward's position was secure. In fact it was weak. The Scots were an ever-present threat; relations with France continued to be hostile; and the Marcher lords resented more than ever the growing Despenser hold in South Wales. By 1326, only one of the great English earls was co-operating with Despenser.

Edward on top, 1322–26

Ordinances cancelled, 1322

The move which led to Edward's downfall came from his wife Isabella, the daughter of Philip IV of France. She had been married to Edward when she was only twelve, and had borne him four children. In her teens she had resented Edward's passion for Gaveston and she was now angered at his dependence on the younger Despenser – who made matters worse by interfering with her estates. In 1325, to help settle a dispute with her brother Charles IV, the new king of France, Edward allowed her to go to Paris; and there she met with English exiles, including the vigorous Marcher lord Roger Mortimer of Wigmore, who had been imprisoned in the Tower of London after the battle of Boroughbridge but had escaped. At some stage, either then or later, he became the queen's lover, and a plot was devised. The first step was to get the heir to the throne, her 13-year-old son Edward, into her keeping. This was done by suggesting that Prince Edward should be invested with Edward II's French lands, and should come to France to do homage for them – a proposal that suited Edward II, who thereby avoided attending to do homage personally. The prince duly crossed to France and performed the homage. Isabella then informed her husband that she and the prince would not return to his court until he had dismissed the younger Despenser.

Queen Isabella

Roger Mortimer

Prince Edward in France

During the following months Isabella betrothed young Edward to Philippa, daughter of the ruler of Holland and Hainault, who provided her with forces for an invasion of England. In September 1326, accompanied by Prince Edward and Mortimer and other exiles, she landed in Suffolk. She announced that she had come to avenge Lancaster and expel the Despensers. Discontented barons and bishops quickly joined her, London rioted in her favour, and Edward was forced to flee to the younger Despenser's estates in Glamorgan. The queen followed with her troops. Within a few weeks they had captured and executed the two Despensers and intercepted the king as he tried to escape by sea.

Isabella's landing, 1326

Execution of Despensers

Early in 1327 the victorious rebels met in a Parliament at Westminster called by Prince Edward in the king's name. There was a very full representation of the Commons, and almost all sections of opinion were agreed that Edward II should be set aside in favour of the young prince. A deputation then went to Kenilworth, where the king was held, to secure his assent. After much pressure, including a veiled hint from a bishop that the crown might otherwise go to Mortimer, the weeping king finally agreed to abdicate.

Deposition and abdication of Edward, 1327

A dreadful fate befell the deposed monarch. While he lived he could be a danger to the victorious Isabella and Mortimer. Three months after the deposition, Mortimer's men took him to Berkeley Castle, in Mortimer's territory. There he was confined to a dungeon and ill-treated in the hope that he might die. Once he was rescued, only to be recaptured. News of a second plot came to Mortimer's ears; and shortly afterwards it was announced that Edward had died, of natural causes. In fact he was almost undoubtedly murdered, and by the most cruel means. It seems probable that to avoid any outward mark of violence on his body his killers thrust a red-hot iron through a horn into his bowels.

Murder of Edward II

Isabella, aided by Mortimer, now held control – rather insecurely – on behalf of the young king. She ordered a specially elaborate funeral for her late husband at Gloucester Abbey – where his splendid tomb soon became a place of pilgrimage. His reign had shown that there were forces strong enough not merely to threaten a king who offended a large part of the baronage – as had happened under John and Henry III – but actually to pull him down.

Edward II *The head from Edward's tomb in Gloucester Cathedral. The effigy is of alabaster, and is surmounted by a most elaborate stone canopy.*

18 King, Parliament, and People

1 Edward III, Scotland, and Parliament

At the beginning of his long reign, which lasted over fifty years, Edward III was fourteen years old and closely controlled by Isabella and Mortimer. He quickly grew to resent Mortimer, and he strongly disliked the recognition of Robert I and Scottish independence. In 1330, with the foreknowledge of the pope and the help of one or two leading nobles, he suddenly struck, arresting Mortimer and declaring himself of age. Isabella was sent off to live in a Norfolk castle; Mortimer, by the judgment of his peers, was drawn and hanged as a traitor.

Edward III takes over, 1330

Edward enjoyed a high reputation in his own time, for his qualities were the fashionable ones of the age. He was chivalrous, courteous, brave, a lover of jousting – at one tournament in London he and his companions challenged all comers – and a successful general. He was also a patron of architecture, learning and literature. A ruler who enjoyed all courtly and military pursuits, and who created the Order of the Garter, Edward found his friends and advisers among the leading earls and barons. He married his children into the great baronial families, and waged war abroad so actively that the barons, having dropped their objection to fighting overseas, had little time or inclination to take part in plots against him at home.

Edward's reputation

The warlike Edward's first concern was to reassert English royal claims over Scotland. His chance came when Robert I was succeeded in 1329 by his infant son David II – a five-year old already married to Edward's sister. In this tempting situation some of the Scottish and English lords whose lands had been confiscated by Robert I – a group usually known as the 'Disinherited' – were able to invade Scotland in 1332, and to establish Edward Baliol, son of John Baliol, as king. Baliol acknowledged Edward III as overlord, but was driven out by the opposing nobility after only four months rule. Edward then came out openly in his support. He besieged Berwick, and won a great victory against a Scottish relieving force at Halidon Hill. Baliol became king again, and Edward took direct control of the lowland shires.

David II, 1329–71

Edward Baliol (Edward I of Scotland)

Halidon Hill, 1333

The Scottish nobles who remained faithful to the young David II now sent him over to France, where Philip VI soon took up his cause. This became one of Edward's grievances against Philip, and helped to lead to war between England and France in 1337 (see Chapter 19). French support for David II then became more open, and after Baliol had again been expelled, David was able in 1341 to return as king to

French support for David II

Neville's Cross, 1346

Scotland. Five years later he invaded England while Edward was in France, but met disaster. At Neville's Cross, near Durham, his forces were overwhelmed and he himself taken prisoner.

Resistance continues –

It now seemed that Edward III might succeed where Edward I had failed. Resistance to Baliol (restored once more) and to Edward III continued, however, under a grandson of Robert Bruce, Robert the Steward, who claimed to act as regent for the captive David II. It was not quelled even by the brutal devastation which Edward III inflicted on the south of Scotland during February 1356 – an episode known as 'the Burnt Candlemas'. The following year Edward tried other tactics. Baliol had by now resigned all his rights in Scotland to him in return for a pension, and the English king decided to release David II and instal him in Scotland. This was on condition of cooperation and the payment of a huge ransom spread over ten years. David, who was childless, was by this time fully prepared to see Edward III, or one of Edward's sons, succeed him in Scotland; and a plan for a union of the two crowns, with Scotland enjoying a separate government, was again drawn up. A Scottish parliament, however, rejected this and when David II died in 1371 it was Robert the Steward – the first of the Stewart line – who succeeded. As Robert II he soon concluded a firm alliance with France, and Edward III was as far from subduing Scotland as ever.

Release of David, 1357

Robert II (Stewart line)

Development of Parliament

Edward's wars with Scotland and France, and especially the latter, speeded on the development of the English parliament. Wars could not be fought without money, and money enough for repeated campaigns across the Channel could only be obtained by grant from Parliament. To put Parliament in the right mood for meeting his demands, Edward made many concessions and many gestures to popular feeling. In 1362, for instance, he chimed in with the growing spirit of English nationalism by addressing Parliament in English. All Edward's Parliaments contained representatives of the Commons, who normally met separately for at least some part of the proceedings. In addition Edward granted many of the growing number of collective 'petitions' from Parliament, and he allowed Parliament to obtain a much greater control over taxation than ever before. He did this not because he wanted to surrender his privileges, but because he found that taxes which Parliament had not consented to – such as some of his attempts to levy extra dues on the export of wool – caused a great deal more trouble than those which Parliament had approved.

Taxation – and concessions

Parliamentary statutes

Parliament also played a part during the reign in law-making, in the form of some important statutes. Among these were two which aimed to restrict papal power in England. The first, the Statute of Provisors, dealt with the practice by which the pope frequently 'provided', i.e. appointed, clergy to positions in England. The clerics thus appointed (and known as provisors) were often foreign and non-resident, which meant that a deputy did the work while the provisor drew most of the revenues. Papal provision was often used to reward officials important

Provisors, 1351

A gold coin of Edward III *Edward III was the first English king to issue a gold coinage. Before that, and for long afterwards, English coinage was based on the division of a pound of silver (Troy weight) into 20 shillings, and those into twelve (silver) pennies. Edward's regular gold coins were the florin, from 1343 onwards, and the noble. The sovereign was not coined until the reign of Henry VII. On this coin, note the built-up platforms, or castles, on the representation of the ship, and the French fleur-de-lys quartered with the English leopards on Edward's shield.*

to the pope, and it was resented in England by all those, such as the king and the cathedral or monastic clergy, who would otherwise have made the appointments themselves. The statute authorised the king to expel papal provisors, which in practice meant that there was usually some bargaining between king and pope when the latter desired to make an appointment.

    The other measure, the Statute of Praemunire (Latin = to warn) forbade resort to courts of judgment outside the realm. The papacy was not mentioned, but the effect was that an expelled papal provisor, for instance, could not now appeal to the papal courts against the king's action. The feeling behind both statutes was all the stronger

Praemunire, 1353

because during most of the fourteenth century the popes were resident not at Rome but at Avignon, where they were thought to be under the influence of the king of France.

Crises with
Parliament – 1340–1

By timely concessions (which he sometimes withdrew later) Edward generally kept on good terms with his Parliaments. There were, however, two great moments of crisis. The first was in 1340–1, when Edward, compelled to break off his campaigning by shortage of money, in a fit of anger arrested his chief ministers. The second came right at the end of the reign with the activity of the so-called 'Good' Parliament of 1376. By this time Edward was becoming old and feeble, and a whole series of grievances had built up. With the Commons taking a leading part, Parliament demanded the removal of some of the king's ministers whom it declared responsible for over-taxation. The result was the trial of half a dozen officials before Parliament, with the Commons accusing them – the beginning of a new process in law which when fully developed (with the Commons as accusers and the Lords as judges) became known as impeachment. This was very important, for it meant that Parliament was claiming that ministers bore some responsibility not only to the king but to the nation as represented in Parliament. Parliament also demanded a reforming council to advise the king, and made attacks on John of Gaunt, Duke of Lancaster, the king's second son.

– 1376
(The 'Good'
Parliament)

Gaunt's revenge

The following year Gaunt struck back. He succeeded in getting the impeachments cancelled, in excluding many of the reforming members of Council, in imprisoning the Commons' Speaker of 1376, Sir Peter de la Mare – the first Speaker of whom there is record – and in securing from a new Parliament a reasonable rate of supplies. Nevertheless what the 'Good' Parliament of 1376 had done was not forgotten. Henceforth it would be difficult for a king to ignore the fact that Parliament had developed fast during the last century, and that the Commons were by now fully capable of taking, on occasion, a leading part in its actions.

2 The Black Death and its Aftermath

The Black Death,
1348–9

Britain in the 1370s was only just beginning to recover from one of the greatest disasters which she, in common with much of the rest of Europe, suffered during the Middle Ages. In 1348 the plague which men called the Black Death reached England. Starting in China, it had entered Europe by way of the Crimea and in the spring of 1348 was active in Italy, Spain and southern France. It then moved into northern France and in August claimed its first victims in Dorset. It spread rapidly through the west country and by November appeared in London. In January 1349 it struck Norwich and the eastern counties and then moved north. It began to die out in the late summer of 1349 but reappeared three times, in less violent form, during the next twenty years. Thereafter plague was a recurrent visitor, casting a deep shadow over late Tudor times, and ending only with the epidemic of 1665 known as the Great Plague.

The Black Death, with its swift onset, its swellings, boils, tumours, and delirium which nothing could relieve, was an epidemic of the two deadliest forms of plague, bubonic and pneumonic.[1] The bubonic variety, which was the more prevalent, first affected black rats, from which fleas carried the infection to human beings. The pneumonic form spread from person to person by germ infection from the breath. Medieval medicine, which knew nothing of germs, was powerless to deal with such maladies; and the treatments attempted, such as bleeding or repentances by fasting, usually had a weakening effect which made the sufferer more likely to succumb.

There are no accurate figures but from local records the extent of the disaster can be guessed. In Britain, probably over a million people died out of a population of between two and three million. The clergy, who were in touch with the poor and the dying, suffered especially severely; very probably nearly one half of their total number did not survive the years 1348–49. In each of the dioceses of Exeter, Winchester, Norwich and Ely, about fifty per cent of the clergy are known to have died in these years; in the dioceses of York and Lincoln about forty-four per cent. Westminster Abbey lost its abbot and twenty-six monks – mortality was particularly heavy in monasteries once the plague got a grip. In Bristol, the total death rate was nearly forty per cent of the population, while at Smithfield, just outside the walls of London, 5,000 plague victims were buried in twelve months – at the worst period at the rate of two hundred a day. In the country some villages, such as Tilgarsley in Oxfordshire and Ambion in Leicestershire, were completely wiped out; in others the few survivors moved their homes to new sites. An army from Scotland, hoping to take advantage of the situation in England, began to move south in 1349 but was itself destroyed by plague when it had got no further than Selkirk.

Despite all its horrors the Black Death seems to have caused no general panic. The war in France, halted by truce in 1347 was being waged again by 1351, and the great wool trade was not totally disrupted. It took several years for the full consequences of the epidemic to be felt, and these were complicated by the poor harvests of the next decade and by three great waves of cattle disease. One thing, however, is quite clear. The plague drastically reduced the amount of labour available. After the Black Death there were fewer workers to till the soil and tend the herds; and so those who survived were in a position to demand higher wages, or fewer burdens of service, or both.

This led to the Government, on the demand of Parliament, attempting to hold wages and prices down to pre-plague rates. A law was passed to this effect – the Statute of Labourers – which also tried to prevent men from leaving the estates upon which they customarily worked. But the Statute had several times to be reissued, which suggests that

Long-term effects

Shortage of labour

Statute of Labourers, 1351

[1] The bubonic form causes buboes, or swellings; the pneumonic form affects the lungs.

it was never really effective. Labourers naturally resented such restrictions – they wanted to be free of feudal burdens and to acquire land of their own; while employers of labour, wanting work done, were often willing to offer wages above the maximum laid down in the Statute. Earlier in the century, when a slump in the wool trade began and the cloth trade was not yet fully established, some landholders had started leasing out their surplus demesne lands, and after the Black Death this practice became more usual. Also there was a move in many areas away from cultivation to sheep farming, for the latter required less labour and it now promised greater profits.

Growth of sheep farming

Peasant discontent

A disaster on the scale of the Black Death hit very hard at the structure of medieval society, and its after-effects gave rise to much discontent. For the first time the common people of England – as distinct from the barons, the gentry and the merchants – began to make their voices heard. Their outcry took violent form early in the new reign, in the Peasants' Revolt of 1381.

Dovecot *From a thirteenth-century Bestiary in the Bodleian Library. Doves were an important source of food in the Middle Ages.*

Beehives *From a Bestiary of about 1200 in the Bodleian Library. Honey was extremely important in the Middle Ages for sweetening and medicinal purposes and for the making of mead. Cane-sugar was grown in the East, and later in Sicily and Southern Spain, but in Britain it appeared only as a rare and costly import.*

19 The Struggle in France

1 The Origins of the Hundred Years War

'The Hundred Years War' is one of those time-honoured terms which expresses a truth, but only roughly. The period of hostility between the kings of England and France to which it refers lasted in fact not 100 years but 116 – from 1337 to 1453; and during this time the fighting was frequently broken by long periods of inactivity, truce, or even formal peace.

England and France in the early 14th century

The background to this lengthy struggle is complicated. In the early fourteenth century, England and France were not yet fully formed 'national' states. The feeling of being 'English' or 'French' was not yet so important that it overshadowed local loyalties such as the feeling of being a Londoner, or a Parisian, or the vassal of a certain lord. Moreover 'France' was a term with more than one meaning: geographically it meant most (though not all) of the land we now know as France; but the kings of 'France' did not yet rule all this directly. For nearly two centuries they had been bringing more and more parts of France – such as Normandy and Anjou – under their direct control, but there were still large regions where the local duke or count, though he acknowledged the king of France as overlord, retained all the real power. Among these almost independent rulers in 1337 was Edward III of England, who as Duke of Aquitaine still controlled the important coastal territories of Guienne and Gascony. These provinces, with their great port of Bordeaux, had a flourishing wine trade with England, and they showed little wish to change the rule of their largely absent Duke for direct control by the French king.

The Hundred Years War was not, therefore, really a conflict between what we regard as England and France. In many ways it is better to think of it – though this is also to over-simplify – as a conflict between the King of England (who had territories in France, was part-French, and normally spoke in French) and the King of France (who was trying to extend his rule over the whole of that country). But in the course of the struggle the two sides, and especially the English, became much more conscious of 'nationality'. Men from different parts of England, or owning allegiance to different lords, began to attach less importance to this kind of difference, and more importance to their common difference from the French. Though they were fighting for the claims of the King of England, they began to think of themselves as fighting for England; and those who stayed at home began to see the conflict

Development of national feeling during 100 Years War

in the same light. In a country as small as England, with the spread of trade and the growth in power of the central government, it was natural that feelings of nationality should develop. They were doing so long before the Hundred Years War, but the experience of a struggle against men of another country speeded on this development, just as feelings of Scottish, Welsh and Irish nationality developed in struggles against Englishmen.

Causes of the war

Among the causes which gave rise to the war in the first place, three were especially important. The first was the fact that the king of France, Philip VI, the first of the Valois dynasty, was prepared to continue the French royal policy of absorbing the great feudal duchies into the kingdom of France. In 1337, following disputes with Edward III, he declared Edward's duchy of Aquitaine forfeited to the French crown. Edward, in other words, had to fight to preserve his French inheritance. The second cause was the help which the kings of France had begun to give the Scots. Edward was anxious to put a stop to this. The third cause was one which historians have often dismissed as unimportant, or as a propaganda move – Edward's claim to the throne of France. But there was nothing at all outrageous about Edward's claim, and although he did not stress it at all times, its existence made peace difficult between the two monarchs. Added to these three main causes there were many lesser ones, such as disputes between English and French sailors and traders in the Channel, and the bad relations between the Flemings (who depended greatly on wool supplies from England) and their count (who supported the king of France). Not to be forgotten, too, are the love of Edward III and his companions for warlike adventures, and the desire of the English for easy plunder, when they found this possible in France.

Edward's title to the French crown

The facts about Edward's claim to the French throne are these. When the last Capetian king of France, Charles IV, died without children in 1328, a claim was lodged on behalf of Edward, whose mother Isabella was Charles's sister. Edward had much the best claim by descent, if the title could pass through a female ancestor. Titles to great fiefs did in fact pass in this way, but the Crown was a very special matter, and as yet no queen had actually reigned in France, nor had a king's title been derived through the female side of the royal family. In any case Edward in 1328 was a youth in no position to enforce his claim, and in the following year he did homage to the new king, Philip VI of Valois (a cousin of Charles IV) for the duchy of Aquitaine. This seemed to settle the matter – for if Edward was pressing his claim, he would not do homage to another as king of France.

1337, Philip VI declares Edward's duchy forfeit. War begins.

Quarrels, however, quickly followed about the frontiers of Edward's territory, the rights owed to the French king, and the support given by Edward to one of Philip's rebellious kinsmen, Robert of Artois. These quarrels led to Philip VI in 1337 declaring Edward's duchy confiscated and to a state of war. A few months later Edward brought his claim to the French throne forward again, declaring that he had

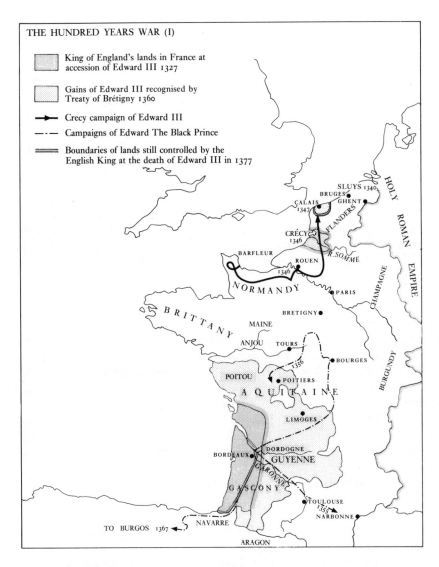

THE HUNDRED YEARS WAR (I)

King of England's lands in France at
accession of Edward III 1327

Gains of Edward III recognised by
Treaty of Brétigny 1360

Crecy campaign of Edward III

Campaigns of Edward The Black Prince

Boundaries of lands still controlled by the
English King at the death of Edward III in 1377

been too young beforehand to assert it properly. It was nearly two years,
however, before the active fighting began.

In 1340, Edward took the next step. He passed from claiming the
throne to actually assuming the title of King of France, and quartering
the fleur-de-lys of France on his shields and standards with the leopards
of England. He did this no doubt because he wanted the greatest possible
help from his Duchy, from the Flemings, and from any other allies he
could find. Nearly all these allies would be subjects of the king of
France. If Edward declared himself to *be* the King of France, as
opposed to merely claiming the throne, the consciences of his allies
would be clearer and their help to him all the greater, in that they need
not regard themselves as rebelling against their overlord. Instead, they
could claim to be supporting the rightful king against a usurper.

1340 – Edward
assumes title of
King of France

2 The Fighting in the Fourteenth Century

Flanders – Edward's
alliance with towns
against the Count,
1339

The early campaigns of the war consisted of little more than raiding – Edward in northern France, the French against English south coast towns and the Channel Islands. The first major battle came in 1340 and surprisingly enough was fought at sea. It followed important events in Flanders, whose Count was an ardent supporter of the French king. In an effort to put pressure on the Count, Edward had banned the export of English wool to Flanders. This wool was vital to the cloth industry of the Flemish towns; and the citizens of Ghent, under the leadership of the brewer and merchant Jacob van Artevelde, combined with those of Bruges and Ypres to drive out the Count. In 1339 Edward made an alliance with this group of towns and the following year an English

Sluys, 1340

fleet under his command sailed into the harbour at Sluys, a Flemish port where a much larger French fleet lay at anchor. The English archers and men-at-arms did great damage as the ships lay grappled together, and the French fleet, consisting of more than a hundred vessels, was almost wiped out. Edward soon returned home because of financial difficulties, but his naval victory gave him for some time the advantage of controlling the Channel.

During the next few years, despite truces from time to time, there was almost continuous fighting on the borders of Gascony. In 1341–2 Edward also intervened in a disputed succession in Brittany. Meanwhile he tried to hold together his allies in Flanders, who were quarrelling and under pressure from the French. In 1345 van Artevelde was assassinated in Ghent, and Edward determined to make a fresh effort in France before his Flemish allies collapsed. Raising an army by 'commission of array', he prepared a great expedition for the following year. Wales, for example, had to provide 3,500 infantry, Sussex 200 archers, and Norwich 60 mounted spearmen.

The Crécy campaign,
1346

In July 1346 the expedition, numbering perhaps 10,000 to 15,000 men, embarked at Portsmouth and landed on the Cherbourg peninsula in Normandy. Edward's movements then led Philip VI to think that he was heading for Gascony. By way of Caen (which he plundered mercilessly) and Rouen, Edward moved up the Seine to within twenty miles of Paris. Here, however, instead of veering south-west for Gascony, he crossed the river and made off north-eastwards to join up with the Flemings. With difficulty he crossed the Somme, hotly pursued by the French – only to learn that his Flemish allies, advancing west to join him, had been defeated by another French force. Edward accordingly halted and prepared for battle with his pursuers, taking up a good defensive position some twenty miles north of the Somme at Crécy.

The Battle of Crécy *A somewhat unrealistic presentation in a fifteenth-century edition of Froissart's Chronicles in the Musée de l' Arsenal. On the left, the forces of the King of France; on the right, those of the King of England. The archers— cross-bows v. longbows—are shown as beginning the action.*

nault qui furent tousiours
delez le roy phle de france

Cy parle de la bataille de
crecy entre le roy dangleter
re et le roy de france

Soldiers looting *From a fourteenth-century manuscript in the British Museum. Such actions by troops were a normal practice, and they caused particular misery in France during the Hundred Years War.*

The English king arranged his army in three 'battles' or divisions, two of these in the front line, one in reserve. Each 'battle' consisted of two projecting wings of archers, with dismounted knights and men-at-arms between. These were dispositions which had already proved their value in Scotland. On the right of the front line his eldest son Edward, known to later centuries as the Black Prince and then a boy of sixteen, was in nominal command; in command on the left, two leading English noblemen; and in reserve, in the rear, Edward himself. His headquarters, in a windmill on a mound, made an excellent viewpoint for control of the battle. Having inspected his men and ordered them to rest and eat, the king awaited the French attack.

Crécy, 26 August 1346   The French forces under Philip VI, who was accompanied by the blind King John of Bohemia and by many of the leading barons of France, were much more numerous than the English. They came up towards Edward's army during the afternoon of 26 August. By then it was too late, Philip thought, to attack that evening; but his knights would brook no delay. As the French moved on, the sky suddenly darkened and a thunder-storm broke. It quickly cleared but now the

French were facing a blinding evening sun. To open their attack they used their mercenary force of Genoese cross-bowmen – who ran out of missiles, and were in any case outshot by the storm of arrows from the English longbows. The Genoese broke, and retreated; and as they fled they were cursed for cowards and cut down by the French knights who now swept in to the attack. Fifteen or sixteen times, despite huge losses, the French horsemen charged, but each time Edward's Anglo-Welsh army repulsed them. Night fell before the French king left the field, and not till the following morning was Edward sure that the battle had ended.

In fact, the French defeat was overwhelming. Some 1,500 of Philip's knights lay dead on the field; and among the killed were the count of Flanders and the king of Bohemia who, blind though he was, had charged forward tied to two knights to guide him. Thousands of the ordinary French soldiers also perished, while English losses were very small. So outstanding a victory at once brought Edward, and the English and Welsh archers, high military renown throughout Europe. It also showed more clearly than before the power of the longbow – though this had already been evident in Wales and Scotland – and so lessened the prestige of the mounted knight, who henceforth began to encase himself in plate armour to such an extent that he finally charged in battle only with difficulty and was often powerless when unhorsed. By comparison with the longbow, the few primitive cannon used in Edward's army were as yet ineffective, though useful for frightening horses.

Though a great victory, Crécy did little to settle the struggle in France. Continuing eastwards, Edward went on to besiege Calais, which thanks to its double walls held out for nearly a year. The French king, disheartened by Crécy and by the defeat of his Scottish ally David II at Neville's Cross, for long made no attempt at relief – and when he did appear, retired without striking a blow. The starving burghers of Calais thereupon decided to surrender. Edward, angered by their long **Calais, 1346–7** resistance, would have hanged their leaders; but their lives were saved, it seems, by the intercession of Queen Philippa. The fortress passed into English hands, the townsfolk were nearly all driven out and replaced by colonists from England, and for the next two centuries Calais was the main English gateway to the Continent, for purposes both of trade and war.

During the next nine years truces were frequent. The Black Death **Black Prince in** took its terrible toll of both countries and prevented any great military **Gascony** effort. In 1355, however, the Black Prince went out to Gascony as his father's deputy. Having made Gascony secure, he tried to move north to join up with an English force from Brittany. Finding the Loire too difficult to cross, he turned south again, and on his way back came up against a greatly superior French army commanded by Philip VI's successor, John II. Battle was joined at Maupertuis, near Poitiers, **Poitiers, 1356** where the Black Prince won an overwhelming victory. In an effort to learn something from Crécy the French knights for the most part fought dismounted. But this was useless except in a defensive position shielded by archers – advantages not possessed by the French at Poitiers. Their defeat was complete, even to the loss of their king, who rushed desperately into the fray and was taken prisoner.

Two years later France was ravaged by the peasant revolt known as the Jacquerie. Despite much brilliant campaigning in 1359–60, however, Edward was unable to press home his advantages. He therefore agreed to negotiate and in 1360 the draft treaty of Brétigny, later confirmed at Calais, brought the war – though only temporarily, as it proved – to an end.

Peace of Brétigny, 1360

By the terms of this treaty, the King of England was to rule a much-enlarged Duchy of Aquitaine in full sovereignty (that is, no longer as a feudal vassal of the King of France) together with Ponthieu, Calais, and one or two other districts in Northern France. John II's ransom was fixed at the enormous sum of three million gold crowns (£500,000 – or about five times the annual revenue of the King of England); and Edward agreed to renounce the title of King of France. This was the high-water mark of English success in the fourteenth century. The triumph, however, was incomplete, for despite defeat in battle French power had not been destroyed.

French recovery under Charles V

The next few years saw a slow recovery in France. King John II was released when the first instalment of his ransom was paid; but one of his sons, who became a hostage pending the payment of the further instalments, broke his parole and fled. The chivalrous French king then voluntarily returned to captivity in London, where he died in 1364. He was succeeded by his son, Charles V, an able ruler who helped his kingdom to regain its strength.

Black Prince in Gascony and Spain

It was not many years before war broke out again. The Black Prince, now appointed by his father Duke of Aquitaine, led a successful but highly wasteful and expensive campaign over the Pyrenees to restore the expelled King Pedro (nicknamed 'the Cruel') to the throne of Castile. In the course of this he won another resounding victory at Najera. To help pay for this expedition, he taxed his Gascon subjects, some of whom appealed to the King of France. King Charles V agreed to hear their appeals and ordered the Black Prince to appear before his Court for the trial. This was a violation of the treaty of Brétigny, under which the French king had no rights whatever in Gascony. Before long,

Renewal of War, 1369

Edward retaliated by assuming once more the title King of France. Charles V then took the next step by declaring Edward's possessions in France forfeited. By 1369 fighting had again set in.

This time, however, the English armies met with little success. John of Gaunt led a great plundering raid across France, but without any lasting benefit to Edward's cause. The Black Prince became ill, and marred his reputation by the manner in which he dealt with rebels in Aquitaine: when at length he recaptured the city of Limoges, he ordered – or at least permitted – wholesale sack and massacre. Above all, the French general Bertrand de Guesclin was able to turn the tide slowly against the English by the policy of avoiding big battles and concentrating on sieges and harassing tactics. By the time Edward III died in 1377, only Calais and a narrow strip along the Gascon coast remained firmly in English hands.

This position remained largely unchanged throughout the reign of Edward's successor, Richard II. At one time the French had recovered well enough to carry out damaging raids on southern England and to threaten invasion. Eventually, however, a truce was concluded. With Richard taking as his second wife, in 1396, the seven-year-old daughter of the French king Charles VI and extending the truce to twenty-eight years, the prospects began to point towards a more lasting peace.

Richard II's marriage alliance, 1396

The deposition of Richard II in 1399, however, quickly ended any such hopes. Fresh causes of conflict soon arose. Within less than twenty years of Richard's alliance, an English king, Henry V, was once again sweeping all before him in France.

Edward III *The head from the effigy by John Orchard on Edward's tomb in Westminster Abbey.*

20 Lollards and Rebels: The End of the Fourteenth Century

1 The Church, John Wyclif and the Lollards

Throughout the Middle Ages, the Church remained supremely important in men's lives. From birth to death people were part of the Church no less than they were part of the manor, the village, the town, or the kingdom. To the Church they came for christening, worship, marriage, burial, guidance, the opportunity to confess their sins and be absolved. To the Church they looked for alms, medical care, education (in favoured cases) and beauty in the form of fine buildings, stained glass windows, wall paintings, statuary, embroidery and music. None of this changed during the fourteenth century. As the century wore on, however, many thoughtful people began to feel that the Church was losing some of her former inspiration and that abuses were creeping in which needed remedy.

To begin with, a number of things lessened the respect felt for the pope. The first of these was when the popes became very closely connected with France. To win its struggle against the Holy Roman Emperors for the control of Italy, the papacy had called in the help of the French king. This alliance, and the turbulent conditions in Rome at the time, led Pope Clement V in 1309 to take up residence at Avignon, a city in the territory of the Count of Provence, but near to that of the French king.[1] From then until 1378 all popes resided here – a period nicknamed by those who disapproved of it the 'Babylonish Captivity', since its seventy-odd years recalled the captivity of the Israelites in Babylon for a similar length of time. In fact, after Clement V the popes at Avignon were not greatly at the bidding of the French kings – but in England and Italy they were thought to be. All the seven popes at Avignon were, however, French, and so were 113 of the 134 cardinals created during this period. During this same time only two Englishmen were appointed cardinals, and no Germans. Such a state of affairs was bound to be resented outside France.

At length in 1378 the pope at the time ordered a return to Rome, only for a far more damaging period to follow. The next pope, Urban VI, quickly quarrelled with his cardinals, who then declared him deposed and elected instead a further pope, Clement VII. Urban, however, did not make way for the new choice. So began a split, or schism, in the papacy which, with various successors to Urban and Clement being

The Church in decline

Weakening of papal authority

– 'Babylonish Captivity' at Avignon, 1309–78

– Great Schism, 1378–1429

[1] In 1348 one of Clement's successors bought the city, and it remained papal property until the French Revolution.

elected by rival factions, continued until 1429. During this .time there were always two rival popes and even – for a spell of six years – three! Clement VII and his successors residing at Avignon were supported by France and her allies, while Urban VI and his successors at Rome were supported by France's enemies. All this made nonsense of the idea of a universal Church under a single head and greatly weakened the authority of the papacy.

A third fact which caused much criticism in fourteenth-century England was the constant need of the popes for money. There was nothing improper about this: the money was genuinely needed for the running of the Church. Of course during the schism, with two popes calling for support, papal demands increased still more. Though these demands were normally met by the clergy, they usually resented them. This resentment was often shared by others not so directly affected. The king felt that the pope was draining away money from his kingdom, while barons and merchants argued that if the proceeds of Church taxation went to the king, instead of the pope, the king would not need to call so heavily on the purses of barons and merchants. *Dislike of papal taxation –*

It was the need of the popes for income which led to the practice of papal provision to vacant sees and benefices. An Italian cardinal, for instance, whose work was important to the pope in Rome, could be rewarded cheaply by the grant of two or three important benefices in England. This was naturally unpopular among the English clergy, who, as national feeling grew, increasingly resented high positions in the English Church being occupied by foreigners. As a rule, too, the foreigner was an 'absentee' – he drew the main revenues of the post, but remained in Italy and paid some English cleric a much smaller sum to perform the duties. This also became widely resented. By no means all absentee clergy, however, were foreigners; English church leaders often held several benefices – a practice later termed 'pluralism' – and employed ill-paid curates to do the work. *– and papal provision*

'Absenteeism' and 'Pluralism'

Another thing which caused criticism of the Church in the fourteenth century was its growing wealth. Monks and friars, for instance, took vows of personal poverty, but this did not prevent the orders to which they belonged, or the monasteries and friaries in which they lived, from becoming in many cases very rich. Over a long period, kings, nobles and other wealthy folk had made gifts or bequests of land and valuables to such institutions or to cathedrals and churches. But as these gifts accumulated so the institution concerned had to give more time to business affairs – to matters like finance and estate management. In this way the very success of the Church tended to make it more worldly, and by the fourteenth century the wealth of the great church leaders and institutions was in all too obvious contrast with the poverty of Jesus and his disciples who had founded the Christian religion. *Growing wealth of the Church*

These facts help to explain the career and teachings of John Wyclif, or Wycliffe. Born about 1320 of a modest land-holding family in Yorkshire, Wyclif spent much of his life in Oxford. He was first and *John Wyclif, c. 1320–84*

foremost a scholar, but in 1374 the Crown appointed him to the
rectory of Lutterworth in Leicestershire, which provided him with an
income (and in later life a refuge). This was probably a reward for
undertaking a royal mission abroad to discuss papal taxation. In his
writings and discourses at Oxford Wyclif increasingly attacked what
he felt were abuses within the Church. He began by criticising the
wealth of the Church and the extreme claims of the papacy, and then
moved on to certain points of church doctrine. The core of his teaching
was that the power of pope or priest depended not simply on his office,
but on his righteousness – on whether he was in a 'state of grace',
without serious sin. If the cleric was well known to be unrighteous, and
the Church made no move to cast him out, the lay power – the king's
government – should confiscate his property and remove him from any
position of church authority.

'Dominion founded on grace'

   This suggestion of state interference angered the bishops, but
Wyclif was fortunate at first in enjoying the support of John of Gaunt,
the overlord of the Wyclif family estates. When the bishops summoned Wyclif to appear before them in London, it was Gaunt who
broke up his first trial, while on a second occasion he was saved from
punishment by the Black Prince's widow. Wyclif reached the height
of his influence in high circles when he was invited to address the
Commons in 1378, to defend a violation of sanctuary committed on
Gaunt's orders. After this the part that he played in public affairs
became less, for his religious views became more and more revolutionary, and this offended his patron Gaunt. From then on Wyclif
poured his full energies into lecturing and writing at Oxford, where he
continued to be regarded as the greatest teacher and scholar of the day.
Though he probably did not, as was once believed, organise missions
from Oxford or Lutterworth, travelling preachers claiming to be his
followers began to spread through the countryside. They became
known as Lollards – a term of abuse probably derived from a Dutch
word meaning 'mumbler' or 'mutterer', applied to certain heretics in
the Netherlands.[1]

Wyclif and John of Gaunt

The Lollards

   At first Wyclif had written only in Latin, but now he began to write
pamphlets in English, such as *The Wicket*. These were widely read.
In 1382 a council summoned by a new Archbishop of Canterbury
condemned twenty-four points in Wyclif's writings and forced the
University of Oxford to expel him and his followers. He then retired
to Lutterworth, where he remained until his death two years later. Had
he survived into the following century he would undoubtedly have been
burned as a heretic. As it was, his corpse was disinterred and burnt
in 1428.

Wyclif expelled from Oxford, 1382

   In his teachings, Wyclif finally attacked not only the wealth of the
Church and extreme claims of the pope and clergy, but also the accepted
doctrine concerning the Mass. This was very dangerous ground. To

[1] The name perhaps caught on from the fact that the wandering preachers may have
'lolled' or leant against trees or buildings while waiting for an audience.

The fox in bishop's clothes *This fourteenth-century wood-carving forms a pew-end in the church of St Michael, Brent Knoll, Somerset. To show a fox dressed as a bishop and preaching to the birds – whom he intended to gobble up – was a satire against greedy and deceitful clergy, and perhaps suggests that there were not a few of them around.*

Burning heretics *From a fifteenth-century French chronicle in the Bibliothèque Nationale, Paris. The scene is meant to be an early thirteenth-century one, and the king present on the left is Philip Augustus. Note the mass gibbet with suspended bodies in the background.*

counterbalance the power of the pope and the clergy he stressed the authority of the scriptures, and argued that men should be able to read these in their native language. The fact that the approved Bible – the Vulgate – was in Latin and that few apart from the clergy were learned enough to read it was, he maintained, totally wrong. He put his beliefs into practice by helping to organise a translation of the Vulgate into English. This proving not entirely satisfactory, in 1386 a less literal translation was published for which the main work was done by his secretary, John Purvey. These, the first translations of the complete Bible into English, were profoundly important in enabling more people to study the Testaments for themselves.

Though they gained a stronghold in Oxford and appealed to some men of influence, on the whole Wyclif's teachings were most widely adopted by the discontented and men of a questioning turn of mind. Since the lower ranks of society had the best reason to be discon-

The Lollards
suppressed

tented, Lollardry tended to flourish most among peasants, labourers, and artisans. This became even more so after the Peasants' Revolt of 1381, which frightened the authorities and upper society of the day into a stricter attitude towards criticism of existing practices. Regular persecution began in the 1380s, and this soon scattered the Lollards – particularly after the Church in 1401 secured the support of the new king, Henry IV, for the passing of the savage statute 'de heretico

'De Heretico
Comburendo', 1401

comburendo' (concerning the burning of a heretic). This brought England into line with most other European countries by setting up a regular procedure for the execution of heretics – who in the past had only rarely suffered extreme penalties. Henceforth, when a bishop's court declared a person heretical and handed him over to the lay power for punishment, the sheriff was to have him killed by burning.

After this, Lollardry went very largely underground. No longer a serious threat to the Church, it still retained an influence which quietly persisted and which later flared up again in other forms. On the Conti-

Continuing influence
of Wyclifism

nent, Wyclif's teachings had already inspired the great Bohemian reformer, John Hus, who was burnt for heresy in 1415. In Britain, they were to inspire many of the leaders of the Protestant movement during the sixteenth-century religious struggles which finally shattered the unity of the Church.

2 The Peasants' Revolt and the Overthrow of Richard II

Richard II, 1377–99

When Edward III died in 1377 he was succeeded by his grandson, Richard II. The son of the Black Prince, who had died before Edward III, Richard was only ten years old when he came to the throne. Born at Bordeaux, he had been brought up in England from the age of four by able and cultured tutors. Since he was too young to rule, a Council was appointed, but the most important figure of the time remained out-

John of Gaunt

side this – Richard's uncle, the ambitious and unpopular John of Gaunt, Duke of Lancaster. By this time John of Gaunt had taken as his second wife a daughter of the deposed King Pedro of Castile and was claiming to be the rightful king of that country. He seems to have done his best, by a policy of conciliation towards his old enemies, to give the new reign in England a good start.

Despite the sensible behaviour of Lancaster, the kingdom was soon

The Peasants' Revolt,
1381

in turmoil. This time the trouble did not come from a rebellious section of the baronage but directly from the ordinary people – a new voice in English history.

General causes –

The causes of the so-called Peasants' Revolt of 1381 were many and varied. The Black Death had led to unsettled conditions in the countryside. There was great resentment at the efforts of the Govern-ment to prop up the decaying manorial system by the Statute of

– Resentment at
villein status and
control of wages

Labourers and other measures: villeins resented doing their customary labour services on the lord's demesne when they needed to till their own ground, and when free labourers were obtaining high wages. The free labourers themselves resented the Government's efforts to keep down these wages. Mingled with these grievances, however, was wider criticism of the existing order of society. This was seen in the attacks of Wyclif and the Lollards on the wealth of the Church; and it was also seen, in its most extreme form, in the teachings of the priest John Ball, one of the rebel leaders. Ball is reported to have preached a sermon to a group of rebels on the text:

– Objections to Church wealth and social system

> Whan Adam dalf, and Eve span
> Wò was thanne a gentilman?

It was normally considered to be God's will that some people should have great riches and power, others only a life of poverty and toil. Ball utterly denied this. His ideas, in a period when custom and traditional authority counted for almost everything, were new and revolutionary.

The Peasants' Revolt occurred, not at the time of greatest general hardship in the fourteenth century, which was probably during the Black Death and the next twenty years, but when things were beginning to be rather better. Froissart, the famous chronicler, went so far as to say that 'the peasants' rebellion was caused and incited by the great ease and plenty in which the meaner folk of England lived'. This was not true; but many of the rebels had had glimpses of better things, and were resolved not to be held down by ancient customs.

– Peasant prosperity?

There can be little doubt that the measures which actually sparked off all this discontent were the poll-taxes (poll = head). Taxation in the past had never been imposed directly on every individual. In 1377, however, to help meet the great expense of the war in France, Parliament approved a grant to the king of a groat (4d.) for every person in the country over the age of fourteen. This was followed by a graded poll-tax two years later. The yield of this being disappointing, in 1380 a third poll-tax was granted, at the extremely high rate of three groats (one shilling) per head. To expect a labourer and his wife to find two shillings, when his earnings might amount to no more than twelve shillings a year, was quite absurd – even though the wealthy were urged to pay on behalf of the poor – and the violent injustice of the tax caused widespread anger and evasion. Many people went into hiding, which in some areas led to household searches, and the tax collectors found themselves with a hopeless task. Because of this, Government officers made a visit of inquiry to some areas, and this was misunderstood as the beginning of yet another tax. By the spring of 1381 the counties as yet chiefly affected, in the south-east, were ripe for revolt.

Immediate cause – poll-taxes

Poll-tax of 1380

The first riots, against the tax collectors, began in Essex in May 1381. They were quickly followed by outbreaks in Kent, and by early June men from the two counties had linked up in Rochester. Thence they moved to Maidstone, where they chose as their captain Wat Tyler – a man of obscure origins (possibly a tiler, possibly an ex-soldier) but of great force of character. From Maidstone they marched to Canter-

Outbreaks in Essex and Kent

Wat Tyler

bury, where they released from the archbishop's prison the wandering priest John Ball. Then on 11 June this mixed force of Kentish and Essex men began to head for London. So far they had attacked tax collectors and justices of the peace, stormed the odd manor house or castle, and burnt manorial documents. Now they claimed to be acting in support of King Richard, to save him from his traitorous and incompetent ministers – and they asked that he should come out to meet them at Blackheath. This point – a distance of some seventy miles from Canterbury – Wat Tyler's men reached in only two days. Meanwhile other groups from Essex, approaching north of the Thames, had reached Mile End to the east of the City, and encamped there.

The young king and his main councillors, who had taken refuge in the Tower, seem to have decided to parley with the rioters at Blackheath. The king set out on the Thames and reached Greenwich, but the mob on the south bank of the river was so great and unruly that he did not land. Instead he returned to the Tower. The frustrated rioters then moved on London itself. They attacked the Marshalsea prison in Southwark and the archbishop's palace at Lambeth, and then, with the help of sympathisers in the capital, stormed over London Bridge. Pouring along Fleet Street they opened the Fleet Prison, burned lawyers' houses, executed lawyers, officials and foreign merchants and finally joined another mob from London itself in destroying John of Gaunt's great palace at the Savoy – one of the finest houses in Europe. The rioters claimed to be acting from the highest motives and not looting. According to one chronicler, a man seen pocketing a piece of silver during the destruction of the Savoy palace was thrust by the mob into the flames.

From the Tower, where he could see the ruin being wrought, Richard now managed to inform the rioters that he would meet them the following day, 14 June, outside the City at Mile End. With a few attendants he made the journey and was respectfully received. Either on his own initiative or on the advice of his Council, he promised everything that the mob leaders demanded. Villeinage was to be abolished, labourers were to be entitled to get what wages they could, and the demonstrators were to be allowed to seize traitors.

Most of the Essex men then began to move homeward, but other forces persisted in the hunt for 'traitors'. A large group broke into the Tower and hauled off the archbishop of London, the treasurer, and other officers to instant execution. Other mobs from Hertfordshire and Middlesex, including one led by a certain Jack Straw, were by now coming in from the north. Tyler's force from Kent and the Londoners themselves were still active.

The next day, 15 June, Richard accordingly confronted a great mob once more, this time at Smithfield. Tyler presented their demands, but it seems in an insolent manner; and the demands themselves, including the abolition of all lordship except that of the king, and the confiscation of the estates of the Church, went far beyond those of the Essex men

John Ball

The peasants at Blackheath and Mile End

Tyler's men enter London

Destruction of Savoy Palace

14 June: Richard's promises at Mile End

Storming of the Tower

Richard at Smithfield, 15 June

at Mile End. All the same, Richard seems to have promised to grant everything, and advised Tyler to trust in his word and go home. Tyler was not to be got rid of so easily. He began to exchange words with the king's attendants. The Mayor of London, Walworth, then pulled Tyler off his horse to the ground, where a squire struck him dead. It was at this moment of crisis, with the mob in a highly dangerous mood, that Richard – according to Froissart – spurred forward crying out 'Sirs – will you shoot your king? I will be your chief and captain. You shall have from me all that you seek. Only follow me to the fields without.' Riding away, he led large numbers off to the north. Meanwhile Walworth gathered troops and volunteers to surround the remainder, who finally dispersed quietly. Richard's courage, his readiness to hand out worthless promises, and the vigour of Walworth, whom Richard promptly knighted, had saved the day for the existing order.

During these same few days and the rest of the month, similar

Richard II at Smithfield *An imaginative illustration to a copy of Froissart's Chronicles in the British Museum. On the right Richard addresses the rebels. On the left, Mayor Walworth strikes down Wat Tyler.*

Riots elsewhere,
June 1381

events were happening elsewhere. In the villages outside London, in Bedfordshire, Sussex, Yorkshire, rioters attacked the houses of officials and great landlords. At St. Albans there was violent protest against the rights of the abbot over his tenants: the townsmen broke into the abbey and burned the documents on which the abbot based his powers. At Bury St. Edmunds mobs sacked the priory and later hunted down and beheaded the prior. At Cambridge townsfolk and peasants stormed the University Church and Corpus Christi College, destroyed the University charters and declared its privileges surrendered to the town. Similar risings occurred in Norfolk and Suffolk. But by the end of June the forces of law and order were in control and Richard even felt strong enough to issue a proclamation cancelling, on the advice of his council, the pardons he had 'lately granted in haste'. He was certainly not lacking in nerve. To a deputation of protest from the Essex men about the broken promises, he seems to have replied, 'Villeins ye are, and villeins ye shall remain.'

The Government in
control

On the whole the Government confined punishment to obvious leaders. Jack Straw, John Ball and several others were executed. Later in the year Parliament confirmed a general pardon – and the cancellation of the king's promises. The whole incredible episode was now over. The rioters had gained nothing except relief from further poll-taxes. The manorial system, already decaying, continued to decay, but no faster than before the revolt. But if the movement had brought no obvious gains to the depressed classes, it doubtless had some effect on the king. A youth of fourteen, he had saved the situation when his elders failed. The knowledge of this may have led to the excessive self-confidence which later helped to destroy him.

Character of Richard

Richard, like Edward II – whose fate he finally shared – and unlike Edward III, was not fitted by temperament to be the leader of the barons. A patron of art, one of the first users if not the 'inventor' of the pocket handkerchief, clever, scheming, and self-assured, he had little time for those who took their pleasures in fighting, in tournaments, and in hunting. Yet he came near to creating the sort of strong monarchy which the Tudors were later to achieve. He failed in part because of his rashness, but probably more because he lacked the essential support that the Tudors possessed, that of a strong middle class.

The opposition
successful, 1386–8

Much against his will, which frequently expressed itself in bursts of violent temper, Richard remained in his teens dominated by his uncles, the Dukes of Lancaster, York, and Gloucester. Lancaster on the whole acted as a moderating influence and it was when he sailed away in 1386 in pursuit of the throne of Castile that disputes between Richard and some of the leading magnates came to a head. Invasion from France threatened, Richard seemed unwilling to lead his country in war, and bands of unpaid troops were roaming through the capital. The opposition demanded the dismissal of the chancellor (Michael de la Pole, Earl of Suffolk) and of several household officials. The king replied that he would not move 'the least boy in his kitchen from his place'. All the same he soon felt obliged to dismiss Suffolk and submit to other demands.

The crisis over, Richard soon strove to recover his lost ground. Fearing that the king was going to bring proceedings against them some of the magnates decided to strike first. Five of them – the Duke of Gloucester and the earls of Warwick, Arundel, Derby and Nottingham – 'appealed' (i.e. accused) five of Richard's friends of treason. Most of the accused, including Suffolk, took to flight, but one of them, Robert de Vere, Duke of Dublin, led an army south from Cheshire to help Richard. The magnates, however, intercepted him at the bridge over the Thames at Radcot, in Oxfordshire, and scattered his force in confusion.

The Lords Appellant

Radcot Bridge

In the Parliament that followed, the Lords Appellant, as they were called, entered arm-in-arm in cloth-of-gold garments and demanded the death of Richard's five servants. The 'Merciless' Parliament, as it became known, condemned all five and many more, and for a year the Appellants were triumphant. None of their victims seems in any way to have been a traitor, or deserved death; but in the Middle Ages the penalties of being on the losing side were severe.

The 'Merciless' Parliament, 1388

A year later, Richard judged the time ripe to hit back. The Scots had won a great victory – known as the Battle of Chevy Chase – over the English at Otterburn, north of Newcastle; the king's new advisers who had forced themselves upon him were discredited; and the idea of peace with France was becoming more attractive. Now twenty-three years old, Richard suddenly declared himself of age and dismissed his enemies from the Council. They were taken by surprise, and for the next seven years Richard was able to rule peacefully. But the quiet was deceptive: both sides were building up private 'livery' armies, Richard

Richard turns the tables, 1388

Richard quarrels with London, 1392–

Richard II *A portrait of the king, of a realistic character, painted during his later years. The artist is unknown. (National Portrait Gallery.)*

himself under the emblem of the White Hart.

The first signs of trouble came in 1392 when Richard quarrelled violently with the mayor and citizens of London. The Londoners had resisted attempts to exact loans for the king, and this led to Richard imprisoning the mayor and sheriffs and for five months keeping the City under royal control. Eventually there was a reconciliation when the Londoners agreed to give the king a 'free gift' of £10,000, but the dispute weakened Richard's hold over the capital, to his later cost.

– and with Lord Arundel, 1394

Shortly after this, Richard clashed openly with the most defiant of the former Lords Appellant, the Earl of Arundel. When Richard's beloved queen, Anne of Bohemia, died in 1394, Arundel failed to join the funeral procession, appeared late at Westminster Abbey for the burial and then asked permission to withdraw immediately. Taking this as an insult Richard seized a verger's wand, knocked Arundel down, and sent him to the Tower for a week. Another example of the king's extreme behaviour followed when he ordered the wing of the palace at Sheen, in which Anne had died, to be burnt down and obliterated.

Truce with France, 1394

In that same year, after an embasssy under Lancaster had paved the way for a long truce with France, Richard began to tackle the problem of Ireland. The Irish chieftains there had been gaining ground and there was little order throughout the whole country. In a visit which lasted till May 1395, the king and his troops achieved a great deal. Richard did not do much fighting, but by conciliation he brought most of the important native chiefs to acknowledge his overlordship. When he returned to England he had stronger forces at his command than ever before, and he seemed as firmly settled on the throne as any of his predecessors.

In 1396, as the symbol of the new friendship with France, Richard married the seven-year-old Isabel, daughter of the French king. The alliance was not popular and it made the king's uncle Gloucester draw closer to the aggrieved Arundel. Scenting danger and feeling himself powerful enough now to pay off old scores, in 1397 Richard suddenly struck at three of the five former Lords Appellant. He had Arundel,

Richard attacks three former Lords Appellant

Gloucester and Warwick arrested, and shortly afterwards 'appealed' them of treason in Parliament, just as they had earlier 'appealed' Richard's friends. A subservient Parliament did what Richard wanted: the peers found all three men guilty. Gloucester had died as a prisoner just before the trial, or more likely been murdered; Warwick was banished, Arundel beheaded.

This left two of the Lords Appellant of 1387–88 still unharmed – Thomas Mowbray, formerly Earl of Nottingham and now Duke of Norfolk, and John of Gaunt's son Henry Bolingbroke, formerly Earl of Derby and now Duke of Hereford. To Richard's great satisfaction, these two now fell out; for Norfolk apparently invited Hereford to ally with him against the king – and Hereford, on his father's advice, reported the conversation to Richard.

Hereford's charges against Norfolk

In the absence of clear proof of the conversation it was decided that the matter should be tried by personal combat – Hereford *v.* Norfolk. All was arranged for the duel to take place before the king at Coventry, and the great nobility of England assembled. The two dukes, in armour and mounted, waited with their lances couched. A trumpet sounded, and they began their charge. But instantly another clamour of trumpets caused them to draw rein: Richard had cast down his staff to stop the duel. After two hours of hubbub, the king's judgment was then announced: Hereford was to suffer exile for ten years, Norfolk confiscation of his property and exile for life. At one stroke Richard had rid himself of the last of his old Appellant enemies of 1388.

Trial by battle

Richard now set out to harass smaller fry who had been in any way associated with the Appellants. In addition to these individuals no less than seventeen counties were fined – for Richard's revenue was not enough to cover the expenses both of government and of his costly tastes. Trouble would certainly have followed these impositions had it not come from another direction. In February 1399 John of Gaunt died and his title of Duke of Lancaster passed to his son in exile, Henry Bolingbroke, Duke of Hereford. Most of Gaunt's vast estates should have passed likewise. But Richard, by an act which was to cost him his throne, now confiscated most of the Lancaster inheritance. At the same time he extended Bolingbroke's sentence to exile for life.

Richard in full power

Hereford Duke of Lancaster, 1399; his estates confiscated

Coming on top of the confiscation of Norfolk's property for treason, this was an act which disturbed many of the great landholders, who feared that their turn might come next. Amidst this, Richard confidently went off to Ireland to deal with a revolt by one of the great chieftains. His rashness was Henry Bolingbroke's opportunity. He left France with a small company and finally landed at Ravenspur, in Yorkshire, to make for his family castle at Pontefract. The great northern lords rapidly joined him, and everywhere the populace greeted him with enthusiasm.

Richard in Ireland

Lancaster lands at Ravenspur

Richard's regent, the Duke of York, quickly submitted to the returned exile, who then marched west to intercept the king on his return from Ireland. His plan succeeded to perfection. Deserted by many of his leading men, Richard soon after landing in Wales found himself besieged in Conway Castle. He made terms, as he thought, with one of Henry's envoys and agreed that Henry should receive the Lancastrian inheritance. He then emerged from the castle – into an ambush laid by Henry.

Richard captured

The last act in the tragedy of Richard II saw the king lodged in the Tower, the Londoners' allegiance transferred to Henry, an abdication extracted from Richard, and the king formally deposed by an assembly called on the model of Parliament. This same assembly then went on to approve Henry's own title to the throne, by right of descent from Henry III. He became Henry IV – the founder of the Lancastrian line of kings. His title was a weak one, and the Lancastrians were to pay dearly for this later.

Abdication and deposition of Richard, 1399

Henry IV

Death of Richard,
1400

Like Edward II, Richard II did not long survive his deposition. Three months later, after an unsuccessful rising in his favour, he died in Henry's castle at Pontefract. There is no proof that he was murdered, but this seems highly probable.

Historians are by no means all agreed about Richard II. The most common view is something like the following. Richard was a gifted and cultured man, a patron of art who rebuilt Westminster Hall, and a ruler whose policy of peace with France had much to commend it. Having at length established himself as the real ruler, and not a figure-head, Richard in the last year or two of his reign became openly tyrannical and more than a little mad, so that finally he deserved the verdict of the assembly that deposed him, that he was 'utterly unworthy, and useless, to rule and govern the realm'.

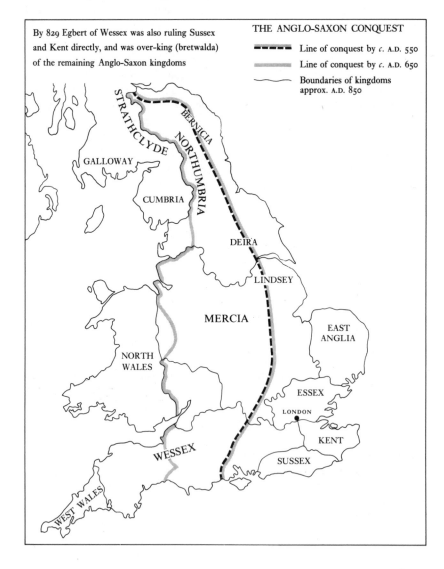

By 829 Egbert of Wessex was also ruling Sussex and Kent directly, and was over-king (bretwalda) of the remaining Anglo-Saxon kingdoms

THE ANGLO-SAXON CONQUEST

▄▄▄ Line of conquest by *c.* A.D. 550

▄▄▄ Line of conquest by *c.* A.D. 650

—— Boundaries of kingdoms approx. A.D. 850

21 Medieval Architecture

I Materials and Methods

Most buildings today are constructed either of brick or else of steel and concrete. Though cheap and easy to obtain, these materials are not normally products of the land on which they stand. For many centuries, however, the materials employed for all but the most exceptional buildings had to be obtained locally. It is this which, quite apart from Local materials the mellowing effect of time, makes so many old village houses and churches fit perfectly into the countryside. It is this, too, which produces their interesting variety – whether the lovely yellowing stone houses of the Cotswolds, the austere grey stone farmhouses of Derbyshire and Yorkshire, the half-timbered houses of Cheshire and Shropshire, or the chalk and flint buildings of the south-eastern counties.

For major buildings in the Middle Ages, especially cathedrals and churches, stone was indeed brought from other parts. Purbeck marble, Imported stone for example, was widely used throughout England for the shafts of columns and pillars, and Caen stone was often brought across the Channel from Normandy and then transported to its site by river. Norwich Cathedral, built at the beginning of the twelfth century, was largely made of Caen stone which was shipped to Yarmouth and then up river to Norwich. But this was expensive, and normally medieval masons had to rely on what they could obtain much nearer the site.

The best building stone was quarried from the belt of limestone which Limestone stretches from the Dorset coast through the Cotswolds to its ending in the Yorkshire moors. Close-grained in texture, it was called freestone because it could be carved easily on any surface; yet it was sufficiently hard and durable to withstand the weather. It was used for many of the finest medieval buildings, and the villages built of it have a mellow beauty all their own. In some other regions sandstone was widely Sandstone employed but its tendency to flake makes it less easy to carve than limestone, and it does not have the same resistance to weather. Other stones harder than these two were also used, in areas where they were easily obtained, and the type of building that resulted from them was normally strong and weather-resistant, with a minimum of decoration. In Flint the chalk districts, however, large flints were used with the chalk to produce interesting decorative effects.

Where there was little easily accessible stone, timber was the main building material. Probably most buildings were originally made from wood, and especially from oak, but few purely timber buildings have Timber

Early English Gothic: the nave of Lincoln Cathedral *Following the collapse of most of an earlier structure in a landslide, Bishop Hugh of Lincoln began rebuilding the cathedral in 1192 in the new style with pointed arches – what we call 'Gothic'. The choir ('St Hugh's Choir') was the first part to be completed: then came the nave (1209–35). Later in the century a rear-choir or presbytery ('the Angel Choir') was built by another famous Bishop of Lincoln – Bishop Grossteste – in a more decorated Gothic style.*

survived: one interesting relic from the Anglo-Saxon period is the timber nave of the church at Greensted near Ongar in Essex, where the original walls, with the logs split and set vertically, are still in position.

Thirteenth-century builders *Drawings by Matthew Paris in the Book of St Alban (Library of Trinity College, Dublin).*

For houses, a frequent method of construction was to build a strong timber frame and fill this in with earth or wattles as a base for a covering of clay or plaster.

Brick, or baked clay, was employed extensively by the Romans in Britain but fell out of use with their withdrawal. Occasionally, however, medieval buildings or parts of them were constructed with bricks obtained from Roman ruins, as at St. Albans Abbey. It was only in the fifteenth century that the use of brick became common. Brick (15th century)

Up to the twelfth century, the axe was the main all-purpose building tool, but this did not permit very delicate shaping or carving. The increasing use of the chisel allowed much greater variation in pattern, and by the thirteenth and fourteenth centuries carpenters and masons had developed all the tools that they needed to produce superb work in wood and stone. As for the problem of building tall structures, this was met by the erection of scaffolding and the use of rope-and-wheel hoists. In view of the hard labour involved in shaping planks, the scaffolding usually consisted of saplings. Tools

Scaffolding

Most buildings of any importance today are designed by professional architects, who depend on the services of surveyors and normally also of structural engineers. When the architects' plans are approved, they are put into the hands of civil engineers and builders, and the finished structure is the work of three or four different professions and many trades. In the Middle Ages, however, there was not this degree of specialisation. It is often said that there were no professional architects, but this is true only in the narrow sense that they were not called 'Architects'
(master-masons)

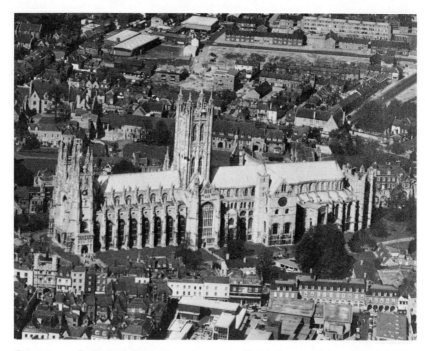

Canterbury Cathedral *Canterbury is a marvellous mixture of the various Gothic styles from the twelfth to the fifteenth century, and even retains some earlier Norman work. After the murder of Thomas à Becket in 1170 it became the chief place of pilgrimage in Britain. Becket's shrine attracted so many valuable gifts that when Henry VIII pillaged it at the dissolution of the monasteries twenty-six cartloads of jewels and precious metals were taken off to the Treasury.*

architects, and that as well as designing structures they were qualified to build them. The architects of the Middle Ages were master masons or builders; and undoubtedly the greatest of them were so much in demand that they finally concentrated entirely on designing and super-vision. They had no time left over to shape or lay stone themselves. Whether they did or did not soil their hands by manual work, however, these master masons worked on the site in control of their team of masons and carpenters, and built their buildings in relation to the land on which they were working. Such men travelled about the country-side with their fellow craftsmen, with the result that many of the medieval buildings in a particular area show a similarity of planning and workmanship.

Famous master masons

The names of several of the great master-masons are known. It was certainly not always local men who were employed on building our medieval churches. After the great fire at Canterbury in 1174, for example, a master-craftsman from northern France, William of Sens, was put in charge of the rebuilding. Master John of Ramsey was probably responsible for the great octagon of Ely Cathedral, while Master William of Hurley worked with him on building its wooden vault. Later in the fourteenth century Henry Yevele, the king's master mason after 1360, was to a great extent responsible for the spreading of the perpendicular style throughout the country. These men were highly-skilled craftsmen and they were highly paid for their services.

When we visit a great medieval cathedral and gaze at the massive pillars and the vaulted roofs high above, we cannot but marvel at the skill of their builders. With the simplest tools, they were able to raise magnificent edifices which have endured now in some cases for nearly nine hundred years. To guide them they had no highly developed system of mathematics for calculating stresses in building; instead they relied for the most part on their own experience and on the practical knowledge handed down by their predecessors. They knew, for instance, in a purely practical way, that they could make a perfect right angle for the corner of a building by marking out a triangle of which the base and vertical sides were 3 feet and 4 feet, and the third side 5 feet.

Every building is essentially the enclosing of a certain amount of space; but how to enclose it is a very complex problem. The earliest stone buildings after the departure of the Romans were probably copies of turf huts, as in Ireland – they consisted of posts with a wooden roof and no walls. Then walls were introduced, but as the buildings got bigger so the problem of roofing developed. Even a timber roof – the normal solution – had its problems, quite apart from that of fire and decay; but a stone roof of course presented far greater difficulties. The problem of holding the stones together was solved by vaulting, but a vaulted roof exerts great pressure not only downwards but also outwards. Therefore walls and other supports had to be sufficiently massive to withstand this double roof pressure upon them.

Gradually the understanding of stress in building grew. The first solution to the problem of stone roofing during the medieval period was barrel-vaulting. The roof was made by a continuous series of stone arches – the stones were mortared together in the first place within a wooden frame – the weight of the centre stones pressing down and helping to hold all the others together. This gave a continuous vault like a barrel cut in half. The stress of such a roof was spread all along the walls, which had to be very thick to withstand it. By breaking the space to be roofed into squares, however, and 'cross' vaulting each square, the thrust could be concentrated at the four corners of the square, and so strong pillars at these points could replace a thick wall. Such vaulting was normally used only to cover fairly narrow areas, like aisles, between an outer wall on one side and internal columns on the other. Later, however, by means of buttresses and other devices, and by new forms of vaulting involving the use of pointed arches, the master masons learned how to concentrate the stress from the roof much more effectively at certain points. Their vaulting had no longer to be based on dividing the space into squares, but could span large oblong areas. Thus, from the twelfth century on, more complex vaulting allowed greater spaces to be roofed over, and as the centuries passed

Building skill

The problems of roofing

Vaulting

and the skill increased, so vaulting became more complex and more decorative until it produced the final splendours of the cloisters at Gloucester Cathedral and the Henry VII Chapel at Westminster. The increase of skill and knowledge enabled the masons to concentrate the stresses at more widely separated points, thus making it possible to dispense with large sections of wall and insert windows in the space gained. So architecture passed through many phases in the Middle Ages, each successive period depending on developments in the principles of construction.

By no means all medieval workmanship, however, was perfect. The chancel arches of many parish churches are not wholly true; and Norman walls are often not as strong as they appear. It is a curious fact that not only the Romans but also the Anglo-Saxons knew how to make stronger mortar than their medieval successors. This weakness in medieval mortar, coupled with the problem of foundations, helps to account for the frequent collapse of buildings in the Middle Ages. The Norman central tower of Ely, for example, fell down in 1322, to be replaced by the great central octagon which is now one of the glories of the cathedral; and when the foundations of Winchester Cathedral were examined in the early part of this century, it was discovered that the whole massive structure was supported merely on logs built over a running stream. The various technical difficulties, however, were steadily overcome, and the whole history of British architecture can show few, if any, finer achievements than the great cathedrals and churches built between 1100 and 1500.

Building weaknesses (margin note)

2 Churches

The great progress in church-building during the Anglo-Saxon period included, as we have already seen, the construction of churches in stone, the use of the two-oblongs plan (chancel for the priests, nave for the congregation) and the development of frontal towers. All this was dwarfed, however, by the progress made under the Normans.

Norman influence in building affected England before the Conquest. One has only to look at the small central tower of Westminster Abbey – one of the few surviving features of Edward the Confessor's church – to realise this. It shows an important Norman development, the building of the tower over the 'crossing' of the church, where nave meets chancel. The downward and outward thrust of such a tower was supported at the front by the nave, at the rear by the chancel, and at the two sides by small transepts which extended the simple two-oblongs plan of a Saxon church into the form of a cross. But once the Normans had actually conquered England, their ideas and energy were of course still more strongly felt. The style of building that they brought with them owed much to the famous monastery at Cluny. It was inspired by the desire for size and grandeur, and the great Norman cathedrals rise wholly dominant over the other buildings around them.

Norman or 'Romanesque' architecture, late 11th and 12th century (margin note)

The Normans firmly established the centres of the dioceses in towns instead of rural places, and much of their work springs from the need for new cathedrals in towns. It may still be seen in the cathedrals of Durham, Ely, Norwich, Peterborough, and Winchester, as well as in the great abbey churches of St. Albans and Tewkesbury. Thick walls; later, massive pillars inside to do much of the work of these walls in carrying the weight of the roof; 'barrel' vaulting of the aisles; rounded arches decorated with particular types of moulding such as chevron or dog-tooth – these were among the characteristics of their architecture. Another notable feature was the way the sides of the nave were often designed in three layers – an arcade of main arches and pillars as the base, a gallery of smaller arches above, and at the top the clerestory or arched windows admitting light. The small windows were often splayed inside to allow the maximum of light but the general effect of the whole building was one of massiveness, heaviness, and solidity.

With the twelfth century, church architecture became lighter in spirit and more ornamental. In doing so it entered one of its finest periods which lasted till the sixteenth century and saw the building of nearly all the major English churches. This was the age of what was later called 'Gothic' architecture – a term of abuse coined in the eighteenth century, when classical styles were fashionable, to describe 'barbarian' architecture not based on Greek or Roman models.

Gothic architecture

The most important new feature in Gothic architecture was the technique of vaulting by means of a framework of ribs (with stone in-filling) forming pointed arches, as opposed to the solid round vaulting of Romanesque architecture. The earliest uses in England of the pointed arch may be seen in Cistercian abbeys, such as those at Rievaulx and Fountains in Yorkshire. This was probably because the Cistercians were closely in touch with France, where 'Gothic' architecture first developed. But the first major work in a fully-fledged Gothic style in England was the choir of Canterbury Cathedral, rebuilt by William of Sens. Other splendid early Gothic works were the nave of Wells Cathedral and St. Hugh's Choir in Lincoln Cathedral, which was followed only a few years later by the magnificent nave. Pointed arches were the answer to the problem of vaulting, and the ribs or framework of the vaulting could be emphasised to form a decorative pattern in themselves. Moreover by concentrating the thrust of the roof at points wider apart than before, ribbed vaulting enabled these points to be reinforced by buttresses, and so permitted the walls and pillars supporting the roof to become more slender. Windows, while still narrow, became much taller – what are known as 'lancet' windows. A splendid example of these is the group known as the 'Five Sisters' in the north transept of York Minster.

New vaulting techniques and the pointed arch

Simplicity, purity of line, strength – these became the characteristics of the first clear form of English Gothic architecture, the style often known as 'Early English'. Contrasting colours of stone were used, especially in the grouped shafts of pillars, and extensive use of Purbeck

Early Gothic architecture in England ('Early English'), late 12th and 13th century

marble can be seen in Canterbury, Winchester, and Chichester. But perhaps the finest cathedral of the Early English period, and the only English cathedral which was built throughout as a unit, is Salisbury, started in 1220 and completed in 1266 – apart from the superb tower and spire which were added in the fourteenth century.

In 1245 Henry III, who was a great patron of building, commissioned an extensive rebuilding of Westminster Abbey. His principal architect was probably a Frenchman, and his work marked a move towards the next phase in Gothic architecture in England – towards the style usually called 'Decorated'. This, though influenced from abroad, also grew naturally out of the Early English period once the builders had mastered the techniques of delicate stone carving and the use of 'flying' buttresses to support the weight of the roof and upper storey. The reconstructed Westminster Abbey was very high, its windows were large and distinguished by their delicate stone tracery, and its vaulting was more complicated than Early English vaulting. The upper storey of the nave was supported by a double tier of flying buttresses on the cloister side.

The next Gothic phase, ('Decorated') – late 13th to 14th century

The move towards a new style can also be seen in the Angel Choir of Lincoln, in the naves of Lichfield and Exeter Cathedrals, and in the choir and west front of York. In all of these there were great windows formed on highly elaborate stone tracery, and by the beginning of the fourteenth century these had become the dominant feature of new cathedral architecture. It was under the inspiration of this new Decorated style that the famous octagon and lantern at Ely were built, when the tower of that cathedral collapsed in 1322. The octagon, replacing the lower half of the tower, was built of stone, but the lantern above it was constructed in wood. The use of elaborate wooden roofing was a new fashion of this period, and it is interesting to note that in the Ely lantern the main timbers are 63 feet long and 3 feet square: the whole of England

Salisbury Cathedral *Built within an unusually short period of time Salisbury is a marvellous combination of fine building and superb setting. Inside, it has suffered from drastic cleaning-up and restoration carried out during the nineteenth century.*

Medieval clockwork *A fourteenth-century clock preserved at Salisbury Cathedral. The earliest recorded clocks in Britain date from the 1280s. This one, which struck the hours, worked in a tower till 1884.*

Westminster Hall *The hammer-beam roof of Westminster Hall, built by Hugh Herland for Richard II 1394–1400, is one of the crowning glories of late medieval timber roofing in Britain. Hammer-beams are so-called from the horizontal parts which project from the wall like the top of a hammer, and reduce the width to be covered by the main arched beams supporting the roof.*

was searched for suitable trees. At many cathedrals the Decorated style, too, was now employed for new towers, chapter houses (the monks' meeting places, often octagonal or decagonal in shape), and cloisters.

The last great Gothic phase ('Perpendicular'), late 14th and 15th century

All cathedrals had their cloisters but amongst the finest are those of Gloucester which, with their fan vaulting – an extreme example of elaborate tracery – were one of the first examples of the last major phase of English Gothic architecture, the 'Perpendicular'. Soaring vertical lines were the strongest feature of this style. Because of progress in vaulting and the greater use of flying buttresses, internal supports could be reduced to a minimum and the walls filled with windows: the great East window of Gloucester Cathedral measures 38 feet by 72 feet, about the area of a tennis court, and occupies the whole breadth of that end of the building. Some of the finest 'open' wooden roofs also come from this period, perhaps the most magnificent being that of

The earliest fan-vaulting: the cloisters at Gloucester Cathedral *This picture in addition to showing some of the vaulting shows also a recess at one side of the cloister containing the lavatorium or washing place of the monks.*

Westminster Hall. In all this work the king's own masons set fashions which were widely followed elsewhere.

Examples of Perpendicular architecture can be seen in several cathedrals and in chapels such as St. George's, Windsor, and that of King's College, Cambridge. The greatest profusion of this style, however, is to be found in the parish churches. For by the fifteenth century the great age of cathedral building was over. The Black Death had brought a shortage of labour and money, and energies became concentrated on the parish churches and on chantry chapels such as William of Wykeham's lovely building at Winchester, where masses might be said regularly for the soul of the founder.

Parish churches

In medieval times the parish church was the centre for the life of the community. The general idea was that the chancel belonged to the clergy and the nave to everyone else; and as the church was normally

Non-religious uses

the only public building, both church and churchyard were often used for non-religious purposes. Plays, the themes of which were always religious, might be presented there; and in the churchyards, where there were few monuments, archery practice might be held and fairs set up, although from time to time bishops or kings tried to stop this.

Variety and number

Some churches were very large, like St. Mary Redcliffe in Bristol, or the great 'wool' churches of the Cotswolds like Northleach and Chipping Campden. Others were tiny, like those of the villages of the Sussex downs. The broad framework of parish organisation in England was laid down in Anglo-Saxon times but it was not completed until the fourteenth century. In the towns parish churches often stand very close to one another; by late medieval times, York and Norwich each had about sixty churches, and in Shrewsbury three parish churches stand within 200 yards of one another.

Styles and plans

Most parish churches were altered and enlarged as time went on, and like the cathedrals they show a complete mixture of styles. The simplest plan was for a nave and chancel, but on to this were often built side chapels, vestries and sacristies. From the fourteenth century onwards Lady Chapels were often added – for it was then that veneration of Our Lady, the Mother of Jesus, became most popular. Great porches were often built, generally on the south side to catch the sun, the upper room of the porch often being used as a schoolroom or a storeroom.

Roofs, painted walls, coloured windows

Inside, the carved timber roofs were often the glories of the churches. The walls were frequently painted, for the church could teach its lessons through pictures. The windows, too, could tell Bible stories – by pictures made in pieces of coloured glass held together by lead. Much of this glass has a richness of colour and texture that has seldom been equalled. Made by mixing various oxides with the molten glass – cobalt to give deep blue, iron to give olive green, manganese to give purple, and so on – it may be seen at its best in the wonderful windows of Canterbury Cathedral or those of the parish church of Fairford in Gloucestershire.

It was not usual in these churches for the nave to have chairs, although for the benefit of the old or infirm there might be stone benches along the walls and round the pillars. The floors were normally strewn with rushes, and light was given by candles or simple oil lamps. The font by the main door symbolised entry to the church through baptism: its sides were often carved, to represent more incidents from the Bible. Increasingly, font covers were made to prevent consecrated water from being stolen, for it was popularly thought to have magic properties.

Screens and roods

The larger the chancel, the farther away the priest was from the congregation; and in the later Middle Ages, the clergy and altar were made even more remote by the building of screens. This is especially noticeable in cathedrals, where the chancel and presbytery are entirely cut off from the nave. Some fine screens exist, such as the Neville Screen in Durham, but many of them were destroyed at the Reformation. With them too were destroyed the roods, the mighty crucifixes, which were set up above the screen to dominate the nave.

The parish churches, like the cathedrals, are an endless source of interest and information. The yew trees in the churchyard, the crosses often standing outside the church porch, the mass clocks sometimes carved into the wall to show the priest when it was time to say his daily services, the finely (and often amusingly) carved misericords – hinged seats in the choir stalls with a projecting shelf underneath so that when turned up they could support the posteriors of aged clergy weary of standing: all of these, in their details, throw some light upon the ideas or habits of our ancestors in the 'Age of Faith'.

3 Castles and Manor Houses

Apart from the cathedrals and parish churches, the greatest surviving medieval buildings in Britain are the castles. There had been fortifications of many kinds before the Norman Conquest, including Alfred's 'burhs', but until the Norman invasion very few stone castles had been built. In late Saxon times there were one or two in Herefordshire, where there were some Norman settlers, and others in Shropshire and perhaps also at Dover. But it was with the Conquest that the great period of castle-building began, and that castles became regularly used both to hold down the conquered country and to help defend it against attack.

The Normans and castle-building

Early Norman castles were simple affairs, put up quickly so as to establish control with the least possible delay. They are called 'motte and bailey' castles, the motte being a mound of earth with a stockade on top and a surrounding ditch at the foot, while the bailey was an open space adjoining the mound, encircled by its own ditch, rampart, and stockade. Wood was the material used for the stockades, and the strength of such castles depended largely on the height of the mound and the depth of the ditch. Remains of this type of castle, now often overgrown but with their basic plan clearly showing, can be seen all over England and along the Welsh border. Siting was of course very important: a water supply nearby and a good field of view were essentials. If a castle was built to defend a town and the town stood on a river, as at Shrewsbury, the castle was placed where the town walls and the river met. Sometimes the main object of a castle was to overawe a town, as with William I's Tower of London – though this was by no means its only purpose.

Once the Normans had established control and the first need for haste disappeared, they began to use stone much more. The first stage was usually to scrap the wooden stockade of the motte and build stone walls instead. This resulted in what is called a 'shell keep' on the mound, with wooden or stone buildings inside it. As most of the mounds were artificial some time had in any case to elapse for the earth to settle down before the weight of a stone stockade could be added.

Stone replaces wood

Stone keeps

When this had been done, the next step was usually to replace the wooden gates and stockade of the bailey in similar fashion.

From the early twelfth century the most common plan came to be a square or oblong stone keep surrounded by a stone walled enclosure. The White Tower of London and Colchester were the only square keeps built before the death of William I; but from the building of the great keep at Bridgnorth on the Severn in 1102 such fortifications became general. Their strength lay in their height and solidity. The walls of the White Tower of London, for instance, are 15 feet thick at their base and rarely less than 10 feet thick elsewhere. Occasionally the plan of the keep was circular instead of square, but this pattern never became as popular in Britain as it did in France.

All these keeps could survive long periods of attack. Their only entrance was on the first floor, with access by an easily defended ladder or stairway; and they generally had their own water supply. As they were intended to be lived in, they were divided into different rooms such as the Hall, the Solar, the kitchens, the storerooms and sometimes the Chapel. The roof was generally battlemented. With the means of attack at the time it was almost impossible to take one of these keeps by direct assault. To starve the garrison out was much the best hope for an attacking force, but this was generally a long process and not often a successful one, especially if the castle was supported by an army outside. Equally, however, it was very difficult for the garrison alone to force the attackers to raise the siege.

Siege methods

One method of attack was to undermine the walls of the keep. Alternatively, the besieging force could try to batter a hole in the structure by the use of a 'ram', a great iron-tipped log suspended on chains or ropes and swung repeatedly against the walls. They could also try to scale the walls by the use of ladders, or they could build a siege tower which could be wheeled into place against the walls, so as to overtop them. The 'mantlet', a large movable shield, could be brought forward to give protection to sharpshooters, while missiles could be hurled by either the 'ballista' or the 'mangonel'. Later, came a more effective kind of catapult, the 'trebuchet'; but before the invention of gunpowder the balance was generally on the side of the defence. It was because of the strength of these castles that kings tried to prevent barons building them without special permission.

Concentric castles

The next great advance in castle-building owed much to the Crusades. From the defences of Constantinople, Acre, Jerusalem and similar fortresses, the Crusaders drew many lessons. They learned, for instance, that great defensive strength could be obtained by a series of concentric walls rising in height towards the inmost wall, with frequent protruding bastions in the walls so that the besiegers would meet concentrated fire from several directions. The Crusaders adopted these ideas in their castles in Syria and the Holy Land, including the famous Krak des Chevaliers. Richard I, slightly earlier, tried out similar plans in Chateau Gaillard, his great fortress above the Seine.

Bastions

In the concentric-type castle, each line of walls had its own narrow but strongly defended gate, and the gates into each ward were arranged so as not to be opposite to each other. If any attackers managed to storm the first line of defence, they found themselves inside a narrow strip of ground facing another even higher wall from whose bastion-towers fierce fire of arrows and other missiles could be directed upon them. If they managed to fight their way along this strip of ground, they were then faced by another strongly defended gateway, so that their task was practically impossible. In Britain one of the first concentric castles was built by a Marcher baron at Caerphilly, in South Wales; the last of them, and the last castles built for purely military purposes, were Edward I's great fortresses at Conway, Caernarvon, Beaumaris and Harlech. In these superbly sited and constructed castles, the place of the keep has to some extent been taken by the great gatehouses. Within the walls, the buildings are arranged to give some degree of comfort.

Edward I's castles in N. Wales

From the end of the thirteenth century, castles began to decline in military importance. As England became more peaceful, so the castle became a fortified place of residence rather than a fortification in which

Fortified manor houses

A Norman castle hall *Part of the Great Hall in the keep of Hedingham Castle. It is 39ft long by 31ft wide, and has a gallery built into the thickness of the wall with arched openings to the hall. Half-way along the hall there is a great arch for the support of the main timbers of the ceiling. This permitted the use of main beams only half the length of the room. The furniture shown is of a later period.*

to survive. Old castles were modified to allow a more civilised life – a process which can be traced even at so important a border castle as Ludlow. In the north, on the Scottish border, the 'peel towers'[1] were still built as a defence against raids; but further south castles such as Tattershall in Lincolnshire and Bodiam and Herstmonceaux in Sussex were built first and foremost as places in which to live. No more royal castles were built, and the fortified manor house became more general – places such as Stokesay in Shropshire and Wingfield in Derbyshire. This decline of the castle was partly the result of social changes but also, after the middle of the fifteenth century, the result of the development of artillery. At Crécy, Edward III's small cannon did little more than frighten the French horses. A century later, the walls of castles were beginning to fall before the impact of cannon balls propelled by the explosive force of gunpowder.

Effects of artillery

It was, however, only the king or the great baron who lived in a castle. Lesser land-holders, if of sufficient wealth, lived in what we know as manor houses. In a village, the manor house generally stands near the church, forming a central group for the life of the community; and it was in the hall of the manor house, where the lord ate with all his household, that the affairs of the village were regulated. It was there that the lord held his court, and there that the rotation of crops and other village matters were decided upon.

In the early Middle Ages, most people did not expect to have any accommodation purely to themselves. It was only in the fourteenth and fifteenth centuries that the desire for privacy developed and that houses began to provide it. Markenfield Hall near Ripon, built soon after 1300, is a good early example. In the 'Nun's Priest's Tale' Chaucer wrote of a widow and her cottage: 'Ful sooty was hir bowre and eek hire hall' [Extremely sooty were her bower and her hall] and this recalls the basic plan of the medieval English house. The hall was where the daily life of the whole household was carried on; while the 'bower' or 'chamber', the inner room, gave the owners some degree of privacy. In using such terms for a widow's cottage (which also showed the basic division between eating room and sleeping room) Chaucer was being gently humorous.

A common pattern of large house

Gradually there developed a pattern for the larger house which was commonly followed until the seventeenth century. Some houses were built of wood, some were half-timbered, some were of stone, and some in the later Middle Ages were of brick. The main structure might be suitable for several purposes: a large rectangular building with supporting columns might equally well serve as a church, as a barn, or as the hall of a house, like the aisled hall of Oakham Castle in Rutland. The main door of such a house would lead into a passageway on one side of which was a wooden screen, generally with two doors in it, leading into the hall. In the wall opposite the screen were normally four doors: one led to the kitchen, and others to the buttery, from which

[1] So-called from an old word for stake or palisade.

A fifteenth-century castle: Herstmonceaux *Though it has strong walls and is moated, this castle in Sussex also shows the new tendency among the nobles to build for comfort. The windows are larger than those of an earlier medieval castle, and the battlements seem to be for ornament as well as for practical use.*

drink was served through a hatch, and the pantry. The fourth door might lead to a minstrels' gallery, which was usually at the end of the hall above the screen, and to the rooms above the kitchen wing. Sometimes the kitchen was separated from the hall but this was generally in castles where the domestic arrangements were being made more comfortable. A very similar plan, including separate kitchens, was employed for the halls of Oxford and Cambridge colleges.

The hall in a great house was a lofty, oblong room open to the roof. At one end was a low dais on which stood the High Table, where the lord of the manor took his meals. He had a special chair, while the rest of the company sat on benches. The tables were normally boards on trestles, placed lengthways down the hall, and there were benches fixed to the walls. Early halls had a central fireplace, as at Penshurst Place, with a louvre in the roof for the smoke to escape, but wall fireplaces with carved overmantels became increasingly common. Windows were set high up, and it became the practice to build a great bay window recess to one end of the High Table. In this recess was placed a sideboard. The floors would be strewn with rushes, and lighting would come from torches dipped in fat. The hall was the centre of the household's life, especially in early medieval times, for here slept many of its members as well as travellers who sought shelter.

The hall

Behind the High Table a door usually led into another passageway which provided the entrance to the cellar and store room underneath the hall, and to the great chamber – the 'solarium' or solar, so-called because its windows were large enough to admit a good deal of sunlight. This was the main private room of the house, the personal quarters of the lord and lady of the manor. Its walls might be painted or plastered, or later on hung with tapestry possibly brought from London or Paris or Arras. Such rooms were large, as may be seen from the solarium in one of the most beautiful of these houses, Haddon Hall in Derbyshire.

The solar

A fifteenth-century manor house *This is a reconstruction drawing by Alan Sorrell of Minster Lovell Hall in Oxfordshire. Impressive remains of the buildings still survive. The Hall, which was built by Lord Lovell in the first half of the fifteenth century, illustrates the new tendency among the nobility to construct residences for comfort and convenience rather than prolonged defence.*

From the late fourteenth century onwards, the demand for greater comfort and privacy led to the addition of further rooms. By modern standards, however, these houses must have been very cold and comfortless: there was little heating and little furniture, the window seats were made of stone and the beds of wood, the sanitary arrangements were primitive in the extreme. The houses grew haphazardly but gradually many took on a quadrangular plan, as again appears at Haddon Hall: a central courtyard with buildings all around and a gatehouse. This plan also became the basis for the majority of Oxford and Cambridge colleges. The earliest of these – Merton College[1] at Oxford and Peterhouse at Cambridge – were founded in the late thirteenth century, and many more followed in the next three centuries.

The houses of the poor were of course very simple. Sometimes in the country they consisted of only one room, used for all purposes including the stabling of animals. Most, however, had the two basic rooms. They were made sometimes of mud, sometimes of timber (using the cruck construction of wooden supports fastened together rather like a capital A) and sometimes of wattle and daub. In the towns stone houses, though not common, were more frequent than in the country. They belonged mainly to merchants and shop-keepers; and a few early

The quadrangle pattern

Colleges

Houses of the poor

Merchants' houses

[1] University College claims to have been founded by King Alfred, but the evidence is unconvincing.

ones still exist, like the Jews' House in Lincoln or Moyses' Hall in Bury St. Edmunds. Such stone houses often had three stories: the business premises on the ground floor, the hall on the first floor, and the chamber on the second. Larger and more comfortable houses were built in the fourteenth and fifteenth centuries, like the merchants' houses backing on to the quayside at King's Lynn, or the houses of the rich cloth and wool merchants at Lavenham.

Household life

For most people, household life remained hard throughout the Middle Ages. Sleeping quarters were uncomfortable and toilet facilities non-existent. The food had little variety. The richer could eat meat and fish, with fowl, game, and venison providing some change from the salted beef of winter; but the poorer could afford little meat and the penalties against hunting and poaching remained very severe. There were no potatoes and no root vegetables, although cabbages, peas, beans, and leeks became more widely grown as time went on. In the richer households, a light meal would be taken at daybreak, followed by the main meal of the day at about 11 a.m. and supper at about 5 p.m.; the poorer generally had only two meals a day. For drink most people had ale, mead, and cider, but wine was also drunk by the rich. In general, people ate off wooden platters, but pottery became more frequent in the fifteenth century, and pewter later.

The lady of the manor, who had the help of a large staff, was responsible for all the domestic arrangements of her manor house. She often took into her household the children of other nobility or gentry, to educate them in the pattern of life, while her own children and especially her sons might be away at some other house. Perhaps here we can trace the origins of the boarding school. Until the fifteenth century there were very few schools except those attached to monasteries, and these did not teach the skills – such as those of swordplay, archery and hawking – that the children of noblemen were expected to learn.

Few of the smaller houses of the Middle Ages survive, but Britain is still rich in medieval cathedrals, churches, castles and manor houses. Their existence today is evidence of the many centuries of stable government and internal peace which Britain has been fortunate enough to enjoy.

Chess *From a fourteenth-century manuscript in the Bodleian Library. Chess is a very ancient game probably originating in India and passing thence to Persia and the Arabs. It seems to have reached Britain during the eleventh century. During the Middle Ages it remained a game for courtiers, not cottagers.*

22 Priests, Monks and Friars

Parish priests

The parish priests of medieval Britain were generally men of little education, not very different from their neighbours. But they had had some schooling, and they knew enough Latin for their main task, the speaking of the services. For their keep, they cultivated the glebe – the part of the village lands set aside for the parson – and they were entitled to some of the annual tithe (the tax for church purposes, amounting to a tenth of each parishioner's annual gain, e.g. a tenth of his crops or newly born livestock). They could also claim fees for conducting personal services such as baptism or burial. Mostly of humble standing, they were the Church's main representatives in everyday life.

The religious houses

Dominating the religious life of medieval Britain, however, were the monasteries and, from the thirteenth century, the friaries. Until the rise of the universities of Oxford and Cambridge, they were also unrivalled as centres of learning. At one time there were nearly two thousand religious houses in Britain, and men could not travel far without seeing a great monastic church or passing over monastic lands.

Monastic training

Many men were attracted to the monastic life. Sometimes their parents would hand them over to a monastery at an early age for care and education, but more frequently they applied for admission of their own free will. The procedure was always the same. On arrival, a would-be monk was housed in a lodging near the entrance to the monastery for four or five days. Then he presented himself on three successive days to the Chapter of the monks, asking for admission. If his request was granted he became a novice. Under the direction of the Master of the Novices, he was then trained in the Rule and in the observance of the religious life and in the customs of the monastery. At the end of a year, provided that his character had been found suitable, he took his vows and became a monk. Those vows were irrevocable, and if a monk attempted to break them he faced the penalties not only of the Church, but also of the king's justice.

Monasticism in Britain

As we have seen (p. 30) monasticism came early to Britain, and at first in the Celtic form, in which the traditions were more of holy individuality than of highly organised communities. After the triumph of Roman practices, however, the Benedictine Rule was everywhere followed. The attacks of the Danes ruined or disorganised many monasteries, but in the tenth century St. Dunstan and others set about restoring the vigour and purity of English monastic life. Their main inspiration came from Cluny, the great monastery in Burgundy which had developed a new interpretation of the Benedictine Rule.

The 'work', apart from religious services, visualised by St. Benedict had been mainly field or manual work, but at Cluny this was largely omitted and all the emphasis was placed on the praise of God. The monks were encouraged to express this mainly in prayer and services – they sang something like 100 psalms a day – but also in works of art. The result was a monastery of impressive appearance and size – the church at Cluny was the largest in Europe until the building of St. Peter's, Rome. The size and beauty of Cluny much influenced the development of monasteries elsewhere. Moreover, when monasteries were founded by groups of monks from Cluny, the new houses remained under the authority of Cluny itself, and so Cluny gave birth to what is called a monastic 'order': the Order of Cluniac Benedictines.[1] By the middle of the twelfth century, Cluny was the head and centre of an order covering more than 300 houses, stretching from Scotland to Syria and containing some 10,000 monks.

There were no Cluniac monasteries in England before the Norman Conquest, but afterwards several were established including St. Pancras Priory at Lewes and the Priory of Much Wenlock in Shropshire (most Cluniac houses were headed by priors rather than abbots, to show their dependence on the Abbots of Cluny). In Scotland a priory was founded at Paisley, and in all some forty Cluniac houses eventually sprang up in Britain. Apart from Cluny itself other great French monasteries such as Bec and Fleury also set the example for the building of huge monastic churches. Many of these churches were also in fact cathedrals – the seat of a bishop, and the chief church in his diocese. About half of the great cathedrals of England were originally or became monastic, the bishop being officially the abbot but the monastery in fact being controlled by his deputy, a prior.[2]

Until the beginning of the twelfth century the Benedictines, or Black Monks as they were called from their black gowns or habits, were unchallenged. After that, several new Orders established houses in England. The most important of these was the Cistercian, founded from the monastery of Citeaux in Burgundy. The Cistercians, called White Monks from their white habits, were an offshoot of the Benedictines. They aimed to restore the full simplicity of early monastic life and to re-create the conditions of St. Benedict's own monasteries at Subiaco and Monte Cassino. The Cluniac Benedictines had taken to building huge churches with costly decorations, and with ambulatories to allow processions during the church services; and their leading abbots had

[1] The ordinary Benedictines, though sometimes referred to as an order, were not really so, since there was no central control of all the Benedictine houses. The monk was a member of his monastery, not a member of an order. From the twelfth century onwards, however, groupings or federations of these monasteries were formed in several countries.

[2] Examples of monastic cathedrals were Canterbury, Durham, Ely and Winchester; of non-monastic, Exeter, Lincoln, St. Paul's (London) and Salisbury. Nearly all the monastic cathedrals were Benedictine.

become very often the chief officials of kings and princes. The Cistercians, of whom St. Bernard of Clairvaux was the most outstanding (although the Order owed much of its organisation to Abbot Stephen Harding, an Englishman from Sherborne Abbey), believed that all this was a hindrance rather than a help to the task of prayer and praise.

St. Bernard of Clairvaux

Early Cistercian churches were extremely simple. They were all built on much the same plan and it was said that a blind Cistercian monk could find his way without much difficulty around any Cistercian monastery. Great stress was again laid, as in St. Benedict's day, on manual labour as a form of worship; the Cistercian motto is *Laborare est orare* (to work is to pray). The first Cistercian house in England was built at Waverley in Surrey in 1128, and thereafter the Cistercians deliberately went out to wild and remote districts, where the ruins of their abbeys may still be seen.

All told, about 100 Cistercian abbeys were established in England during the twelfth to thirteenth centuries. Among them were the great Yorkshire abbeys of Fountains, Rievaulx, and Jervaulx, and the Lancashire abbey of Barrow; in Wales there were many houses such as Whitland in the south and Valle Crucis on the border near Llangollen. Tintern, too, was one of the great Cistercian monasteries, and so was Melrose in Scotland. From their settling in remote places, and from their belief in field work, the Cistercians came to be great agriculturists and heavily engaged in livestock raising and the wool trade. For this they depended largely on the work of their lay brothers – workers who took vows and lived in a separate part of the monastery but were not monks or priests.

Cistercians in England

Agriculture

At the same time as the Cistercians, the canons regular (from *regulus*, a rule) began to establish themselves in England. Most monks were not ordained priests but the canons regular were: they were communities of priests who, like monks, lived by a rule, yet carried out the normal priestly work of pastoral care and conducting services, usually in a cathedral or collegiate church. Soon there were three principal Orders of these canons regular. They were the Augustinian or Austin Canons, who lived by a so-called Rule of St. Augustine, and who eventually had nearly 200 houses in Britain and Ireland; the Premonstratensians, who took their name from the mother house at Prémontré in France, and who had over thirty; and the Gilbertines, who had twenty-seven. The Gilbertines, called after their founder St. Gilbert of Sempringham,

Orders of Canons Regular –

Augustinians, Premonstratensians, Gilbertines

The ruins of Fountains Abbey *The great Cistercian Abbey of Fountains, Yorkshire was founded in 1132 under Henry I and destroyed in 1540 under Henry VIII. This aerial photograph shows clearly not only the ruins of (2) the abbey church but also the site of (2) the infirmary, (3) the abbot's lodging (4) the rere-dorter (5) the dorter (6) the chapter house (7) the cloister (8) the warming house (9) the frater or refectory (10) the kitchen (11) the lay brothers' dorter and frater (12) the lay-brothers' rere-dorter (13) the lay brothers' infirmary and (14) the guest house. A stream—the Skell, difficult to see in the photo—passes along the whole site on the side of the living quarters.*

were the only purely English order. Their special feature was the 'double' house for canons and nuns, with the nuns owning the property. Both sexes shared the same church, but lived quite separately; even in the church there was a stone screen between the priests' and the nuns' choirs. When the nuns were called upon to represent their convent at a meeting of the Order's chapter, or governing body, they travelled there in closed carts.

The military Orders

Other Orders well known in Britain during the Middle Ages included the two great military Orders, the Knights Templar and the Knights Hospitallers, formed during the Crusades. Both Orders comprised those who took the full vows of monks for life, and others who took lesser vows or served for a term of years only. Both Orders became very wealthy, for they used their international connections to act as bankers and money-lenders. This proved the undoing of the Templars. When Philip IV of France fell heavily in their debt, he had charges of heresy and immorality laid against them, and after confessions had been extracted from leading Templars under torture he induced Pope Clement V to suppress the Order (1312).

The Carthusian Order

In 1181 the first Carthusian house was established in England, at Witham in Somerset. The Carthusians, so-called from their original monastery at Chartreuse, Grenoble, were founded by St. Bruno of Cologne towards the end of the eleventh century. They were the most austere of all the Orders: each monk lived apart from his fellows in a separate cell with a small patch of garden, meeting only two or three times a day in the monastic church for services and once or twice a week in the refectory for a meal or other recreation. The rule of silence was almost total. Naturally, this Order never became as popular as the others, only nine houses altogether coming into existence in England. More than any other Order, the Carthusians succeeded in preserving through the centuries all the original purity of their practices.

Orders of Friars (13th century)

The twelfth century was the golden age of English monasticism and after this there was a slow decline. A new religious development, however, occurred in the thirteenth century, with the arrival of the friars. Their task, unlike that of the monks, was to go out into the world. They took their name from the Latin word 'frater' meaning 'brother', and there were two principal Orders. The Dominicans who arrived in

Dominicans

England in 1221 were founded a few years earlier by St. Dominic, a Spaniard, whose life was spent in the struggle against heresy, at first in Spain, later in the south of France. It was here, at Toulouse, after Pope Innocent III had sanctioned an actual military crusade against the heretics of this region, that Dominic organised a body of comrades to specialise in preaching and in expounding the true faith. His movement, which rapidly grew into the great Dominican Order, was closely parallel

Franciscans

to that of the Franciscans, founded by St. Francis of Assisi at about the same time. The central idea of St. Francis was actually to imitate the daily life of Christ – not only the preaching but the ministering to the sick, the poor and the downtrodden. He and his earliest disciples believed that to do this properly they must themselves be poor. These ideals made a wide appeal, and soon the Franciscans too were a great Order with missionary friars in all parts of the known world.

From their habits the Dominicans were called in England the Black Friars, and the Franciscans the Grey Friars. Both Orders quickly became very popular after their arrival in the early 1220s, and each soon established fifty or more friaries. They settled mainly in towns, for they wished to preach in the poorest and most squalid surroundings that they could find; they lived by begging, for at first they were forbidden by their Rules to own anything, either personally or as a community. Complete poverty as regards corporate property soon proved unworkable, however, and friaries began to be as well endowed as monasteries. To these friaries the friars did not 'belong', as monks 'belonged' to a monastery. The friars 'belonged' only to their Order and might be moved from one friary to another as their superiors thought best. The friary was not their retreat but their temporary headquarters for missionary and pastoral effort in the outside world.

The friars in England

There were several other orders of both monks and friars, including the Carmelite Friars and the Austin Friars. Nearly every major Order had a companion Order of Nuns, although there were many fewer

Nuns and nunneries

Poor Clares in choir *From a psalter of Henry VI in the British Museum. Poor Clares were a sister order to the Franciscan friars. Founded by St Clara with the encouragement of St Francis, they were nuns who lived in convents of special poverty and austerity, and they did not go out into the world in the manner of friars. They are shown here with psalter-books; nuns were not expected to sing the services by heart, but monks usually were.*

St David's Cathedral *Of the many buildings which made up the great religious centre in Pembrokeshire the cathedral and some impressive ruins of the Bishop's Palace are what chiefly remain. This view of the Cathedral nave shows its happy blend of different but related styles – Norman arches and columns, a fourteenth-century choir screen, and a superb sixteenth-century wooden ceiling covering the beams above.*

nunneries and they served rather different purposes: they were often used as places of education for girls and homes for widows or spinsters. Some, however, maintained a high standard of religious life. The **Franciscan tertiaries** Franciscans also very early developed a wing known as the Tertiaries, or third order. These were men and women who embraced Franciscan ideals and tried to put them into practice while remaining in their ordinary posts and households.

With regard to sites, Benedictine monasteries were generally built in or near towns, and their size was often limited by previous building or the space available. Such Orders as the Cistercians, however, who built in remote rural places, were not restricted in this way. The great abbeys of Yorkshire were built in a region which had been devastated by William the Conqueror, and there was plenty of land available. The precinct wall of Jervaulx enclosed a hundred acres; that of Fountains, ninety.

Stone and water The essentials for any monastic site were a good supply of stone and water. For the first the monks often tried to get possession of quarries, and for the second they normally built near a stream. The sites of most Cistercian abbeys are very similar: a wooded valley with a stream running through it. In fact the idea of 'water' often appears in the names of these Abbeys, as in Fountains and Rievaulx (i.e. the valley of the Rie). The monastery buildings were often sited to fit in with the flow of the stream, which had to serve many purposes. It was important that these purposes were served in the correct order: first the water had to be used for drinking and perhaps brewing, then for cooking, then for washing, then for laundering, and then for carrying away sewage and refuse. It had to be channelled off to the parts of the monastery where these activities were carried on, though sometimes drinking water was brought from a separate and purer source such as a hillside spring.

Dominating every monastery was its church, towering high above all the other buildings. The great churches of the eleventh and twelfth centuries, such as those of Westminster, Winchester, Durham, Gloucester and Tewkesbury, all show the idea of magnificence copied from Cluny.

Monastic churches

The centre of monastic life was the cloister, and this was normally built on the warm southern side of the church, though sometimes the site, as at Canterbury, did not allow this. Originally the cloister, with its square of grass in the middle called the 'garth', was a simple passageway covered in from the weather; but later it became part of the architectural design of the church and such a magnificent cloister as that of Gloucester resulted.

The cloister

The north walk of the cloister, alongside the nave, was used for work and study – and very cold it must have been in winter. Along the east walk of the cloister were placed the Chapter House, where the whole community met every day, and one or two other smaller rooms such as the parlour (where a certain amount of conversation was allowed) or a room with a fire burning in it in cold weather. Above these was the monks' dormitory, or dorter, with a lavatory called a reredorter, at the end farthest from the church. The dorter had two staircases leading from it – the night stairs, leading into the church, the day stairs into the cloister. On the walk opposite the church were placed the dining-room or 'frater' and the kitchen, both as far away as possible from the church and the area of the cloister set apart for study. Finally, on the west walk were the store rooms under the control of the cellarer, and it was in this part of the cloister walk that the Master of the Novices taught them the Rule and customs of the monastery.

Monastic rooms

Other buildings lay outside this central cloister block. The infirmary, where sick and aged monks were treated, was a monastery in miniature with its own chapel and frater. The abbot had a separate lodging spacious enough for him to entertain important visitors. In the great courtyard which was entered from the outside through a gatehouse, could be found the bakehouse, the brewhouse, a mill, the almonry from which alms were given to the poor, a chapel, the guesthouse, and stabling for visitors' horses: the abbey of St. Albans, for example, had stabling for over three hundred horses. Most Benedictine houses were built according to this plan. The Cistercians altered it somewhat because of their system of lay-brothers, who had their own dorter and frater in the western part of the cloister. The Carthusian plan again was

Other monastic buildings

different, for a Charterhouse had to be constructed so that each monk could live for the most part separate from his fellows.

Monastic officials

The work of the monastery was normally divided into different departments and individual monks were made responsible for them. Amongst the most important were the Precentor who was responsible for the singing, the Sacrist who looked after the church fabric and monuments, the Kitchener who was in charge of meals, the Cellarer who kept the stores, the Infirmarer who looked after the old and sick, the Master of the Novices, the Fraterer who was responsible for the dining-room, and the Almoner who gave out alms. Then there were the monks, such as the Forester and the Wooller, who looked after the more commercial activities of the monastery; and lesser officials like the Porter and the Parchmenter.

Non-spiritual tasks

Most of the monasteries in the days of their prosperity ran efficiently. But this sort of organisation meant that many individual monks could not easily devote themselves to the spiritual life as laid down by St. Benedict, nor could they observe the full discipline of the monastic day. The Abbots were tenants-in-chief and had public duties to perform: we even find Abbot Litlington of Westminster in 1386 going off with his armour to oppose a rumoured French invasion. Many of the heads of the various services had to travel to the outlying estates of the monastery, and from reasons of this kind monasteries could gradually become heavily involved in worldly tasks.

Monastic meals

St. Benedict had originally planned that about four and a half hours a day should be spent in prayer and praise, and the monastic routine was arranged around the order of the services. We have already seen how these were arranged in pre-Conquest days (pp. 75–6), and the routine did not greatly vary afterwards, except that the Cluniacs often occupied as much as eight hours of the day in services. Something, too, has been said of the monks' meals. The rule of silence was followed

A thirteenth-century dispensary *From a manuscript at Trinity College, Cambridge.*

A leper *From a manuscript in the British Museum. Leprosy was a common and dreaded disease throughout the Middle Ages. This poor woman is begging – her cry is 'Sum good my gentyll mayster for God sake' —and in accordance with regulations she carries a bell to warn people of her approach.*

during these, except that one of the monks read aloud from a lectern. As they ate, the monks had to ask the servers for what they wanted by signs; they had to keep their arms and elbows off the table and they were not permitted to gaze around. Originally their food was simple, such as bread, fish, and eggs, and sometimes cheese and fruit. Enormous numbers of eggs were eaten: for example, at Durham the cellarer bought 44,140 eggs during the year 1333–4, but until about 1300 no meat was allowed. During the fourteenth century that rule was partly relaxed, especially in Benedictine houses.

It was not very surprising that over the centuries standards began to decline. Many of the monasteries became extremely wealthy: Christ Church, Canterbury owned twenty-one manors in Kent alone, Bury St. Edmunds a total of 170. If monasteries had famous relics, or were centres of pilgrimage, they grew wealthy on the offerings of the visitors. The friaries also, once the early rule of complete poverty had been abandoned, soon became as rich as the monasteries: the friars still lived by begging and gifts but they appointed friars who were called 'limitours' to beg in a particular district systematically, and very unscrupulous many of them were. We have already seen how the Cistercians and the Gilbertines helped to establish the wool trade. The wealth they drew from it is evident from the great Yorkshire abbeys.

But although monastic revenues were large so also were the expenses, and many monasteries found themselves in debt, first to Jewish and then to Italian moneylenders. Knights, or later money, had to be found for the king; continuous building was a strain on resources; an increasing number of lay servants had to be paid; hospitality and alms-giving became very costly services. The greatest expense in this last direction was not of course the distribution of left-over food to the poor at the gate, but the custom that pilgrims and other travellers could lodge for two days free at a monastery. Birkenhead Priory complained con-

Monastic expenses

tinually about the cost of hospitality to passengers waiting for the ferry across the Mersey; while the expenses of a visit from royalty, which sometimes lasted several weeks, could be quite crushing. When Humphrey Duke of Gloucester, for instance, was entertained for a fortnight in 1423 at St. Albans Abbey, he brought some three hundred followers. With the labour shortage following the Black Death, monasteries tried to save expense by renting out an increasing part of their lands; and from the fourteenth century they also supplemented their revenues by selling guarantees of food and shelter in old age.

Functions of the monasteries

The monasteries of the Middle Ages performed many functions besides fostering a life of prayer and praise. Inns, hospitals, schools, strong-rooms, centres of learning and art – they were all of these, as well as engaging in farming and acting as great landlords. But from the mid-thirteenth century, monasteries entered a slow decline. Many monks

St Andrews *A seventeenth-century print. It was at St Andrews, already a seaport and the seat of a monastery and a bishopric, that Scotland's first University was founded in 1411.*

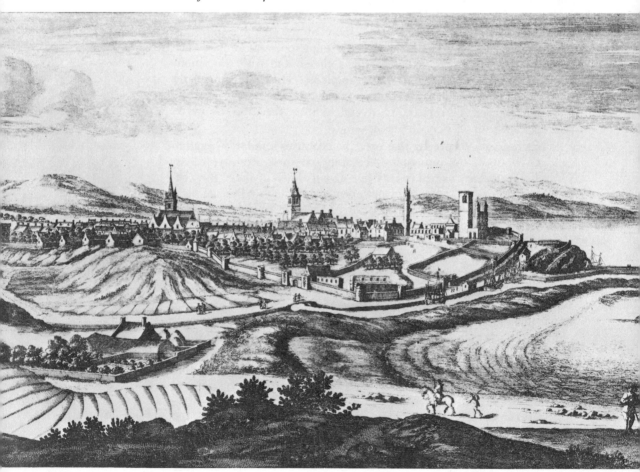

allowed their own standards to drop; and monasteries in towns were often very unpopular because of privileges such as the right to levy tolls. We have seen how the local townsfolk attacked the great abbeys at St. Albans and Bury St. Edmunds during the Peasants' Revolt. Also, as time went on, the growth of colleges at Oxford and Cambridge, with teachers who were clergy but not monks, challenged the monastic monopoly of learning. Thought and habits changed and fewer men entered monasteries.

The decline sets in (*c.* 1250)

Universities

Early in the fifteenth century, by which time national feeling had become stronger, the Commons petitioned Henry V, who was about to renew war with France, to dissolve those priories which were tied to monasteries in France and to take over their revenues. This saved the Commons' own pockets and the 'alien priories' were duly dissolved. Part of the money obtained in this way was later used for the establishment of

Dissolution of alien priories, 1414

Chastisement *From a twelfth-century manuscript in the Library of Durham Cathedral. Corporal punishment was very generously applied in British schools and households until fairly recently.*

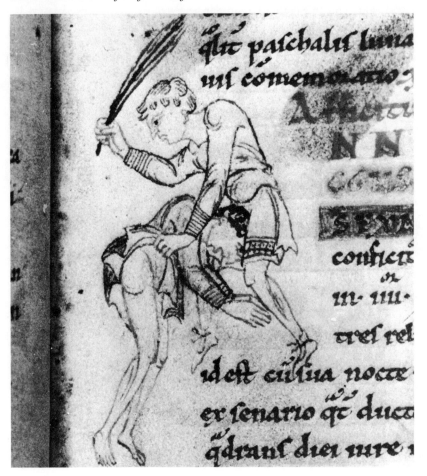

almshouses and schools: Henry VI, for example, used some of it for the sister foundations of Eton College and King's College, Cambridge. The Government suppressed other small monasteries at the end of the fifteenth century; and early in the sixteenth Cardinal Wolsey, for the building at Oxford of Cardinal College, or Christ Church as it later became, used money obtained from the suppression of twenty priories, three nunneries, and an abbey.

Wolsey's dissolutions

This was the prelude to the later monstrous actions of Henry VIII, who coveted the wealth of the monasteries and resented the fact that many of them owed allegiance directly to the Pope or refused to accept his new laws concerning religion. Under the pretext that they were hopelessly corrupt, between 1536 and 1540 he dissolved all monasteries, nunneries, friaries, and chantry foundations. In this he was abetted by nobles, townsfolk and others anxious to share in the spoils. In possibly the greatest act of robbery and vandalism ever perpetrated in England, the monasteries were broken up and their great churches, unless they were also bishops' cathedrals, pulled down and sold as building materials.

General dissolution under Henry VIII, 1536–40

So these great medieval institutions disappeared from English and Welsh soil; and in Scotland a similar series of events followed later. It is only in recent times that monasticism has been recreated in Britain, and then only on a small scale. But the ruins of many of the great abbeys remain to remind us of their past wealth and splendour, and of the religious devotion which inspired their foundation.

A cellarer *A cellarer in a monastery was a monk who kept the keys of the cellar and looked after the wine and ale – which were needed in good quality for visitors. This cellarer, from a manuscript in the British Museum, appears to be enjoying his office.*

23 Towns and Trade

1 The Growth of Towns

To the Romans, town life was the peak of civilisation – a view not shared by the more primitive Anglo-Saxons. As we have seen, the Anglo-Saxons destroyed or neglected to the point of decay the towns of Roman Britain. Gradually, however, they developed towns of their own, mainly at important points of communication such as harbours, river crossings or the junctions of country tracks. Often a town grew up when such a place was made into a fortified strong-point, whether by the Wessex kings or by the Danes or Norsemen. By the end of the Anglo-Saxon period there were more than seventy towns in Britain, with a revived London by far the greatest.

Sometimes the origin of these towns appears in their names, as in the endings 'port', 'ford' or 'bridge'. 'Burh' was Old English for a fortified point or shelter, and in the form of 'borough' or the Scottish 'burgh' this has become one of our regular words for 'town'. It may be seen either in such places as Edinburgh or else in towns with the ending 'bury', like Canterbury ('the burh of the men of Kent'). Danish towns are sometimes revealed in the ending 'by', as in Derby. And when, as time went on, the old Roman sites were re-occupied and rebuilt, their origin as Roman fortified places may often be seen in the ending 'chester' or 'cester' (from the Latin 'castra', a camp), as in Manchester or Leicester. There was, too, an Old English word 'cheaping' which meant 'buying' or 'bargaining', and this can be found in the names of some Anglo-Saxon market towns, such as Chipping Campden and Chepstow, as well as in the London street of Cheapside.

Many English towns, then, have their roots in an Anglo-Saxon past. When the Normans came, they built their churches and abbeys and cathedrals in these places because they already existed, and often they built their castles to dominate or protect them. Sometimes, however, they built a castle in a good defensive position, and then tried to create a town nearby to serve the castle. At first, some of the older towns suffered from the Norman presence but very soon they overcame local difficulties and resumed their growth. The ports in the south and south-east, for instance, greatly benefited from the increased contacts with France and the Low Countries.

By modern standards all the towns of medieval Britain were very small. The total population of England and Wales just before the

Citizens receiving a charter *Town life became increasingly important with the growth of trade, and this fifteenth-century Flemish manuscript shows one of the greatest moments in a town's life—when it received a charter of privileges, with limited rights of self-government, from the ruler or local lord.*

Medieval small towns

Growth of coastal ports

Black Death cannot have exceeded 3½ million, with another half-million in Scotland, and for long afterwards it was smaller. Of these, the great majority dwelt throughout medieval times in isolated farmsteads, hamlets, or villages, living from and working on the land. In the twelfth century the largest towns after London included York, Gloucester, Coventry, Norwich, and Winchester. Apart from Coventry and Winchester these were all accessible by river from the sea. As overseas trade expanded, so the coastal ports grew – places like Newcastle, Hull, Boston, King's Lynn, Southampton, and Bristol. In Scotland, Edinburgh, St. Andrews, Dundee, and Aberdeen flourished likewise, with Stirling and Perth important as gateways to the Highlands. Some of the northern English shires, however, had very few towns: Liverpool and Manchester in the fourteenth century were still tiny villages, while Newcastle, Durham, and Carlisle, though important towns, lived under constant fear of attack from the Scots. London remained overwhelmingly the greatest town and port and its citizens enjoyed very special privileges; but compared with some cities on the Continent it was small, being only one half the size of Paris and one third the size of Venice or Milan. As trade increased during the Middle Ages, however, several other English towns grew quite wealthy. We can still see from this the merchants' houses and warehouses at King's Lynn, or the splendid late medieval church of St. Mary Redcliffe, Bristol.

Travellers *From an early fifteenth-century English manuscript in the British Museum. For safety's sake it was usual for travellers, such as travelling merchants and pilgrims, to journey in company.*

The townsmen of the Middle Ages had usually to protect themselves against the claims of powerful local lords. Often this was done by securing a charter of privileges from the lord himself. But the best way for a town to preserve and if possible extend its independence was to obtain, if it could, a charter from the King. This would give it the status of a royal borough, including limited rights of self-government and a guarantee of market and trading privileges. Such royal charters became more and more frequent after the twelfth century. Before that, only a few towns such as London and the Cinque Ports had them, and their charters became the models for those towns which obtained them later. By the beginning of Henry III's reign there were some 200 towns in England, and about half of those were boroughs by charter from the crown.

Charters and borough status

Gradually a customary pattern of town law developed. Kings such as Richard I and John found the issuing of charters a convenient way of raising money or winning support – London got self-governing privileges in these reigns – and they and their successors were not above cancelling a charter and then reissuing it on payment of a further sum. All burgesses – the inhabitants sharing full borough privileges – were freemen, paying rent and not services for their houses and plots; and it was the town charter which generally freed them, or confirmed their freedom, from vassal duties and manorial dues. It also gave them complete control over their market, the right to levy tolls on strangers from other places, and the right to hold a borough court to settle trading disputes. Often, too, they could make arrangements themselves for the collection of taxes instead of suffering the intrusion of the shire officials. Towns were very jealous of their independence and, as we have seen already, a runaway serf who could live uncaptured in a town for a year and a day and was accepted by the inhabitants, became a free man.

Charters granted by barons or abbots

The towns which obtained charters from the king were usually the larger ones. It was generally the smaller ones, within the lands of some great baron or monastery, who sought similar charters from their local lord. Haverfordwest, for example, secured a charter from the Earl of Pembroke. All charters, however, finally depended on the approval of the king.

London

London, by which is meant the area we now call the City of London, was always in a special position. Bounded to the east by Aldgate and the Tower, to the west by Ludgate, to the north by Holborn, and to the south by the Thames, it was by far the richest and most important trading centre, and the king with his palace at Westminster was always in close contact with it. Relations between the king and the local authorities in London were by no means always friendly; we have seen how Richard II quarrelled with the Londoners, and how they supported his supplanter Henry Bolingbroke.

Guildhall of the Merchant Venturers, York The size and quality of their Hall help to give us some idea of the wealth and importance of the York cloth merchants. The roof is a fine example of fourteenth-century 'open' timber roofing. On the dais at the far end of the hall are the group's official scales and weights.

Within the boundaries of a borough the burgesses could make local laws – what we call 'by-laws' – and they had their own officials. In late Anglo-Saxon towns the chief official was the port-reeve, who was the urban counterpart of the 'shire-reeve'; but from the late twelfth century the office of mayor (a title taken from France) became more frequent. London had certainly obtained its own chosen mayor by 1193 (and probably by 1191), King's Lynn by 1204, Bristol by 1217. The wealthiest burgesses became the most influential and often they were called aldermen; from the thirteenth century on, we find town councils coming into existence, but the tendency as time went on was for the aldermen to acquire greater power and to leave the councils and the lesser citizens with little say in town affairs. In the thirteenth century there was often – though never in London or Norwich – one large trading gild, sometimes called the Gild Merchant, for all traders in the borough. This controlled the town in matters of trade, and in many other respects as well, so that it was often almost indistinguishable from the town government.

When Bishop Poore, in the thirteenth century, moved the cathedral from its hilltop site in Old Sarum down into the watermeadows of the Avon, the new town of Salisbury that he planned was laid out on a regular gridiron pattern. However, such a degree of town-planning, though also to be found in Edward I's Welsh boroughs and Kingston-on-Hull, was exceptional in the Middle Ages. Most towns grew haphazardly, and originally there was a good deal of space between the houses. A tradesman would live and work and sell his goods all on the same premises, and generally the members of the same trade congregated together. That is why so many medieval towns have street names like Fish Street or Milk Street or Poultry. The Shambles in York was where the butchers lived and worked. For some idea of what a street in a prosperous late medieval town looked like, we can still study the Pantiles in Winchester and the Rows in Chester.

Outside the walls or ramparts or ditch surrounding the town, the townspeople often had their open fields, particularly in the early Middle Ages. These they cultivated in strips like any manorial labourers, for as travel was so difficult they had to grow their own food. Within the towns, the streets were seldom paved or cobbled and there was very little drainage. Refuse was dumped in the open, some of it being carried away in channels which ran down the centre of the street. The smell, especially in summer, must have been horrible and in such conditions there was an ever-present risk of disease. Fire was another danger when houses were built of wood and had thatched roofs instead of tiles;[1] before it was rebuilt in stone in the twelfth century even London Bridge was burned down – as the nursery rhyme reminds us. In London and in the countryside between it and Westminster, buildings were made increasingly of stone – for example, John of Gaunt's fourteenth

Borough officials

Mayor and aldermen

Gild merchant

Town planning

Trade quarters

Town fields

Housing materials

[1] See pages 199 and 216.

century palace of the Savoy. For most town houses, however, wood remained the commonest material until the seventeenth century.

Town building

Apart from the houses most towns had few buildings other than churches, monasteries, or houses of canons or friars. In the later Middle Ages, a few of the richer gilds in the more prosperous towns had their own separate halls; the Merchant Adventurers had one in York, and the great gilds of London, which later became the rich and powerful Livery Companies, had them in London. In most of the larger towns, too, there would be at least one inn or hostelry of some sort. But without lighting or drainage, and with few or no paid officers to preserve law and order, medieval towns must have been unpleasant places in which to live.

Citizens' duties

The burgesses had certain responsibilities towards their town. A statute of 1388, for example, ordered that at harvest time journeymen – the trained craftsmen who were not masters – and apprentices were liable to help to 'cut, gather and bring in the corn'. It was also the duty of burgesses to help to keep the streets and walls or ramparts in repair and to maintain order in the town if need arose. In addition they had to help defend the town if it was attacked. In times of emergency they could be summoned to arms, as at Hereford, by the tolling of the town bell.

2 Crafts and Commerce

Variety of trades

A list made in one town in 1440 gives us some idea of the variety of crafts and trades that the burgesses followed by that date. Amongst many others it includes grocers, drapers, tailors, brewers, bakers, shoemakers, goldsmiths, blacksmiths, butchers, tanners, dyers, carpenters, and glovers. Many of these would have a stall in front of their house, on which they would set out the goods for sale, while inside the house itself would be the workroom and storeroom. Often a shutter in the front of the house would be let down to form a display stand. Since few people could read, each trade had its sign, and if there was no stall this sign would be hung up outside the house to indicate the goods for sale within.

The streets

At busy times the narrow streets of a medieval town must often have rung with a great deal of noise. Traders cried their wares to attract custom, beggars kept up a clamour for alms, and from in and around the inns would come the boisterous voices of drinkers. Travelling musicians, the clatter of horses' hooves, and the cries of children being beaten or animals slaughtered, might all add to the din. On Feast Days and Holy Days the normal commerce would stop, but there might instead be processions or pageants staged by one of the gilds. Some towns like Chichester and Coventry had cycles of biblical plays which were presented regularly on travelling carts or in churchyards, and the goings and comings in connection with these must have created much noise and bustle (see p. 250).

It was on the weekly market day (for which the citizens tended to favour Sundays though the Church did not) that the town was normally at its busiest. A fourteenth-century poet has described the scene:

> . . . Many a butcher, brewer, tailor, and tinker,
> Wool-weavers, linen-weavers, toll-takers in the market . . .
> Cooks and their men were crying 'Pies hot, all hot!
> Good pork and good goose! Come, come and dine!'
> Taverners told the same tale: 'A drink of wine for nothing,
> White wine, red wine, to wash the roast meat down'.

The market satisfied the needs of those living in the town and its immediate neighbourhood. Probably it had once been held in the nave of the church; then it moved out into the churchyard, and then to a site somewhere in the town.

Always, however, the market remained under the protection of the church, and the stalls were set up around the market cross. A thriving market ensured the prosperity of the town and market rights were very jealously guarded by the townsfolk; those who sold goods there had to pay dues which were strictly enforced. There was also plenty of provision for punishing sharp practices by the tradesmen. A baker whose

Fifteenth-century shops *This French manuscript, in the Bibliothèque de l'Arsenal, shows (l. to r.) tailors, furriers, a barber, a grocer.*

loaves were underweight might be condemned to the pillory, and a butcher who sold bad meat might have his whole stock burnt under his nose. One punishment is recorded for a man who sold bad wine: he was condemned to drink some, and have the rest poured over his head.

Fairs

Several towns became the sites of great fairs which were held each year, generally in the late summer months when travelling was easier. Some of these fairs still survive, like the Goose Fair in Nottingham and St. Giles Fair in Oxford. To such fairs came merchants from great distances: in John's reign, for instance, merchants from Flanders, Spain, Scotland and Germany are recorded as attending the fair at St. Ives in Huntingdonshire. Many important fair sites, as at Bristol and Boston, could easily be reached by water; it was through the fairs that much of the longer-distance trade of medieval England was at first carried on.

Gilds

In a medieval town all craftsmen were members of what was called a gild. In some of the larger towns, such as London, each craft had its own gild – there were at least a hundred by 1430 – but in small places there was generally only one gild, or sometimes two, covering all the trades. A craft gild was not like a modern trade union, where all the members are employees; in a gild everybody active in a particular trade or craft was a member, whether master, journeyman, or apprentice.

Craft gilds had many objects. Among other things, the members were joined together for religious and social purposes, even though there were often separate gilds entirely concerned with these matters.

Religious and social functions

Each craft gild had its patron saint, such as St. Martin for the Saddlers or St. Joseph for the Carpenters, and on the feast day of their saint they held a great religious service. Each member of the gild paid an annual subscription and the money so collected was used for the relief of sick or distressed members of the gild and their families. Later on, some of the London Companies like the Grocers and the Skinners helped education by endowing schools, while many others founded almshouses.

Trade functions

The foremost object of the craft gilds, however, was to protect the standards and privileges of the trades or crafts concerned. They ensured, for example, that the correct measurements of cloth were made, and that lead and tin were used in the right proportions in the making of pewter. (A continuation of this sort of practice into our own time is the hall-marking of approved silver by the Goldsmiths' Company.) The gild was also responsible for the training of new craftsmen. If a boy wanted to learn a craft, he was apprenticed for a period of about seven years to a master of that craft; he worked in the master's workshop and learned all the skill of his trade. At the end of that period, if he had satisfied his master, he became a 'journeyman' (from the French 'journée', meaning 'a day'), that is, a fully-trained craftsman paid by the day, and not yet set up as a master. When a journeyman had saved up enough money, he could apply to the masters of the gild for permission to set up his own workshop. In a craft gild, they would want some proof of his skill; and so he had to produce a piece of work which

Late medieval iron miner *As shown in the memorial brass to Robert Greyndour, in the form of his crest, in the church of All Saints, Newlands, Glos.*

was called his 'master-piece'. If this satisfied them, they would then recognise him as a master of the craft, entitled to employ his own journeymen and apprentices.

As time went on, however, the masters became more and more reluctant to admit new masters. They kept them out by forcing up the fees for admission to mastership. By the fourteenth century there was thus an ever-increasing gap between wealthy masters and employee craftsmen, and this eventually helped to undermine the whole gild system. A similar development took place in the great trading gilds, with merchants outside trying to break the monopoly of the privileged groups.

Growing power of wealthier masters

In London, the growing power of the wealthier masters, who tended to become wholesalers in place of practising craftsmen, led in the fourteenth and fifteenth centuries to the gilds becoming what we know today as the Livery Companies. Wealthy, dominating the life of the city, controlling its government, they built themselves Halls and insisted that on certain occasions members should wear a particular Livery or uniform. The expense of this often deterred journeymen from becoming masters, or drove out the poorer masters. By the end of the fifteenth century, twelve great Companies were outstanding in London: the Mercers, Grocers, Drapers, Fishmongers, Goldsmiths, Skinners, Merchant Taylors, Haberdashers, Salters, Ironmongers, Vintners, and Clothworkers. They all exist today, though largely for social and charitable purposes – for only a small proportion of the liverymen are nowadays connected with the trades concerned.

The London Livery Companies

The Hanse

The most powerful group of foreign traders in London during the later Middle Ages were the merchants who belonged to the Hanse, or Hanseatic League – a trading association covering many ports and towns in northern Germany. They controlled much of the Baltic trade and some of them had their London headquarters in what was called the Steelyard, near London Bridge[1]. Owing to their power and favoured position, which began under Henry III, they were very unpopular amongst the London merchants, who especially resented the fact that the English had no such privileges in Germany.

The rise of great merchants

In the later Middle Ages merchants sometimes became very wealthy and began to rank with the great landowners. For the poll-tax of 1379 the Lord Mayor of London had to pay the same as an earl; aldermen the same as barons. William de la Pole of Hull (fourteenth century) was the first businessman to found a noble house; his son became the Earl of Suffolk. And we have all heard of Sir Richard Whittington, a poor boy who became three times Lord Mayor of London. One of the reasons for

[1] The site, which belonged to the surviving towns of the Hanseatic League until 1853, became the site of Cannon Street station. The name has nothing to do with steel, but comes from the German word for sample.

Left: Spinning and weaving *The cloth trade became very important in the fourteenth century. This fourteenth-century French manuscript in the British Museum shows the processes of carding (separating out the staples from the tangled wool) spinning (with distaff and spindle) and weaving (on the hand-loom).*

Right: Dyeing *From a fifteenth-century French manuscript in the British Museum.*

the growing influence of such merchants was that they had enough money to lend large sums to the king. Up to the reign of Edward I, the Jews had been the great money-lenders; and after their expulsion the Italians, and especially the Florentines, took their place, but as Englishmen became wealthier their kings had less need of foreign capital. Just as Edward I had repudiated his debts to the Jews, so Edward III repudiated all his debts to the Italian banking houses, many of which never recovered from the blow. From this time on English kings relied almost entirely on English wealth for borrowing as well as for taxation.

In the House of Lords to this day the Lord Chancellor, who presides, sits upon a large square seat without back or arms known as the Woolsack. Stuffed with wool and covered with red cloth, it is the age-old symbol of the trade upon which so much of English prosperity has been based. English wool was famed in the Middle Ages and the weavers of the Continent sent their agents to England to buy it to supply the looms of Flanders, Germany and Italy. The Cistercians were the first great capitalists of the wool trade and they grew wealthy on their Yorkshire sheep farms. The Cotswolds also were a great centre of

The wool trade

production, and many lovely churches (such as those of Northleach and Chipping Campden) stand as evidence of the prosperity which resulted. At first most of the wool was exported, but slowly a cloth industry was established, chiefly in the eastern part of the country. Though this was a domestic affair, several towns became prominent in the industry, notably Salisbury, Coventry, York and Norwich.

In the thirteenth century, however, a minor industrial revolution took place. For the first time, extensive use began to be made of water-power in the fulling, or finishing, of the cloth. The cloth industry then

Rise of cloth industry

Early fifteenth-century ship *A model in the Science Museum, South Kensington, based on a ship shown in the seal of the Duke of Bedford, c. 1426. Note the front and rear platforms, or castles, the single mast, and the stubbiness of the hull.*

The fulling mill

began to concentrate in the areas where there was most water-power – in the Cotswolds, the Pennines, and the Lake District. New organisation was required, and we can trace the emergence of the capitalist clothier, a man like Jack of Winchcombe who employed many people in the production of cloth. Great quantities were produced for use both at home and for export: the weavers of Salisbury, for example, produced 6,600 rolls of cloth in one year. Much of the traffic on the roads of medieval England must have consisted of merchants' pack-horses laden with bales of wool or rolls of cloth. The decline of the one trade, and the rise of the other, can be seen in the export figures. In the 1350s, England exported each year on the average roughly 32,000 sacks of wool and less than 5,000 cloths (each 24 by 2 yards). In 1485 England exported about 10,000 sacks of wool and 50,000 cloths.

The main ports of England were on the east and south coasts – that is, they were close to the Continent. They included places such as Newcastle, Hull, Boston, King's Lynn, London, Sandwich, Winchelsea, Rye and Southampton. Bristol was important for the trade with Spain, western France and Ireland. All these ports handled a steadily growing volume of trade, and so did the Scottish east coast ports of Leith, Dundee and Aberdeen. One of the major imports throughout the Middle Ages was of wine, especially from Bordeaux; but we can also find record of imports of tar, furs and timber from the Baltic; of cloth and metal work, including arms and armour, from Germany; of leather, bow staves, olive oil and fruit from Spain; of linen from Cambrai; of cloth from Flanders; of tapestry from Arras; of jewels, spices and silks from the far-away lands of the east, imported through the great Italian traders. By way of exports, in addition to wool and cloth there were hides, tin, lead, coal, grain, dairy produce, fish and salt.

Imports and exports

These goods were mainly carried in small, blunt-nosed, broad-beamed ships called 'cogs', driven by a single square sail and steered by a modified oar on the starboard side. But as the cargoes grew so did the ships, although the ships of the Channel would never compete in size with the great oared vessels of the Mediterranean. By the fifteenth century, ships were beginning to be larger, to be built up in front against the weather, and to carry two masts and three sails, including a 'leg-of-mutton' or lateen sail at the rear which enabled the ship to sail closer to the wind than before. It was in these improved ships that the great voyages of discovery were made in the latter part of the fifteenth century.

Improved shipping

So the foundations of commercial enterprise were laid in Britain and the basis of later wealth established. It was to be some time, however, before overseas commerce became Britain's life blood. Though Marco Polo journeyed from Venice to China in the mid-thirteenth century, it was not until the late fifteenth century that Vasco de Gama and others opened the all-important sea-route to the East. At the same time Columbus's voyages across the Atlantic began the movement westward. The power and trade of European countries, and especially at first of Spain and Portugal, then began to press outwards into a wider world. But in what we call the Middle Ages, horizons were still limited. Though Britain's more distant future was to lie with her towns, her overseas trade and her industries, for centuries to come the main occupation of all the British peoples was still to be agriculture.

24 Language, Literature and Art

1 Language and Literature

The Anglo-Saxon base of modern English

Modern English is largely a simplified form of Anglo-Saxon or Old English, built up by additions from other languages. Of these, French and Latin have contributed the most, for they were the other languages used in England during the Middle Ages. The Celtic languages spoken in much of Scotland, Ireland, Wales and Cornwall have not influenced modern English to anything like the same extent.

Effects of Norman Conquest

As we have seen (p. 61) by the eleventh century there was a common tongue in England – Anglo-Saxon or Old English. It was spoken with considerable local variations of dialect, and it had already produced great literature. Latin was the language of the Church, of learning, and of converse between educated men of different countries. When the Normans conquered England, they introduced the other element of French, itself derived from Latin. For two or three centuries after the Conquest the Normans spoke among themselves the kind of French (we call it Norman French) they had brought over with them. Meanwhile the English in their households and everyday work continued to use their native language. Conquerors and conquered needed, however, to communicate. Englishmen educated or clever enough to take up

Norman French

positions in court or castle therefore learned to speak Norman French fluently, and to act as the barons' agents in dealing with the people. Similarly the Norman masters, living surrounded by their English subjects, eventually came to speak and understand the English tongue well enough, even though their own continued to be the language of upper society. The Normans also extended the use of Latin, which became generally employed for official documents such as laws, charters and Treasury accounts. Domesday Book, Magna Carta and the pipe rolls of the Exchequer were all compiled in Latin.

It has often been pointed out that the use of French in upper society, and of Anglo-Saxon in lower, could be guessed from some of our common terms for animals and food. Many of the animals tended by the English peasants have kept names from the Anglo-Saxon. 'Ox', 'swine' and 'sheep' are examples. But their flesh, eaten at the tables of the Norman barons, has names taken from the French – 'beef', 'pork' and 'mutton'.

Influences of French romances and poetry

In the first two centuries after the Conquest, when Anglo-Saxon was a 'depressed' language used by a subject population, no literary masterpiece seems to have been written in the native tongue. Songs, poems and romances of great interest were beginning, however, to be written in France, and particularly in the south. The subject of these was often courtly or ideal love – the selfless service of a chosen lady – and this became part of the growing code of chivalry. Before long, such poems were to inspire imitations in English. Meanwhile, nearly all the outstanding writing in England was in Latin. All the monastic historians, for example, wrote in Latin: men such as William of Malmesbury, Roger of Wendover, Matthew Paris, and Geoffrey of Monmouth, in whose works we find the first English references to the legend of King Arthur.

Latin writings

During the thirteenth century there were poems of considerable merit written in what must now be called Middle English. One was *The Owl and the Nightingale*, a dialogue between two birds representing austerity and love. With its use of rhyme, it showed the influence of the new French poetry. But it was in the fourteenth century that the really great change occurred, and that English began to come once more into its own, as both the literary and the truly national language.

The 14th-century changes

There were probably two main reasons for this. One arose merely from the passing of time and King John's loss of Normandy: the descendants of the Norman conquerors in England gradually lost their family connections with France. They had in any case by this time frequently intermarried with well-born people of English descent, and they thought of themselves as subjects of the King of England. The other reason was the long series of wars between England and France begun in the reign of Edward III. In the Hundred Years War, as it was later called, national feeling grew on both sides; and before the struggle was over the nobility of England ceased to speak the same language as their enemies across the Channel. The first King of England to use English as his everyday speech was Henry V (1413–22), but well before this a number of important official changes had been made. In 1362, for instance, a statute ordered the use of English in the law courts, and the following year the Chancellor opened Parliament in English for the first time.

Greater official use of English

This upsurge of the native tongue was seen not only in its greater use in government, education and upper society, but also in a new wealth of English literature. During the second half of the fourteenth century John of Trevisa, for example, made fine English translations of earlier historical works written in Latin, and the poet John Gower turned from writing in Latin and French to writing in English. In 1377 *The Travels of Sir John Mandeville* was translated into English: this supposed pilgrimage of a knight of St. Albans to Jerusalem gave an excuse for many colourful descriptions of geography and animals. And not long after this, in the 1380s, came Wyclif's translation of the Bible.

14th-century literature

Although the main fashion was by now for rhymed poems of chivalry in the French style, some of the greatest poems of fourteenth-century England were written in the Anglo-Saxon pattern of alliterative verse.

Knight and lady in Garden *From a fourteenth-century manuscript in the British Museum. 'Courtly love', involving selfless devotion and services by the knight to his chosen lady, was a fashion of chivalry during the eleventh–fifteenth centuries, and formed the subject of many poems and stories.*

Froissart presenting his work to Richard II *From an edition of the Chronicles in the British Museum.*

Langland's 'Piers Plowman'

To a large extent this is true of the famous poem *Sir Gawain and the Green Knight*, though this also has occasional rhymes. An outstanding writer of alliterative verse was William Langland, who seems to have been born about 1330 in the neighbourhood of Malvern. He was the author of a long poem which exists in three different versions. It is in two parts, of which the first is called *The Vision of William* [i.e. Langland] *concerning Piers the Plowman*. The poet fell asleep, he tells us, one sunny May morning in the Malvern Hills and in his dreams saw 'a field full of folk'. The events in his dreams are an allegory – i.e., there is a deeper meaning to them, as in *Pilgrim's Progress*. But, as Langland recounts them, so he recreates for us the world of the fourteenth century. Here, for example, in modernised English (for the original is in the West Midland dialect) is a tavern in London:

Then in goes Glutton, and great oaths welcomed him.
Cis the sempstress sat on the bench,
Walt the gamekeeper and his wife drunk;
Tom the tinker and two of his 'prentices,
Hick the hackneyman, Hogg the needler,
Clarice of Cock Lane and the parish clerk;
Parson Piers of Pray-to-God and Pernel the Flemish woman,
Daw the Ditcher and a dozen more of them;
A fiddler, a ratter, and a Cheapside scavenger,
A ropemaker, a lackey, and Rose the retailer,
A watchman and a hermit and the Tyburn hangman;
Godfrey the garlic-seller and Griffin the Welshman,
All early in the morning welcomed Glutton gladly
To try the good ale.

Langland's poem concerns the search for truth and understanding, but it was also a satire. In it he attacked wealth and corruption, bribery and idleness, insincere clergy (especially friars) and dishonest lawyers. His hero was Piers the Plowman who worked hard and honestly to grow crops and to cultivate the land, and it was in the guise of the Plowman that he portrayed Christ.

A greater poet than Langland – and one of the greatest poets in English literature – was his contemporary, Geoffrey Chaucer. Born the son of a London vintner about 1340, Chaucer was at various times valet and esquire to Edward III, controller of the customs, clerk of the works, commissioner of roads, a justice of the peace, and a member of Parliament. He married a sister-in-law of John of Gaunt, fought in France (where he was taken prisoner and ransomed), and was employed by the king on several missions abroad. On these journeys he became acquainted with foreign literature, and his own works show the influence both of French and of Italian writers, especially Boccaccio. *Chaucer*

Chaucer wrote in Middle English in the East Midland dialect, which because it was the speech of London and the most advanced part of the country, finally developed into our modern English. His work is full of human understanding and kindly humour, and thanks to his powers of vivid description his characters are wonderfully real. In his famous work the *Canterbury Tales*, a group of pilgrims are travelling *The Canterbury Tales* in springtime to the shrine of St. Thomas à Becket in Canterbury. In the Prologue to the 'Tales' Chaucer begins by telling how he fell in with this party, twenty-nine strong, at the Tabard Inn in Southwark, and he goes on to describe his companions. He starts with the highest in rank:

A Knight ther was, and that a worthy man,
That fro the tymë that he first bigan
To ryden out, he lovéd chivalry,
Trouthe and honour, fredom and curteisye.

All told, he was a man faultless in speech and deed, 'a verray parfit gentil knight'. With him was his gay and jolly son, the Squire, a 'lusty bachelore':

> Singinge he was, or floytinge[1] al the day;
> He was as fresh as is the month of May.

The company included a large number of churchmen. There was a Prioress called Madame Eglantyne, of very refined appearance and manners and extremely tender-hearted:

> She was so charitable and so piteous
> She woldë wepe, if that she saw a mous
> Caught in a trappe. . . .

In contrast to the delicacy of the Prioress was the vigour of the amply-built Monk – 'a lord full fat and in good point' – who much preferred hunting to the discipline of the cloister. An amiable and sly Friar – 'the bestë beggere in his hous' – compared badly with a poor Parson who truly practised what he preached:

> But Christës lore, and his apostles twelve
> He taught, and first he folwéd it himself.

A fierce and drunken Summoner – an official of the Church Courts – and a Pardoner carrying false relics, were two more of the clerical characters.

Among the laymen, there was a plausible Merchant, so well apparelled that no-one would have known he was in debt, a worthy and good-natured Ploughman, a Cook and a Sea-Captain, a Weaver and a Serjeant at Law. All these and many others are described with vivid, detailed, and humorous accuracy. The Miller was an especially rum-bustious character, broad-shouldered, a great wrestler, with big black nostrils and a wart on his nose from which grew a tuft of red hairs. Like many other millers of the time he was a swindler and he also had a liking for a dirty story. For broad, earthy humour, however, he was almost, if not quite, matched by the Wife of Bath, who had had five husbands, not counting 'other companye in youthe'.

The plan of the Canterbury Tales was that each of these pilgrims should tell two stories on the way and two on the way back. It was a gigantic undertaking and Chaucer never completed it. But the tales that were told were absolutely in character; whether lofty and chivalrous from the Knight, gay and kindly from one of the Prioress's priests, or coarse and vulgar from the Miller.

Chaucer wrote many other poems which add up in bulk to about the length of the Canterbury Tales, but they do not match the latter in brillance. His influence can be seen in several writers of the early fifteenth century including King James I of Scotland, who during his long captivity in England wrote some admirable poetry. It also appears in another Scots poet, William Dunbar, who wrote one of the most vivid descriptions of London.

15th-century Scottish poets

> . . . Sovereign of cities, seemliest in sight,
> of high renoun, riches and royaltie.

[1] Fluting

Geoffrey Chaucer *The poet as seen in the early fifteenth-century Ellesmere manuscript, which has pictures of the various pilgrims as headings to the tales they tell.*

Of the prose writers in the fifteenth century, probably the greatest was Sir Thomas Malory, whose *Morte d' Arthur* (1469) was a retelling of the Arthurian legend in a style which was at once simple yet musical and full of poetic feeling.

Malory

In addition to the works of the greater writers, there were also large numbers of popular songs and poems, few of which from the earlier periods have come down to us. From the fifteenth century, however, we have a great deal, including carols and ballads. Carols had originally been songs to accompany a round-dance, but gradually they became religious in their theme and separated from the dance. The ballads

Carols and ballads

usually told stories and among those which have survived are the Robin Hood stories, the Nut-Brown Maid, the Ballad of Chevy Chase, and Sir Patrick Spens. All these must have been repeated countless times.

Drama

Among the great literary developments of the Middle Ages was drama. Medieval drama seems to have started in the church, where the priests tried to represent symbolically the story of such festivals as Easter and Christmas. Then the plays moved out into the churchyard, and thence into the streets and open spaces, where they were mainly taken over by the gilds. Such drama became very popular, and cycles of plays were written for annual performance. Four of these cycles, in their final fifteenth century form, survive from York, Chester, Wakefield,

Miracle plays

and Coventry; the York cycle contains forty-eight plays, the others rather fewer. The plays of each cycle were usually presented in one day, often on the Feast of Corpus Christi or at Whitsun, the performance starting in the small hours of the morning and ending at nightfall. The whole cycle was Biblical, and spanned stories from the Creation to the Last Judgment. Where possible, each gild had its appropriate play: the shipwrights, for instance, might show the story of Noah, and the goldsmiths the adoration of the Magi.

The actors in these plays were ordinary people, who were paid a certain amount for their day's work. One account from Hull from the year 1483 goes like this:

> To the minstrels, 6*d*.
> To Noah and his wife, 1/6*d*.
> To Robert Brown playing God, 6*d*.

Scenery was confined to an occasional backcloth, but there were costumes for important parts and stage properties. In the fourteenth and fifteenth centuries the plays were acted round the town, being performed on carts or platforms on wheels called pageants. Sometimes these carts were divided into two tiers, the lower acting as a sort of dressing room, the upper as the stage: sometimes there were three, the different levels representing Heaven, Earth and Hell. Frequently Hell was shown as a great hole, or else a dragon's mouth, from which smoke issued. Simple, boisterous, and humorous in parts, these miracle or 'mystery' plays – from the French 'mistère', meaning profession or craft – were one of the great delights of the medieval townsman.

Morality plays:

Slightly later than the miracle plays came the Morality plays, which dealt with qualities such as Truth, Knowledge, and Good Deeds. The most famous surviving play of this kind is called 'Everyman' and it

'Everyman'

comes from the fifteenth century. It tells how Everyman is summoned by God to make full account for his life. All his friends, such as Fellowship, Goods, Knowledge, Strength, and Beauty, and all his relations desert him as he sets off to face his Maker; only Good Deeds will accompany him on his journey. In such ways were Christian principles taught to the mass of the people.

2 Painting, Sculpture, and Music

In the Middle Ages the greatest patron of art was the Church. Bishops vied with one another to make their cathedrals beautiful, and nearly all parish churches had their walls covered with paintings to instruct the congregation in the Bible story. Several kings – Richard II for example – were also patrons of painters and illuminators, as were some great noblemen like the earls of Warwick, but even here the work they commissioned was mostly religious. Not until the late fourteenth and fifteenth centuries do we begin to feel that the artist's interest in human beings and the things of this world may be overtaking his interest in Christianity.

Not very much medieval English painting still exists, and what survives is mainly of two kinds: wall painting and illumination of manuscripts. There also exist a certain number of panel paintings – i.e. on wood – but there are no pictures on canvas. The halls and rooms of medieval barons and wealthy merchants were hung not with pictures but with rich cloths and tapestries.

The two finest surviving panel paintings from medieval England both date from the end of the fourteenth century. They are the portrait of Richard II in Westminster Abbey, and the Wilton Diptych, or two-

Panel paintings

Richard II *A formal portrait on wood of the king when young, from Westminster Abbey. It is one of the earliest masterpieces of painting to survive in this country. The artist is unknown, but may have been French.*

Wall paintings

panelled painting, showing Richard II kneeling and holding out his hands to the Virgin and Child. The wall paintings, too, which were so common a feature of the parish churches, have nearly all disappeared – from the effects either of time, or of the seventeenth-century Puritans, or of the nineteenth-century church restorers. Fortunately enough work has survived to leave a clear impression of how such paintings must once have looked. From the fifteenth century, for example, we have pictures of the Last Judgment and of the Virgin: following the Black Death, people were much occupied with ideas of Death and Judgment, and the Virgin Mother of Christ was worshipped as one who might provide a bridge between God and sinful man. We also have pictures of St. Christopher – for it was commonly believed that those who looked on his likeness would be safe from death that day. In some places church paintings survive which seem to have been done purely for the purposes of decoration, such as the leaf design in the chapel of Haddon Hall. Perhaps the finest surviving fifteenth century wall-paintings in England are those in Eton College Chapel, where the influence of Flemish art is very clear.

The colours of the paintings in most parish churches were very restricted, being often limited to ochre, red, grey and white. This was probably because the surfaces were large, and these were the cheapest pigments. Some of the wall pictures connected with the court, however, were painted in brighter and more varied colours – partly, no doubt, because the kings liked them that way, partly because they could afford to be lavish. The subjects of court paintings, too, were no longer always religious. In the fourteenth century, with the age of chivalry, heraldic designs and battle scenes became very popular: the Painted

Mummers *From a fourteenth-century manuscript in the Bodleian Library. 'Mumming' comes from a word which means both to mutter and to be silent, and mummers were men and women in disguise (often wearing animal heads) who took part in jollities during festive seasons such as Christmas. In Scotland they were known as 'guiscards'. The habit had very ancient origins. The outrageous conduct of some mummers finally persuaded Henry VIII to ban the wearing of masks and disguises.*

Chamber at Westminster was decorated with them, as many a baronial hall or great chamber elsewhere must also have been. Few of the painters are known. Many must have been local craftsmen, and we hear of them only through occasional references in account books.

Before the invention of printing, all books were copied out by hand. This was a lengthy and laborious process, and apart from church libraries only the very wealthy could possess books. Much of the work was originally done in monasteries, but later on groups of professional copiers and illuminators established themselves. Lettering was usually in the Carolingian script – a simple, graceful and legible style, like our modern Italic handwriting – and very often the first capital letter was made the centre of an intricate design. The paints used were of vivid colour, the workmanship was often exquisite, and the pictures give us fascinating glimpses into the life of the times. For even if the books were of a religious nature, the pictures as time went on included many things that took the artist's fancy: people, animals, flowers, grotesque creatures, intricate patterns of leaves. Monkeys appear frequently, doing all sorts of unexpected things like driving a wagon or teaching other animals. By the fourteenth century, farmers are shown working in the fields, women weaving and washing clothes, knights fighting. In the St. Omer Psalter, produced in the fourteenth century in East Anglia, we can clearly recognise pictures of peacocks, rabbits, water-fowl, monkeys, bears, stags, hedgehogs, snails, pigs and unicorns, as well as of people climbing ladders, cutting down trees, and sawing logs.

Illuminated books

The centres for this sort of illumination before the Conquest were the great monasteries and cathedrals like Bury St. Edmunds and Winchester. Later York, Canterbury, and St. Albans had thriving schools of illuminators, while in the fourteenth century East Anglia produced the finest books. By the fifteenth century, when the French and the Flemings took the lead, much of the vigour and originality of the English illuminators had departed. It was the development of printing, however, which dealt the death-blow to this form of art.

Woman and man dancing *From a thirteenth-century Bible in the Bodleian Library, Oxford.*

Sculpture

Closely connected with the designs used in book illumination were those used in medieval stone-carving or sculpture. Again the Church was the great patron, and it is in cathedrals and churches that the bulk of our medieval sculpture can be seen. Again much was destroyed by the Puritans in the seventeenth century, but again there was much that survived, for it was often part of the structure of the building.

The Anglo-Norman masons did not make much use of detailed sculptural decorations. Their building was plain and functional, and decoration tended to be confined to simple repetitive patterns like dog-tooth or chevron moulding over doorways or moulded arcading on the walls. The great period of English medieval sculpture began in the thirteenth century, when with improved building techniques, decoration was applied everywhere. The capitals of pillars, for instance, were carved into detailed and complicated designs: perhaps the finest example of work of this sort can be seen in the leaf carvings of the Chapter House at Southwell Minster. Again, the vaulting of the roof was often tied together with a series of elaborately carved bosses, as in Westminster or Tewkesbury. Very often cathedrals were given massively sculptured west fronts with statues of saints standing in a series of niches: Wells and Exeter were two cathedrals decorated in this way. Great reredoses were carved and erected behind high altars, and frequently these were decorated also with precious metals and jewels.

Colour

Practically all this riot of decoration was coloured – a fact hard for us to visualise, since we are accustomed to churches in completely plain stone.

Tombs and effigies

Within the churches were the tombs of the eminent, and here again the artistry of the medieval sculptor came into play. For these tombs, marvellously detailed effigies were carved, usually in marble or alabaster (for which work English craftsmen were famous). Occasionally an effigy was cast in bronze or brass, like the wonderful figure of the Black Prince in Canterbury, or those of Henry III and Queen Eleanor (the wife of Edward I) in Westminster. Such figures give us a detailed picture of the dress and armour of their time; they are not as a rule personal portraits, but represent types – the knight with his feet resting on a lion, his lady with her head on a cushion and her feet on her dog, and so on. The Temple church in London, for instance, is rich in effigies of crusaders.

Memorial brasses

Many of the stone tombs and effigies were painted and gilded, but sometimes memorials took the form of flat brasses inset into the floor. These became very popular in the fourteenth century and can be found all over England but especially in the eastern half of the country and in the Cotswolds. The earliest surviving one, that of Sir John Daubernon in the church of Stoke D'Abernon in Surrey, dates from 1208. The figures on these brasses, engraved in the sheet-metal, like the statues show in minute detail the costume and armour of the period.[1]

[1] It is possible to make attractive rubbings of these brasses, using paper and a stick of shoemaker's heel-ball. Before doing so, one should get permission from the vicar of the church.

Man with toothache *This grotesque on a capital in Wells Cathedral, Somerset (twelfth–fourteenth centuries) is one of many splendid carvings within the building – which is also unique in Britain for the number and quality of its figure-sculptures outside, on the west front. This particular carving is above the tomb of a bishop, whose relics consequently came to be regarded as possessing powers over this painful – and before modern dentistry, all too frequent – complaint.*

It is possible to see medieval sculpture in other places than churches, as in the case of Edward I's Queen Eleanor Crosses. But the great bulk of sculpture was done to beautify places of worship and the same is true of wood-carving. When pews were placed in churches in the fifteenth century they were often elaborately carved; earlier, there were choir stalls such as those in Chester cathedral, which astonish by their intricate detail. There were also carved wooden covers for fonts, and the hinged seats in the choir stalls – the misericords – were often carved with details of domestic life or with grotesque shapes of animals.

Wood-carving

Churches were also beautified by stained glass. Originally only white glass was produced in England: the coloured glass for St. Stephen's, Westminster, for example, was bought from the Hanse merchants, and that for Exeter Cathedral from Rouen. But English glaziers learned the techniques of making coloured glass by adding metallic oxides to the molten mixture – iron oxide for greens, silver oxide for yellows – and by the fourteenth century there were flourishing gilds of glaziers in London and York. As windows grew larger, increasing quantities of glass were required and very often their basic colouring was made lighter so as to allow more light into the church. Each small piece was fitted into a design and then fixed to its neighbours by strips of lead, for medieval glaziers had not the technical knowledge to produce glass in large sheets. York has perhaps the most complete series of medieval coloured glass windows, but examples of fine work can be found in churches throughout the country, such as Fairford in Gloucestershire. Medieval glass was very vivid in its colouring, but with the fifteenth century the skill in making it began to die out, and the richness of the best medieval work has never quite been matched in later centuries, though in very recent years considerable advances have again been made.

Stained glass

A brass rubbing *This rubbing was done from the fourteenth-century memorial brass to Sir Richard Malyns and his wives at Chinnor, Oxfordshire.*

Fourteenth-century embroidery *Part of the magnificent Syon Cope, now in the Victoria and Albert Museum. Underneath the Crucifixion, this shows St George killing the dragon. The cope – a semi-circular cloak worn by clerics for procession – came from the monastery of Syon in Devonshire. It is worked in coloured silks and silver and silver-gilt thread on linen.*

Embroidery

England also remained famous during the Middle Ages for its embroidery work, 'opus anglicanum'. The vestments of the priests continued to be embroidered in rich and detailed designs, in gold, yellow, green, white and blue. They were worked at first by nuns, and later by professional embroiderers.

Jewels and precious metals

In addition to colours in churches there was also the brightness of jewels and precious metals. When the commissioners of Henry VIII removed the gold and jewels from the shrine of Becket in Canterbury their loot filled twenty-six carts. Henry III's shrine for Edward the Confessor in Westminster was of gold, surrounded by golden statues, and decorated with precious stones. Here, too, is one description of part of Winchester Cathedral:

the nether part of the High Altar, being of plate of gold, garnished with stones: the front above being of broidering work and pearls, and above that a table of images of silver and gilt, garnished with stones. Behind the high altar, St. Swithin's shrine, being of plate, silver and gilt garnished with stones.

Music

Though we are all aware of medieval architecture, we tend to overlook medieval music, since we very rarely hear it performed. Yet it was extremely important both for its place in the general life of the Middle Ages and for the advances it made in the whole art and science of music. Moreover, it was an honoured subject of study in the universities and other places of higher learning.

Church music

In medieval Britain, as elsewhere in Europe, there was an immense amount of music. It played, of course, a very large part in the church services and there were many special schools of song for the training of the clergy in the art of plainsong, or Gregorian chant, in which psalms and prayers were delivered. After the sixth century this chant was based on eight modes, or scales of notes, inherited from the Greeks and approved by Pope Gregory the Great. It spread throughout Europe, but apparently there were different techniques of singing it, for one of the versions of the Anglo-Saxon Chronicle records that after the Norman Conquest the new Norman abbot of Glastonbury, Thurstan, quarrelled with his monks over this matter. Apparently he stationed archers in the upper parts of the church who shot arrows at the monks when they persisted in singing Mass in their accustomed manner.

Plainsong

Plainsong was originally sung entirely in unison, the various voices doubling the tune at their natural intervals. Gradually, however, a freer treatment crept in, with one of the voices – the tenor, or holding voice – sustaining the main line of the melody while others, such as the basses, might sing merely accompanying notes. Alternatively, the treble or alto line might be much more ornamented, and coincide with the tenor line only at fixed points. From this, greatly enlarged ideas of harmony and composition developed, so that by the sixteenth century music was entering an entirely new phase. None of this chant was accompanied by instruments, except that in some large churches organs were used, from an early date, to supply a firm base for the singing.

Musicians *From a fourteenth-century manuscript in the British Museum. The instruments being played are (top to bottom): handbells, a portative organ (i.e. one carried about), bagpipes, hurdy-gurdy and tabors (drums).*

One organ of which we have record, a giant instrument installed in Winchester Cathedral in the tenth century, must have made an enormous din as it led the singing. It had two manuals, played by two performers, and each with twenty notes. Each note had ten metal pipes, making altogether 400 pipes – for which the services of no less than seventy blowers were needed.

Apart from that of the Church, most of the music of the Middle Ages can be described as folk-music. It was not for the most part composed by people whose names are known. It consisted of a mass of songs and dance-tunes, sung and played on all sorts of occasions – there were work-songs as well as leisure-songs – and in all sorts of places from the king's court to the streets and ale houses. Such songs could vary from love lyrics in the *troubadour* tradition to ballads commemorating popular heroes, or rounds such as the famous thirteenth century piece 'Sumer Is Icumen In'. From an early date the Welsh were recognised as exceptionally skilled in part-singing.

Folk music

Instruments

Among the instruments were stringed ones for bowing, like the fiddle or viol (ancestor of the violin), stringed ones for plucking (such as the harp, the guitar and the lute) and wind instruments of many kinds. These included two forms of trumpet – of the forty-two instrumental musicians employed at Henry VIII's court fourteen were trumpeters – various kinds of horn, the shawm (an ancestor of the oboe) and a large range of pipes, not forgetting the bagpipe (which was popular in England well before it became so in Scotland). Other instruments included the dulcimer, the tabor (a drum, usually played with one hand to accompany a pipe played with the other), the portative or portable organ (played with one hand while the other worked the bellows) and a form of hurdy-gurdy, in which a wheel, turned by a handle, scraped like a bow against variable strings. By the end of the fourteenth century there had also come into existence the earliest virginals, a small keyboard instrument from which was later to be developed the spinet and the harpsichord.

Many medieval musicians – or minstrels, as they were often called, from a French word – lived a wandering life, playing their instruments and singing their songs from village to village. They were welcome not only because of their musical ability, but also because they brought news of the outside world – sometimes, indeed, recounted a recent event in the form of a ballad. Other musicians had more permanent posts, being attached to cathedrals or to the houses of great noblemen, or sometimes to municipalities.

The kings and the Chapel Royal

In fondness for music, the later medieval kings of England gave a great lead, as did King James I of Scotland. A special body of clergy and musicians known as the Chapel Royal was attached to the English court from an early date – the existing records go back to 1135 – and this became a centre of musical development. Richard II and his supplanter Henry IV were both addicted to music, Henry V composed pieces and sent for the musicians of his Chapel when he was in France, and Edward IV maintained in the Chapel – apart from the twenty-six clergy – thirteen 'minstrels', eight choir boys, and a 'wayte' or musical night watchman employed to sound the hour from time to time on his horn. Under Richard III the Chapel Royal was authorised to take its pick of choir boys wherever it found the best voices. With the monarchs so keen it was not surprising that the fifteenth century should show very great advances in the art of musical composition, or that England should produce, in John Dunstable (c. 1390–1453), her first great composer – a man known throughout Western Europe for the beauty and skill of his vocal music.

25 The Lancastrians and the War with France

1 The Troubles of Henry IV

The man who overthrew Richard II and founded the Lancastrian dynasty was a famous warrior at the height of his powers. Before his death fourteen years later, at the early age of forty-six, he was already worn out from illness and the problems he encountered as king.

Henry IV, 1399–1413

Any king of medieval England had a hard task. At home, he had to deal with violent and ambitious barons, clergy who claimed special privileges, and wealthy merchants who were beginning to feel important. Outside England, he had to defend his possessions in France and keep a watchful eye over the Welsh, the Scots and the Irish. With a large revenue, all this might not have been too difficult; but the estates of the Crown having grown smaller as grants of land were made to followers, kings found it impossible to govern from their own resources and the recognised feudal payments. To fill the gap they had to rely on taxation, which could only be collected easily if it had been approved by Parliament – and Parliament usually tried to impose conditions, such as the dismissal of a hated counsellor, before it met the royal wishes. In this way kings escaped from one set of difficulties only to run into another.

Standing difficulties of government

Besides these standing problems of later medieval monarchs, Henry IV had others of his own. Many of them sprang from the fact that he was a usurper: his claim to the throne, though approved by Parliament, was not a strong one by descent. Also he was indebted to certain nobles for their help in overthrowing Richard II. These men expected Henry to reward them lavishly and to heed their advice.

Special problems of Henry IV

Trouble arose very quickly. Some of Richard II's supporters tried to seize Henry at Windsor. He escaped; and shortly afterwards, whether by coincidence or design, Richard II died in captivity. Before the end of 1400, Henry was also up against the French, the Scots and the Welsh – who in Owen Glendower, or Glyndor, found a new and brilliant leader.

Henry's early troubles

A landowner probably descended from the old Welsh princes, Owen had studied law at Westminster and seen service with Henry. Wrongfully accused of treason by his English neighbour in the Marches, Lord Grey of Ruthin, Owen resisted Grey's efforts to arrest him. Henry backed Grey and the affair led to a general rising in Wales, during which Owen captured several great castles. Three times in three years Henry attacked him, only to be beaten back. Calling himself Prince of Wales, by 1403 Owen had gained control over most of the country. He was also part of a formidable alliance against Henry in

Revolt of Owen Glendower begins, 1400

Revolt by the Percys

which the Welsh were joined by Scots, French and rebellious English.

The leading English rebels included the Earl of Northumberland and his redoubtable son Henry Percy, known as Hotspur. The Percys had helped Henry IV against Richard II, and had defeated a Scottish invasion at Homildon Hill in 1402. Dissatisfied with their rewards, they allied with the defeated Scots and with Owen Glendower. They planned to link up with Owen, but the king was too swift. While one English force held back Owen near Carmarthen, Henry IV and his sixteen-year-old son, Prince Henry of Monmouth, intercepted the Percys and the Scots near Shrewsbury. In the battle which followed, the rebels were crushed and Hotspur killed.

Battle of Shrewsbury, 1403

Despite this triumph, Henry's troubles went on for many years. Glendower, the French, the Earl of Northumberland – all continued to defy him. However, in 1406 he also enjoyed one stroke of good fortune: the young heir to the Scottish throne, Prince James, travelling by sea to France, fell into English hands. Although he soon succeeded to the Scottish throne as James I, he was held captive in England for the next eighteen years.

In Wales the skill and iron determination of young Prince Henry gradually wore down Glendower. One of the final blows came in 1409, when the English recaptured Harlech Castle and took several of Owen's family prisoner. The Welsh leader himself remained undefeated in the field and he never surrendered. He rejected a free pardon offered later, and he died obscurely around 1415. A man of culture who had called a Welsh parliament at Machynlleth, negotiated with the kings of France and Scotland, and planned the foundation of two universities, he had been a worthy champion of Welsh independence. It had taken a soldier of genius and the resources of a far larger country to subdue his movement – the last great Welsh rebellion.

Prince Henry subdues Wales

2 The Conquests of Henry V

Weakness of France under Charles VI (1380–1422)

Orleanists (later Armagnacs or Dauphinists) and Burgundians

In his closing years Henry IV faced a problem of a different kind. This arose from the growing weakness of France under Charles VI, who was subject to fits of insanity. In this situation his leading relatives vied with each other to dominate him and govern in their own interests. At first the two great rivals were Louis Duke of Orleans and John 'the Fearless', Duke of Burgundy. The latter was the overlord of great territories which covered not only what we now think of as Burgundy, but also most of present-day Holland, Belgium and Luxembourg, and a good deal of north-eastern France. Before long Burgundy hired assassins to kill Orleans, and in 1407 civil war set in between the two factions. The supporters of Orleans, now known as Armagnacs from their new leader Bernard of Armagnac, pinned their hopes on the young Dauphin Charles, and gradually they began to get the upper hand over the Burgundians.

This conflict tempted both parties to seek English help. Small

Henry IV and his Queen *From the alabaster effigies in Canterbury Cathedral.*

Henry V *From a portrait by an unknown artist in the National Portrait Gallery*

English forces were sent to France in 1411 and 1412, but as Henry IV favoured the Armagnacs and Prince Henry the Burgundians, the English intervention was half-hearted. When Henry IV died in 1413 the way was clear for his warrior son to act as he wished. This bold and confident young man of 25 at once put forward again the claim of the royal house of England to the throne of France.

Since the Dauphin and the Armagnacs could not accept this claim, Henry made an agreement with the Duke of Burgundy (whose Flemish weavers depended on supplies of English wool) and prepared to mount an invasion. With liberal supplies from Parliament, he brought his navy up to a strength of thirty vessels and hired or commandeered hundreds of transport craft. He also collected together over 10,000 soldiers – English, Welsh, Irish, German, and Dutch – of whom about 2,500 were mounted men-at-arms, the remainder archers. Nearly all of them were got together through a system of indentures, or contracts, by which leading subjects undertook to provide the king with so many men in return for a given sum. The king remained responsible for all overseas transport, but not for weapons, armour, horses or food. To

Accession of Henry V in England, 1413

His claims to throne of France

Henry organises the invasion

avoid disputes between contingents, pay was to be standard: that of the mounted men-at-arms varied from 13*s* 4*d* per day for a duke to 1*s* a day for an esquire, while that of the archers was 6*d* a day. All these sums were high by the standards of the time.

Henry sailed from Southampton for the Seine in August 1415. He first besieged Harfleur, the fortress which guarded the entry to the river. In five weeks he captured it, but disease, casualties, and desertions took an appalling toll of his army.

With his forces reduced by at least a third, Henry decided to march to Calais, about one hundred and fifty miles away. It was the one town remaining to the English crown in France, and a good port for re-embarkation. On his way, near the village of Agincourt, he had to meet the challenge of a much larger French army; and here, on 25 October 1415, St. Crispin's Day, Henry fought one of the most famous battles in English history.

The small English force waited for the French attack. This served them well, for heavy rain overnight had affected the ground between them and the French. Twice the French pushed forward, their knights trying to move dismounted in armour across the heavy fields. Twice they were repulsed with terrible losses by the mixed English formations of long-bow archers and dismounted men at arms. A third assault was threatening when a group of French camp-followers broke into the English camp and ransacked the tents. Fearing that he was attacked by cavalry from behind, Henry issued a grim order, resented by his troops, to kill all prisoners except the high-born (whose ransom went to him). The French made no further assault, and Henry was able to resume his march to Calais. English losses in the battle seem to have been no more than 500 dead, while the French amounted to some 7,000, including many great nobles.

In 1417 Henry again invaded Normandy. In two years he took most of the major Norman towns and finally captured the capital Rouen after a gruelling six months' siege. During this, food became so scarce among the defenders that dogs were sold for ten shillings and mice for sixpence. By now Henry was at odds with Burgundy, and his progress had so frightened the opposing French factions that they agreed to negotiate with each other. For this purpose the sixteen-year-old Dauphin and his followers arranged to meet Duke John on the bridge at Montereau, forty miles south-east of Paris. The result was tragedy. Whether by previous plan or not, the Dauphinists suddenly assaulted the Burgundians, and one of them brought an axe down on the head of Duke John.

The murder of Burgundy so enraged his son and successor, Duke Philip 'the Good', that he quickly concluded a full alliance with Henry V. As Burgundy had now for some time controlled Paris and the persons of the mentally sick King Charles VI and the Queen (who conveniently disowned the Dauphin as illegitimate), his action was decisive. The Treaty of Troyes which he concluded with Henry gave the English king almost all he wanted. Henry was to marry Katherine, the daughter of Charles VI, and was to be recognised as heir to Charles. While Charles lived, Henry would be Regent and would share in the government of France. He would retain all his conquests, including Normandy, until he became King of France, when Normandy would revert to the French crown.

Henry heir and Regent of France

Only the north and east of France accepted these arrangements. The rest refused and looked to the 17-year-old Dauphin Charles as the rightful Regent. Having married Katherine and enjoyed one day's honeymoon, Henry was therefore quickly off on his campaigns again. By December 1420, Henry, Burgundy and their puppet Charles VI were riding into the famine-stricken city of Paris, and Henry celebrated

Opposition under Dauphin Charles

Henry in Paris, 1420

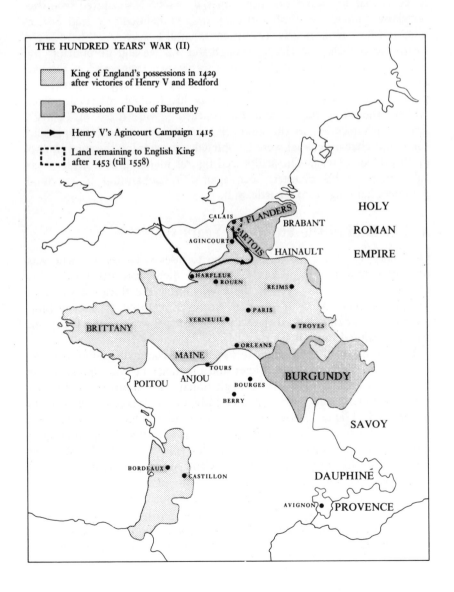

THE HUNDRED YEARS' WAR (II)

King of England's possessions in 1429 after victories of Henry V and Bedford

Possessions of Duke of Burgundy

Henry V's Agincourt Campaign 1415

Land remaining to English King after 1453 (till 1558)

Christmas in the Louvre. He then set off for England with Katherine, to have her crowned Queen and to go on triumphant procession through the country, but by June 1421 was back in France. He sought out the Dauphinists, hanged the garrison and drowned the fugitives from a castle which resisted him, and then concentrated on reducing the fortress of Meaux, which commanded the Marne forty miles east of Paris. Seven months of determined effort won him this prize, but in the course of it he contracted a disease which was to prove fatal. At the height of his glory and in his thirty-fifth year, Henry V found himself too weak to ride a horse.

Little more than three months after the surrender of Meaux Henry was dead. To transport back to England the remains of the warrior king, it seems that his body was dismembered, his flesh separated from his bones by boiling, and flesh and bone then embalmed in a lead casket. The journey took nearly two months and everywhere there were sorrowing crowds; for Henry, though too warlike and humourless for our modern taste, was much admired in his own time, even in France, as being not only a great soldier and organiser but also a firm, just, and pious ruler. The last scene of all was his funeral in Westminster Abbey, the most magnificent for centuries, with three of Henry's finest warhorses led to the altar. Some years later Henry's splendid tomb and chantry chapel were completed, overtopping the monuments of all previous kings. The sculptured figures included one of Henry at full gallop on his charger, seen against a background of executed prisoners hanging from a castle wall.

3 The End of the Hundred Years War

On Henry V's death the throne passed to his son Henry VI, who was only nine months old. When Charles VI died soon afterwards, this infant became, in the eyes of the English and the Burgundians, also king of France. Most of France, however, refused to accept him. Instead they acknowledged the wily if seemingly weak young Dauphin, who proclaimed himself Charles VII.

For the English, the Regent in France and commander-in-chief was the Duke of Bedford. As a soldier and organiser he was almost in the class of his brother Henry V, though much more humane. At first he was able to continue the war successfully, and he made every effort to govern well. His task, however, was almost impossible, for he had not only to conquer two-thirds of France but also to deal with repeated resistance in the areas he occupied. Charles was in much the stronger position, but his forces were war-weary and his supporters divided, and he had lost the confidence to make an all-out effort.

It was partly through the example of a woman that this confidence returned. At Domrémy in Lorraine there was growing up the girl who was to live in history as St. Joan of Arc. Intensely pious, and hearing, as she thought, the orders of God spoken to her by the voices of three

Joan of Arc at the stake *From a fifteenth-century manuscript in the Bibliothèque Nationale. The cleric to the right of Joan has a cross to hold before her eyes as she burns.*

saints, she became convinced of her divine mission to save France. After many rebuffs she at length secured admission to the court of the still uncrowned Charles VII, and such was her fervour that he finally decided to make use of her. In 1429, dressed in a coat of mail and bearing a sword which she claimed had been sent to her by God, she rode with Charles's commander and 5,000 men to the relief of besieged Orleans.

The presence of Joan inspired Charles's troops to new efforts. They forced the English to break off the siege and saved Orleans. Two further victories then nerved Charles to follow Joan's next advice. At her behest he fought his way to Rheims, the traditional seat of coronation, and with Joan standing by was crowned with the full, ancient ceremonial of the kings of France.

Joan, however, was not without enemies on her own side. Many of Charles's nobles resented her prominence and many churchmen disliked her independence and her claims to direct inspiration from God. The result was that, when she was captured by the Burgundians in 1430, Charles made no attempt to ransom her. Prompted by some of their leading clergy the Burgundians sold her to the English, who regarded her as a witch and were bent on destroying her. Brought

Relief of Orleans, 1429

Coronation of
Charles VII in Rheims

Joan captured, 1430

before the Inquisition on a charge of heresy, she at length gave way under pressure and disowned her visions. This saved her from death but not from a sentence of perpetual imprisonment. In prison, she was trapped into wearing male clothes again and then accused once more of heresy. Condemned now to be burnt, she withdrew her previous recantation and perished bravely at the stake in the market-place of Rouen. As the smoke and flames engulfed her, one English onlooker is said to have cried out 'We are lost, for we have burnt a saint'.

Burning of Joan, 1431

The war was not yet lost to the English but the supporters of Charles VII, despite their continuing quarrels, were now fighting with far greater hopes of success. The decisive event came in 1435 when the Duke of Burgundy, offended by various English actions, deserted the English alliance and came to an agreement with Charles. Shortly afterwards, the death of Bedford robbed the English of a great leader; and when Charles re-organised his army and developed better artillery he was well on the way to victory.

Death of Bedford. Burgundy recognises Charles VII, 1435

Despite the folly of Henry VI's Council in soon declaring war on Burgundy, the struggle still continued for many years. At length in 1450 Charles's troops freed all Normandy from English control, and soon followed this by capturing Guienne. An English effort to retake Guienne was defeated in 1453, and by the close of that year Calais alone remained to the English crown of all its former possessions in France.

French capture Normandy and Guienne, 1450–1

No peace treaty marked the end of the Hundred Years War. The English clung to Calais for another century, and English monarchs claimed to be kings of France for another three and a half centuries, but the struggle had been settled for good and all in the 1450s. In the course of the conflict the English had acquired military glory and plunder; but these brought no lasting benefit, and they had been won only at the cost of great suffering to France and her people. Edward III, Henry V and other English leaders had treated opponents of high rank with chivalry, and so helped to give the war a kind of surface glamour; but the realities beneath were the burning villages, the starving and disease-ridden towns, the maimed soldiers, the violated women and the slaughtered prisoners.

In the long run, France gained more than England from the war. Though her countryside suffered greatly, the conflict finally welded the provinces and peoples of France more closely together. In the course of the struggle, districts which began by feeling loyalty to the King of England as Duke of Aquitaine or former Duke of Normandy, ended by feeling loyalty to the King of France as their protector against hated foreign invaders. What began by being a feudal war between the French king and his great vassal the Duke of Aquitaine, who also happened to be the King of England, ended by being something like a war between two nations, the French and the English.

26 The Yorkists and the Struggle for the Throne

1 The Struggle for the Throne

Henry VI's minority came to an end in 1437, when he was fifteen. During these years a Council of chief officials and magnates carried on the government of the country fairly well. Behind the scenes, however, the rivalries were fierce, and they flared up dangerously after the death of Bedford in 1435. On the one side were Humphrey, Duke of Gloucester, the king's younger uncle, and another member of the royal family in a different line, Richard, Duke of York. On the other side was the Beaufort family, descended from John of Gaunt. Their biggest disputes were over the war in France.

When the Duke of Burgundy became reconciled with Charles VII, most of Henry's advisers began to think that England too should make peace with France. Headed by the Beauforts this peace party had a policy which appealed to the religious and unwarlike Henry VI. In 1445 they were able to go some way towards their goal, at the same time strengthening their hold over the king, by arranging for a two-year truce accompanied by a marriage between Henry and a French princess, the sixteen-year-old Margaret of Anjou. The truce, however, had a price: the English would have to give up Maine. The Duke of Gloucester, rash and ambitious though a great patron of learning, opposed this strongly – and his was the popular view among the English ruling classes. Arrested in 1447, he died four days after his arrest. This left the Beaufort group in full control, with one of their supporters, the Duke of Suffolk, as the king's leading adviser.

With the king more interested in education and religion than in government, however, there was no firm authority at the centre. Though trade and towns continued to expand, troubles grew and the country became divided. The crown was in debt; many of the barons were keeping private armies (often recruited in the first place for the French wars); and pirates in the Channel were attacking English ships and raiding coastal villages – the Government had sold most of Henry V's navy to save expense. The final humiliation came when Charles VII renewed the war in France and in 1450 recaptured Normandy.

Popular discontent now came to a head and vented itself on royal officials. At Portsmouth, a group of soldiers lynched the Bishop of Chichester. In the Channel, sailors from a mutinous royal ship intercepted the Duke of Suffolk, who was departing into forced exile. They bundled him into a small boat and there beheaded him with six strokes of a rusty sword.

Henry VI's minority, 1422–37

Truce with France and marriage with Margaret of Anjou, 1445

Beaufort influence supreme

Decline of royal authority

Loss of Normandy, 1450

Disorders

Henry VI *From an anonymous painting in the National Portrait Gallery.*

Next followed a rising of the Kentishmen. Before long it came under the leadership of Jack Cade, a man of uncertain origin who had served in the French wars and married well. The rebels, who included some substantial landowners, marched on London, where they terrorised the streets and executed Lord Saye, the royal Treasurer. Though their demands included the abolition of the Statute of Labourers, their main cry was for better government. 'The King's false Council', they said, 'has lost his law, his merchandise is lost, his common people is destroyed, the sea is lost, France is lost, the King . . . oweth more than any King of England owed'. The misbehaviour of the rebels, however, quickly forfeited them the sympathy of the London citizens, and under promises of reform they withdrew from their positions at Southwark and Blackheath. Cade himself eventually quarrelled with his followers and fled into Sussex, where he was wounded and captured. He died in the cart bringing him to London for execution.

Cade's rising differed from the Peasants' Revolt of 1381 in that it was mainly directed not against landlords but against the king's advisers and officials. At first it also had 'respectable' support. Its suppression by no means ended the unrest. Among the incidents which followed, a mob dragged the Bishop of Salisbury from the church at Edington, in Wiltshire, and killed him outside.

The scene was now set for the struggle that was to overshadow all others – the struggle for the throne. Henry as yet had no children; and following the deaths of his uncles the likely heir was now Richard, Duke of York. In some ways York had a better claim to the throne by

Cade's rebellion, 1450

York v. Beauforts

descent than had Henry VI himself; he was also of good reputation and popular with the merchants and the lower classes. Many of the magnates, however, were jealous of him, and to the Beauforts he was a hated rival.

Before the Beauforts could remove York, the king in 1453 had a sudden attack of insanity. York now became officially Regent. Very soon afterwards, however, Queen Margaret gave birth to a boy, Edward, who became the heir to the throne. York acknowledged this, but the headstrong queen insisted on treating him as an enemy and a possible supplanter of her son.

York Regent
Birth of Prince Edward

During 1454 the king recovered, but he was now even less interested in power than before. Though all at Court respected his simple goodness, very few respected his desire for peace and quiet. The queen and the leading Beaufort, the Duke of Somerset, now held the reins, and they quickly dismissed York's friends from office. Fearing more violent action, York then took up arms, and with his followers confronted Somerset at St. Albans. Somerset refused to negotiate, the armies clashed, Somerset was killed, and victory went to York.

Queen Margaret and Somerset in power

Civil war: Yorkist victory at St. Albans, 1455

Four years of uneasy truce then followed, with York and his friends in the positions of power. But the quarrel simmered and the queen was only biding her time. In 1459 she felt strong enough to challenge York's position and fighting broke out again. York fled to Ireland, but thanks to his supporter the Earl of Warwick, who crossed from Calais and beat the royal forces at Northampton, was soon able to return. With the king a prisoner – Warwick had captured him at Northampton – York now formally claimed the throne. Thenceforth the division was hard and fast: York and his supporters – the Yorkists – against the supporters of the existing king and queen – the Lancastrians.

York lost no time in seeking out the remaining Lancastrian forces. He engaged them at Wakefield, in Yorkshire, though they were in much greater numbers than his own, and he paid for his boldness by his own defeat and death. No quarter was asked or given in this fierce encounter. As Lord Clifford, whose father had been killed by the Yorkists at St. Albans, stabbed York's son the Earl of Rutland, he exclaimed: 'By God's blood, thy father slew mine; and so will I do thee, and all thy kin.' From now on, this was the spirit of the war among the barons.

Lancastrian victory at Wakefield, 1460: death of York

Early in the following year, Queen Margaret met and defeated at the second battle of St. Albans another Yorkist army commanded by the Earl of Warwick. This Lancastrian victory released Henry VI. The seven-year-old Prince of Wales was allowed to decide the fate of the king's guards, and he condemned them to death. As they were led away to execution, one of them said: 'May the wrath of God fall on those who have taught a child to speak such words.'

Lancastrian victory at St. Albans, 1461

Despite her victory the Queen made no attempt to occupy London. This gave a Yorkist army, commanded by Warwick and by York's eldest son, the Earl of March, the chance to slip in and seize possession.

York's son claims
throne as Edward IV,
1461

March, who was only nineteen years old, now claimed the throne as
Edward IV and was accepted as king by the London citizens and a
Council packed with Yorkists. Tall, handsome, able, and a born soldier,
he then led his army north in pursuit of the Lancastrians and in a
whirling snowstorm won a great victory at Towton Moor, in Yorkshire.

Yorkist victory at
Towton, 1461

Henry, Margaret, and the Prince of Wales all fled to Scotland. Nothing
came of Margaret's efforts to invade from the north in the following
year, and in 1465 Yorkist forces captured the fugitive Henry VI near
Clitheroe. Henceforth he was a prisoner in Edward's hands.

During this long period of confusion Parliaments were still called,
but they merely carried out the wishes of the faction in power at the

The role of
Parliament

time. In 1459, when the Lancastrians dominated Parliament, the Lords
began the bad practice of introducing bills of attainder, or condemnation,
against defeated opponents. By these, the leaders of the losing side were
condemned to death without a proper trial by the simple process of
passing a parliamentary bill. With the Yorkists supreme, Parliament now
also obligingly passed an act declaring all the Lancastrian kings to be
usurpers.

Edward IV, 1461–83

By upbringing, Edward IV was a soldier and a man of action. But he
was also a patron of learning and art, an accomplished dancer, and a
lover of pleasure. Having won his way to the throne, he set out to enjoy
life. But at the same time he dealt cleverly with the many problems he
had inherited – problems such as continued support for Henry VI,
general lawlessness, large royal debts, and difficulties in trade and
foreign affairs. By his skill in handling all these matters, Edward proved
himself as able a ruler as he was a warrior.

Warwick 'the
king-maker'

Edward could not have gained the throne without the help of his
cousin Warwick and Warwick's family, the Nevilles. Their rewards
were accordingly lavish. In addition to his great estates, Warwick himself was allowed to hold the offices of Lord Chamberlain, Constable of
Calais, Constable of Dover Castle, Warden of the Cinque Ports, and
Warden of the Scottish Marches. This, however, did not prevent him
later falling out with Edward over the policy to be adopted towards
France.

Though the English crown had lost everything in France except
Calais, there was still no peace between the two countries. Warwick
thought that the long drawn-out war should be ended and give place to
an alliance, with Edward marrying a French princess. Warwick actually
started negotiations to this end. Edward, however, had other commit-
ments. In 1464, during a hunting expedition, he had taken shelter for
the night in a castle where he met the owner's niece, the young and
beautiful widow Lady Elizabeth Wydeville (or Woodville). Shortly

Edward IV marries
Elizabeth Woodville,
1464

afterwards, though her father and her husband had both been Lancastrians, Edward secretly married her. When Warwick became involved in negotiations with France, Edward had to reveal his marriage,
and this came as a sharp blow to the Earl.

The quarrel with
Warwick

Other blows soon followed. Edward began showering honours on members of his wife's family, the Woodvilles, whom the greater nobles regarded as upstarts, and he dismissed Warwick's brother from the Chancellorship. Equally humiliating, he allowed Warwick to begin negotiations again for an alliance with France, only to counter this by arranging a marriage between his own sister and the Duke of Burgundy. All this drove Warwick to plot against the king. With the support of the Duke of Clarence, one of Edward's brothers, who was angry at the promotion of the Woodvilles, he took up arms against Edward. For a short time he and Clarence were in control, which they celebrated by the execution of two of the leading Woodvilles. Then Edward forced them to flee abroad, where they took refuge in the court of Louis XI of France. And at the French king's prompting they made up their earlier quarrel with Henry VI's refugee Queen, Margaret of Anjou.

Warwick's rebellions, 1469–71

This set the scene for another invasion of England. In September 1470 Warwick, Clarence and a group of Lancastrian exiles landed at Dartmouth and forced Edward, in his turn, to flee the country. He found refuge, not surprisingly, with his brother-in-law the Duke of Burgundy. The victorious rebels freed Henry VI from the Tower, and installed him again on the throne. He remained only a figurehead, and for a year Warwick himself – 'the king-maker' – was the real ruler of the country.

Warwick and Clarence invade, Sept. 1470

Restoration of Henry VI, 1470–1

Six months later Edward was back again, with forces supplied by Burgundy. He landed at Ravenspur in Yorkshire and at first claimed only his rightful family estates. Once in the Midlands, however, he proclaimed himself king again, and then moved on to meet the opposing Lancastrian forces. They gave battle outside London, at Barnet, and there, in a confused struggle in fog, Edward triumphed and Warwick fell. Shortly afterwards Edward defeated the other main Lancastrian army – Queen Margaret's – at Tewkesbury. In this battle, and in executions afterwards, there was a great slaughter of Lancastrian leaders including Margaret's son the Prince of Wales.

Return of Edward, 1471

Edward's victory at Barnet, 1471; death of Warwick

Tewkesbury, 1471: death of Prince of Wales

The direct line of Lancaster was now extinct except for the pathetic Henry VI, who had again been lodged in the Tower. On the day that Edward re-entered London, Henry VI very conveniently died. Some said later that he perished by the hand of Edward's brother Richard, Duke of Gloucester, though there seems no evidence for this beyond the fact that Richard was present at the Tower that evening. Edward's other brother, Clarence, had earlier deserted his alliance with Warwick and had fought for Edward at Barnet and Tewkesbury; but the king found it difficult to trust him and finally had Parliament condemn him as a traitor. He, too, died in the Tower of London, probably by being drowned in a bath of water – not, as Shakespeare would have us believe, in a butt of 'malmsey' (Madeira) wine. This deed, too, was later ascribed to Richard of Gloucester.

Death of Henry VI, 1471

The big challenges to Edward's authority were by this time over. The Lancastrian claim lived on, however, in the person of the young Henry Tudor, Earl of Richmond. His mother, Margaret Beaufort, had

The Lancastrian claimant – Henry Tudor

a claim derived from John of Gaunt; while his father, Edmund Tudor, who had been executed by the Yorkists, was the son of Henry V's widow Catherine and a Welsh gentleman, Owen Tudor. Henry Tudor, however, was an exile in Brittany. In England, Edward IV could at last enjoy the fruits of victory undisturbed.

2 The Yorkist Monarchy

Continued lawlessness, 1461–71

During the earlier part of Edward IV's reign lawlessness and disorder were rife in England. The armed struggle which began among the leading nobility in 1455 set a bad example, and throughout the country great landowners repeatedly took the law into their own hands. In 1469, for instance, the Duke of Norfolk claimed Caistor Castle, which had been left by will to the head of the Paston family in Norfolk. With a force of 3,000 men, he laid siege and took possession. This incident is vividly described in the Paston letters, written to and by members of the family – a correspondence which supplies one of our best accounts of life in fifteenth-century England. Many lords continued to keep powerful armies of retainers, and all too often these were used to overawe judges or juries and secure an acquittal when one of the lord's men was charged in a local court.[1]

Restoration of royal authority

Improvement in royal finances

All the same, Edward IV did a very great deal to restore the power of the monarchy, especially in the second half of his reign. For one thing, he improved the royal finances and wiped out the Lancastrian debts: he was the first king since the twelfth century to die leaving a fortune. This wealth he built up in a number of ways, including the collection of 'benevolences' or forced gifts from the wealthy, and wholesale confiscations of land (e.g. the Duchy of Lancaster and the Warwick estates) from defeated opponents. He even managed to make money from his foreign policy. Unlike the Lancastrian kings, he fought no wars in France. He several times threatened to, and collected cash for the purpose; and finally, after making an alliance with his brother-in-law, Charles the Bold of Burgundy, he actually invaded France in

[1] The practice of granting food and clothing to retainers was known as *livery*; that of upholding retainers if they were in trouble with the law was known as *maintenance*.

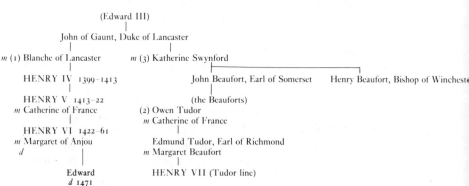

THE HOUSE OF LANCASTER

King's College Chapel, Cambridge
Fan-vaulting and perpendicular architecture are at their finest in this late Gothic masterpiece. The College was founded by Henry VI. The Chapel was begun in his lifetime, came to a lengthy halt, was then continued under Edward IV and Richard III and finished under Henry VII and Henry VIII.

1475. But having brought his army in through Calais he quickly met the French king, Louis XI, at Picquigny, and agreed to retire again in return for a large sum of money and a pension. This was treachery to Charles the Bold, but profitable to Edward and England.

Treaty of Picquigny, 1475

Another source of Edward's wealth was that he engaged in trade, which he did through royal agents. In 1466, for example, the articles shipped in the king's name included 6,000 sacks of wool, 20,000

Edward IV and trade

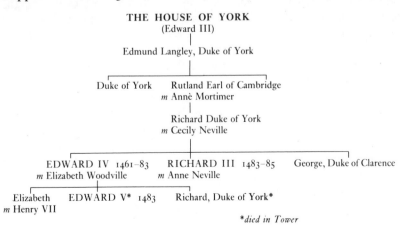

THE HOUSE OF YORK
(Edward III)

Edmund Langley, Duke of York

Duke of York   Rutland Earl of Cambridge
                 m Annè Mortimer

Richard Duke of York
m Cecily Neville

EDWARD IV 1461–83   RICHARD III 1483–85   George, Duke of Clarence
m Elizabeth Woodville   *m* Anne Neville

Elizabeth   EDWARD V* 1483   Richard, Duke of York*
m Henry VII

*died in Tower

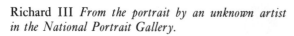

Richard III *From the portrait by an unknown artist in the National Portrait Gallery.*

woollen cloths, and 10,000 blocks of tin. Edward did everything he could to encourage trade and to win the support of the merchant class, and this was one of the reasons why he could normally rely on the friendship of London.

Edward and Parliament

Although Edward did not try to suppress Parliament he summoned it only six times between 1471 and 1483. There would have been nothing unusual in this before the reign of Edward III, but from then on Parliament had been called with great regularity in the effort to secure grants for the king. Since Edward was not involved in foreign wars and hence much better off, he felt no need to call Parliament to the same extent as his recent predecessors.

Edward was thus able to carry on government more and more through royal officials without referring to the great magnates assembled in Parliament. Once he could fill it with his own choices, he developed the work of the King's Council, especially in dealing with cases brought

The King's Council and its offshoots

before it. Branches of the Council were also set up to run the Mortimer estates in the Welsh Marches, and, under Richard of Gloucester, to keep order along the Scottish border. In these can be seen the beginnings of the later Councils of Wales and of the North. All told, Edward re-established the power of the monarchy and developed its governing organs to such an extent that his reign marked a fresh turn in English

The Yorkist monarchy

history. It was on the foundation laid by the Yorkists that the Tudors were later able to erect the strongest monarchy ever known in Britain.

Edward V, 1483

Edward died in 1483 and was succeeded by his son Edward V, a boy only twelve years old. Unfortunately several of the upper nobility bore him ill will because of his 'upstart' Woodville blood, and because

Richard of Gloucester: opposition to Woodvilles

he was under the control of his mother and her relations. They looked instead to Richard of Gloucester, Edward IV's brother, who at the beginning of the reign found himself squeezed out of his intended position as Protector by the Queen Mother and the Woodvilles.

Richard's reputation was thus far fairly good, and nothing like the later Tudor version of it enshrined in Shakespeare's *Richard III*. He had proved himself a good soldier and governor and had remained loyal to Edward IV during the latter's troubles with Warwick and Clarence. It does not even seem that Richard was crook-backed, as early Tudor accounts made him out to be. So he was not without support when, early in the new reign, he intercepted the young king and his Woodville uncle Lord Rivers on their way to London, seized control of the monarch, and declared himself Protector. Queen Elizabeth herself took refuge in Westminster Abbey; but Richard was prompt to arrest and execute as traitors her leading relatives.

Richard's reputation
Richard Protector,
1483

Richard was now in a very tempting position. Between him and the throne there were only his two young nephews, Edward V and Edward's young brother, Richard, Duke of York. Both of these were in his power. Very quickly, Richard declared that Edward IV's marriage had been invalid as he had earlier been betrothed to another woman – a betrothal was often regarded at this time as equivalent to marriage – and that Edward's children were therefore illegitimate and had no title to the throne. In July 1483 he then had himself crowned as Richard III. Soon afterwards, the crime with which his name has always been associated took place – the murder of Edward V and his brother in the Tower. How they died no-one knows, but the murder was strongly rumoured by the autumn of 1483. It was probably their bodies which were found in 1674 when alterations were made in one of the Tower stairways.

Coronation of
Richard III, 1483

Murder of the two
princes, 1483

From the time of his nephews' disappearance and suspected murder, Richard III met opposition from noble families disgusted by his actions. According to Sir Thomas More:

Opposition to
Richard

his eyes whirled about, his body privily fenced, his hand ever on his dagger, his countenance and manner like one always ready to strike again. He took ill rest at nights, lay long waking and musing; more wearied with care and watch, he rather slumbered than slept.

This was written by a man seeking to justify the claim of Henry Tudor to the throne, and could be unfair to Richard.

The first rising against Richard came in October 1483. It was frustrated by bad weather and by Richard's prompt reaction. Richard was not incompetent and he made several efforts to win popular support. But in 1484 his only son died, and in the early part of 1485 his Queen – Anne Neville, daughter of the 'kingmaker' – died also. Richard was now alone, hated by many, feared and distrusted. Moreover, there was a rival claimant whose chances were now much better: Henry Tudor, Earl of Richmond, the heir to the Lancastrian inheritance. Around him, first at the court of Brittany, then elsewhere in France, the opposition to Richard gathered.

Buckingham's rising,
1483

In August 1485 Henry sailed from the port of Harfleur with about

2,000 French mercenaries. He was a cautious man, but he knew that he must take great risks. Wisely he landed at Milford Haven, in Pembrokeshire, a county of which his uncle was earl. Here he could display the red dragon of Wales, stress the Welsh side of his ancestry, and gather supporters before Richard could attack him. Very typical of Henry's foresight was his betrothal to Edward V's sister, Elizabeth of York. This enabled him to appear as one who brought reconciliation between the historic enemies – the houses of York and Lancaster.

Within a fortnight Richard confronted Henry at Bosworth Field, in Leicestershire. The battle lasted only two hours, and despite Richard's much larger forces ended in complete victory for Henry. The key role was played by Lord Stanley, whose son was a hostage in Richard's hands. Outwardly loyal to the king, he stationed his forces at such a point that if he chose he could desert Richard and join Henry. This he did, and it sealed Richard's fate. Seeing defeat inevitable, Richard resolved to die fighting. He plunged into the thick of the fray, his crown on his head, and fell attacking the group around Henry himself. Plunderers quickly stripped his body, which was later thrown over a horse and carried to Leicester for burial. Meanwhile Stanley had placed the crown of England, retrieved from a bush into which it had rolled, upon the head of the victor. Within the briefest time Henry VII, as he became, was sending off letters far and wide to announce his accession and convey his orders.

Trouble by no means ended in 1485, but Bosworth eventually proved to be the deciding battle of the struggle later called 'The Wars of the Roses'. The White Rose was in fact the badge of the Yorkists at the time, but the Red Rose was a device of Henry Tudor produced only in the final stages. In the whole conflict, probably not more than 30,000 people died, and at Bosworth only 200 or so. The longest campaign lasted for only three months. On the whole the life of the country was therefore little affected except in the areas where battles were fought or through which the armies marched. The barons, however, paid heavily for their wars. After one victory Edward IV is said to have cried out: 'Spare the commons, kill the lords!', and this was normal practice. Between 1455 and 1485 there died in the fighting or in deaths, murders and executions resulting from it, three kings, a prince of Wales, nine dukes, one marquis, thirteen earls, and twenty-four barons.

Despite the crimes that he probably committed, Richard had shown abilities as a ruler. He remained popular throughout in the North where he held the Scottish border firm and secured a valuable truce. It seems that he also tried to encourage trade, and to stop the intimidation – except by his own servants – of judges and juries. Despite his mistakes, he did much to continue the stronger and more efficient style of government introduced under Edward IV. The 'new monarchy' of Henry VII, about which a great deal has been written, was in many ways a successful carrying further of work which the Yorkists had already begun.

Marginal notes:

Henry Tudor lands in Wales, August, 1485

Defeat and death of Richard III at Bosworth, 1485

Henry VII King, 1485–1509

'The Wars of the Roses'

Heavy losses in peerage

Richard III as a ruler

The Yorkist monarchy

Conclusion: the End of an Era

In the period covered by this volume, people were not of course conscious of living in 'the middle ages'. That term was invented in the eighteenth century by historians who, looking backwards, thought that the history of Europe could be divided into three great periods. They considered these to be the Classical or Ancient (ending with the fall of Rome in the fifth century), the Modern (beginning with the geographical and other discoveries of the fifteenth century), and the Medieval (the thousand years or so of the 'middle ages' between the Ancient and the Modern). Nowadays, many people think that better divisions could be made: that it would be better to consider the Modern Age, for instance, as beginning with the new scientific ideas of the seventeenth century, or the growth of steam power and the factory system in the eighteenth and nineteenth centuries. Obviously there is nothing hard and fast about these divisions. They were adopted, and are still used, because they are a way of breaking down a vast stretch of time into convenient and more manageable periods.

Historical periods

Whether we agree or not that the changes in the fifteenth and sixteenth centuries were so great as to make the best dividing line between the medieval and the modern, we can at least see that very important changes were then taking place. In Britain, though the accession of Henry Tudor to the English throne has often been taken as a dividing line, a far greater break with the past came under his son, Henry VIII, when the English Church was separated from Rome. In Scotland, the similar break came a little later, at the time of Mary Stuart and John Knox. But though these make the best dividing lines around this time in Britain, it is clear that well before then many centuries-old beliefs and practices were crumbling.

In agriculture, for instance, the manor was becoming less important as villeinage died out and money rents or wages replaced personal dues. Landowners, too, were beginning to consolidate their holdings and enclose them, often with the idea of turning from ploughland to pasture – so saving labour and cashing in on the growing cloth trade. In the towns also there was great change. Many of the older ones were decaying, sometimes because of their rigid gild regulations, but others free from such restrictions were emerging. As a whole, merchants were gaining in wealth and in prestige; and their fortunes were enabling them to play an increasing part in local and national affairs.

15th-century changes –

– in country and towns

Late fifteenth-century ship *A model in the Science Museum, based on a manuscript c. 1485. As compared with the earlier fifteenth-century ship (p. 242), note the greater length in proportion to breadth, and the additional masts and sails. The lateen (from* Latin*) or leg of mutton sail on the rear or mizzen mast enabled such ships to sail much closer to the wind when tacking than their predecessors, and helped to bring about the great discoveries of the late fifteenth century.*

– discoveries and new trade routes

Besides growing in volume, trade was also being carried further afield. At the eastern end of the Mediterranean, it became more difficult, for the Turks in 1453 captured Constantinople and overthrew the Eastern Roman Empire. But this was soon counter-balanced by the extension of trade westwards, and by the opening of new sea routes to the east. During the fifteenth century the Portuguese, the Genoese and the Spaniards began to voyage out into the Atlantic, and down the west coast of Africa. By the end of the century, Columbus had discovered the New World of the West Indies and Central America, others had traced most of the eastern coast of North and South America, and Vasco da Gama had sailed beyond the Cape of Good Hope to India. Large-scale trade did not at once result from these discoveries, but they widened men's horizons, and eventually they gave Britain a place near the centre of the trading world.

– growth of nation states

There was another change at this time common to a large part – though by no means all – of Western Europe. As conditions became more settled, and feudalism and rule through local barons declined, so

Early printing—a woodcut *This picture of a blacksmith with his anvil and tools appeared in one of the early English printed books—Caxton's 'Game and Play of the Chess' (c. 1483). It is a woodcut, printed from an incised wooden block.*

feelings of nationality increased; and where the kings were powerful, and sea or hills and mountains provided fairly clear boundaries – as with England, France and Spain – *national* states developed. Much of the history of Europe in the next four centuries concerns their rivalries.

Nowhere, however, was the pace of change greater than in men's minds. This came about partly because of the growth of schools and colleges. Fifteenth-century Britain, for instance, saw Henry VI's foundation of Eton College and King's College Cambridge, the foundation of several other Colleges at Oxford and Cambridge, and the foundation of three Scottish universities – St. Andrews, Glasgow and Aberdeen. But ways of thought also changed, because the subject-matter of higher education was enlarged to include the whole range of classical literature instead of just a limited number of approved texts. In Italy the movement known as the Renaissance – the 'rebirth' of interest in the whole range of classical Greek and Latin art and literature – had long been gathering force; and soon this interest was to grip scholars and artists all over western Europe.

– interest in mankind

The results were far-reaching. Classical sculpture, for instance, had gloried in the beauty of the human body, but medieval sculpture had usually disguised or distorted the body to serve religious ends. Now once again sculptors began to present man and man's achievements as interesting or beautiful in themselves. Similarly, scholars who examined classical manuscripts closely, or studied the early history of the Church, now frequently came to the conclusion that some of the claims of the popes had been based on forged documents, or that the practices of the

– criticism of the Church

Church in the fifteenth century were in many ways corrupt compared with those of the fourth and fifth centuries. So the movement of the Renaissance, coupled with the growth of national feeling and the power of kings and other rulers, led by degrees in the sixteenth century to the movement known as the Reformation. In this, while scholars and religious men tried to reform the doctrines or practices of the Church, kings and princes often took the chances arising from such criticism to increase their own power or wealth. In England, and in parts of Germany and Scandinavia, the rulers wrested control over the Church

– leading to the Reformation (16th century)

from the Papacy, and themselves became heads of national or local churches. Henry VIII's dissolution and robbery of the monasteries in England, in the name of reform, was an act typical of its time.

Students at university *The growth of universities was one of the great cultural developments of the Middle Ages. This fourteenth-century sculpture of students listening to a lecture comes from the tomb of an Italian professor of law at Bologna.*

Much of this was in the near future as the fifteenth century drew to its close. But if we seek the forces behind such great changes, we must not forget two technical developments. The first, beginning in the fourteenth century, was of gunpowder and cannon. Kings quickly seized control of this new arm of war, confronted with which the feudal baron in his castle eventually became powerless. The second technical development was that of printing. For many centuries the Chinese had printed from carved wooden blocks, a block to a page – Marco Polo mentions their printed paper money – but they had no knowledge of movable type or a printing press. When Johannes Gutenberg established his printing press with movable metal type at Mainz in 1450, he began a revolution which had the most profound results. From Germany the invention spread rapidly all over Europe; by 1474 an Englishman, William Caxton, was printing in English at Bruges, and by 1476 he was established at Westminster, under the patronage of Edward IV. Before his death fifteen years later, he had printed nearly a hundred books. The Reformation could not possibly have spread as it did without the greater circulation of Bibles and pamphlets brought about through the invention of the printing press and movable type.

In 1485 Britain, like the rest of western Europe, stood on the edge of great changes. In the course of the next century, these changes – including the rise of national states, the shattering of western Christian unity, the spread of learning and the spirit of free enquiry, and the growth of a powerful merchant class with large reserves of capital – transformed much of men's lives. That is why historians have so often seen in the fifteenth and sixteenth centuries the closing of one epoch and the opening of another, the end of the medieval world and the beginning of modern times.

Technical development:

– gunpowder

– printing

The passing of the medieval world

A fifteenth-century cannon *Mons Meg*, at Edinburgh Castle. *Forged in Flanders, this was brought to Edinburgh about 1450. Such weapons, which fired balls of iron or stone, spelled the eventual end of baronial independence based on fortified castles.*

Suggestions for Further Reading

These are intended for young readers, but books marked * may be too advanced for those under 14. For films, etc., teachers are recommended to consult *Handbook for History Teachers* (Methuen—revd. ed. 1972), which also contains bibliographies.

Reference

Oxford Junior Encyclopædia. Children's Britannica
W. REES Historical Atlas of Wales
W. O. HASSALL Who's Who in History 55 B.C.–1485 Blackwell

General histories and sources

* ARTHUR BRYANT *The Story of England, Vols. I & II* Collins
* R. L. MACKIE *Short History of Scotland* Oliver and Boyd
 I. M. M. MACPHAIL *History of Scotland for Schools, Vol. I* E. Arnold
 D. FRASER *Looking at Welsh History, Vols. I & II* Univ. of Wales Press
 W. C. DICKINSON ed. AND OTHERS *Source Book of Scottish History, Vols. I & II* Nelson
 W. O. HASSALL ed. *How They Lived, Vol. I* Blackwell
 They Saw It Happen, Vol. I Blackwell
 EDITH RICKERT *Chaucer's World* O.U.P.
* R. I. PAGE *Life in Anglo-Saxon England* Batsford
 M. & C. M. B. QUENNELL *Everyday Life in Anglo-Saxon Times* Batsford
* J. SIMPSON *Everyday Life in the Viking Age* Batsford
* O. G. TOMKEIEFF *Life in Norman England* Batsford
* J. J. BAGLEY *Life in Medieval England* Batsford
* M. A. ROWLING *Everyday Life in Medieval Times* Batsford
 A. DUGGAN *Growing Up with the Norman Conquest* Faber
 Growing Up in the Thirteenth Century Faber
 R. ARNOLD *Kings, Bishops, Knights and Pawns* Longman
 M. & C. M. B. QUENNELL *History of Everday Things in England, 1066–1499* Batsford

Jackdaw folders (Cape) on Alfred, 1066, Domesday Book, Becket, Magna Carta, The Peasants' Revolt, The Black Death, Agincourt, Joan of Arc, Richard III, the Merchant Adventurers, and Caxton.

Special aspects and periods

 C. HIBBERT *The Search for King Arthur* Cassell *(Caravel)*
 L. DIAMOND *How the Gospel Came to Britain* O.U.P.
 D. LEATHAM *The Church defies the Dark Ages* O.U.P.
 F. R. DONOVAN *The Vikings* Cassell *(Caravel)*
 N. DENNY & J. FILMER-SANKEY *The Bayeux Tapestry* Collins
 MARJORIE REEVES *Alfred and the Danes* Longman *(Then and There)*
 The Norman Conquest Longman *(Then and There)*
 The Medieval Town Longman *(Then and There)*
 The Medieval Village Longman *(Then and There)*
 The Medieval Castle Longman *(Then and There)*
 The Medieval Monastery Longman *(Then and There)*
 R. J. MITCHELL *The Medieval Feast* Longman *(Then and There)*
 The Medieval Tournament Longman *(Then and There)*
 J. C. HOLT *Magna Carta* Longman *(Then and There)*

W. K. RITCHIE *Scotland in the Time of Wallace and Bruce* Longman *(Then and There)*
        The Days of James IV of Scotland Longman *(Then and There)*
G. SCOTT THOMPSON *Medieval Pilgrimages* Longman *(Then and There)*
        Wool Merchants of the Fifteenth Century Longman *(Then and There)*
D. JACOBS *Master Builders of the Middle Ages* Cassell *(Caravel)*
G. R. KESTEVEN *The Peasants' Revolt* Chatto & Windus
G. HINDLEY *The Medieval Establishment* Wayland Pictorial Sources
        Medieval Warfare Wayland Pictorial Sources
P. CUNNINGTON *Your Book of Medieval and Tudor Costume* Faber
MICHAEL RAINE *The Wars of the Roses* Wheeton
W. DOUGLAS SIMPSON *Castles in England and Wales* Batsford
ALAN SORRELL *Living History (Buildings)* Batsford

Biographies

M. R. PRICE *Bede and Dunstan* O.U.P. (Clarendon)
H. R. LYON *Alfred the Great* O.U.P. (Clarendon)
R. WINSTON *Charlemagne* Cassell *(Caravel)*
D. WALKER *William the Conqueror* O.U.P. (Clarendon)
E. L. G. STONES *Edward I* O.U.P. (Clarendon)
G. WILLIAMS *Owen Glendower* O.U.P. (Clarendon)
M. RUGOFF *Marco Polo's Adventures in China* Cassell *(Caravel)*
JAY WILLIAMS *Knights of the Crusades* Cassell *(Caravel)*
        Joan of Arc Cassell *(Caravel)*
* M. W. LABARGE *Simon de Montfort* Eyre & Spottiswoode
F. E. HALLIDAY *Chaucer and his World* Thames and Hudson
G. UDEN *The Knight and the Merchant (Rivers and Caxton)* Batsford

Historical fiction

RUDYARD KIPLING *Puck of Pook's Hill* Macmillan
ROSEMARY SUTCLIFF *Sword at Sunset (Arthur)* Hodder & Stoughton
GEORGE FINKEL *Twilight Province (Arthur)* Angus & Robertson
        The Long Pilgrimage (Vikings) Angus & Robertson
HENRY TREECE *Viking's Dawn (Vikings)* Puffin
ALAN BOUCHER *The Sword of the Raven (Vikings)* Longman
FRANCES CASTLE *The Sister's Tale (Ireland)* Bodley Head
C. WALTER HODGES *The Namesake (Alfred)* Bell
        The Marsh King (Alfred) Bell
HENRY TREECE *Hounds of the King (Harold)* Bodley Head
* HOPE MUNTZ *The Golden Warrior (Harold)* Chatto & Windus
HENRY TREECE *Man with the Sword (Hereward)* Bodley Head
ROSEMARY SUTCLIFFE *The Witch's Brat (twelfth century London)* O.U.P.
E. M. ALMEDINGEN *A Candle at Dusk (monastery)* O.U.P.
GEOFFREY TREASE *The Runaway Serf* Hamish Hamilton
VIOLET BIBBY *The Mirrored Shield (apprenticeship)* Longman
RHODA POWER *Redcap Runs Away (fourteenth century)* Cape
RONALD WELCH *Bowmen of Crecy* O.U.P.
        Sun of York O.U.P.
* ANYA SETON *Katherine (wife of John of Gaunt)* Reprint Society

Index